TECHNIQUES OF MANAGEMENT ACCOUNTING

TECHNIQUES OF MANAGEMENT ACCOUNTING

An Essential Guide for Managers and Financial Professionals

DAVID W. YOUNG

McGraw-Hill

New York   Chicago   San Francisco   Lisbon   London   Madrid
Mexico City   Milan   New Delhi   San Juan   Seoul   Singapore
Sydney   Toronto

1 2 3 4 5 6 7 8 9 0 AGM/AGM 0 9 8 7 6 5 4 3

ISBN: 0-07-138486-3

This publication is designed to provide accurate and authoritative information in regard to the subject matter covered. It is sold with the understanding that neither the author nor the publisher is engaged in rendering legal, accounting, or other professional service. If legal advice or other expert assistance is required, the services of a competent professional person should be sought.

—From a Declaration of Principles jointly adopted by a Committee of the American Bar Association and a Committee of Publishers

McGraw-Hill books are available at special quantity discounts to use as premiums and sales promotions, or for use in corporate training programs. For more information, please write to the Director of Special Sales, Professional Publishing, McGraw-Hill, Two Penn Plaza, New York, NY 10121-2298. Or contact your local bookstore.

Library of Congress Cataloging-in-Publication Data
Young, David W.
    Techniques of management accounting : an essential guide for managers and financial professionals / by David W. Young.
        p.   cm.
    ISBN 0-07-138486-3 (hardcover : alk. paper)
    1. Managerial accounting.   I. Title.

HF5657.4 .Y68 2003
658.15'11—dc21   2002152446

 This book is printed on recycled, acid-free paper containing a minimum of 50% recycled de-inked fiber.

CONTENTS

This book is the result of a confluence of two forces. It began several years ago when I prepared an interactive, self-paced text on management accounting that was designed for students at the general MBA and undergraduate levels. Then, about 2 years ago, when asked to teach a module on management accounting in Boston University's Executive MBA Program, I took a chance and used the text there. The students, all of whom had at least 10 years of managerial experience, found it quite helpful. That experience led me to believe that the material could be used for a more experienced audience.

The second force occurred in 1999 and 2000, during a sabbatical leave, when I prepared a text on cross-functional management. That text, called *Leadership in Action*, was designed to answer the question, "When an organization begins to manage across its traditional functions, exactly what kinds of matters do senior and line managers need to address?" In preparing this text, I frequently found myself putting management accounting into a broader strategic and organizational context than is usually the case. The context included topics such as conflict management, motivation, culture, authority and influence, strategy formulation, and customer management. Most of those topics rarely, if ever, are addressed in the management accounting literature, yet they all are key issues for *users* of management accounting information.

When McGraw-Hill indicated its interest in a book on management accounting targeted toward users, I saw the two themes merging, the result of which is this book. Because of this merging of themes, the book is nontraditional in three respects. First, it downplays the *preparation* of management accounting information (which some readers may question in certain chapters), focusing instead on the use of that information by senior and line managers. Second, it links management accounting with other organizational processes and activities; this takes place throughout the book, but especially in Chapter 11. Third, it is interactive; it asks the reader to prepare solutions to problems not because readers will have to do so in their daily activities but because this is the best way to learn the material and understand what kinds of decisions accountants make that can affect the information available to managers for decision making. Thus, with the knowledge gained from this book, managers and analysts should be better able to interact with their accountants.

Interacting effectively with accountants is not a trivial matter. In many organizations senior and line managers defer to the accountants' decisions because of insufficient knowledge to question the accountants. One of the goals of this book is to help senior and middle managers know enough to ask the *right* questions and know if they are getting reasonable answers. Of perhaps even greater importance, a key goal is to help managers know when they should delegate decisions to their accountants and when they should make the decisions themselves.

ACKNOWLEDGMENTS

This book has benefited from the input of a wide variety of individuals, both academics and practicing managers. Some of the most useful input came from my colleague and friend Anthony Hourihan, Professor of Banking and Finance at University College in Dublin, Ireland, and a consultant to financial institutions in Asia, Africa, Europe, the United States, and Latin America. He gave me extremely valuable feedback on the *Leadership in Action* manuscript. If he had the slightest suspicion that in so doing he also had contributed to the preparation of an *accounting* text, he would cringe in agony. Bob Anthony, the widely acknowledged dean of management control and my coauthor of a text oriented to nonprofit organizations, also provided invaluable input to the *Leadership in Action* text that also benefited this text. Leslie Pearlman, a former doctoral student of mine, made some major contributions, always questioning my approach and helping me sharpen the focus. Sheila McCarthy, a former MBA student at Boston University and now a colleague, also helped in many ways, moving from accepting what I said as gospel to questioning everything.

Several other people who reviewed the *Leadership in Action* text contributed inadvertently to this book. They include Diana Barrett, Senior Lecturer at Harvard Business School in Boston and my partner in The Crimson Group, Inc.; Douglas Grant, a former undergraduate student and teaching assistant at Boston University, now completing the MBA program at MIT; Robert Goldszer, MD, MBA, Director of Specialty Services and vice chair of the Department of Medicine at Brigham and Women's Hospital in Boston, and a former student in several executive education programs as well as Boston University's Executive MBA Program; Laura Roberts, a former MBA student at Boston University and now Principal at The Museum Group in Cambridge, Massachusetts; Robert Simpson, DSW, another former student and now chief operating officer of SPHS Behavioral Healthcare in Springfield, Massachusetts; Martin Charns, DBA, Professor and Director of the Program on Health Policy and Management at the Boston University School of Public Health and a teaching colleague in many endeavors; Alan Edelstein, CPA, retired partner and director of Alan Edelstein and Associates and a longtime contributor to the Accounting Department at the Boston University School of Management; and Ron Cook, CPA, my cousin, and President of The Connecting Point in Las Vegas, Nevada. Finally, Ela Aktay and Ann Wildman of McGraw-Hill Professional provided useful advice throughout the process, and Ruth Mannino did a great job of coordinating the editing effort.

Two institutions also have contributed to the book. Boston University granted me a sabbatical leave for the spring semester 2000 during which I prepared some of the content of this text. I am especially grateful to Michael Lawson, Boston University's Senior Associate Dean, for his efforts in making that happen. The University of Ferrara in Italy provided an academic home for me for three weeks in spring 2001 during which, despite the incredible Italian food, the academic camaraderie, and the general *vita bella* of Italy, I was able to prepare a first draft of the text. I am indebted to Professor Stefano Zambon for his efforts in making that happen.

Despite all these contributions to the effort, the responsibility for any errors, omissions, or shortcomings in the text remains my own.

David W. Young
Arlington, Massachusetts
February 2003

Introduction

This book was written for senior and midlevel managers who use management accounting in their day-to-day activities but do not aspire to become management accountants. It assumes no prior formal exposure to management accounting concepts or techniques, and although it demonstrates several techniques in some detail, its primary emphasis is on the *use* of management accounting information, not its preparation. Thus, the book's goal is to help managers be more effective in a business environment in which an understanding of management accounting is important to success. Moreover, the book aims to give readers an improved ability to communicate with their organizations' accountants to ensure that the management accounting information provided to line managers and others is as useful as possible for decision making.

Management accounting information can be divided into three areas: full cost accounting, differential cost accounting, and responsibility accounting. Exhibit I-1 lists the book's specific learning objectives in each of those areas. As it indicates, many of the learning objectives are either behavioral or organizational in nature, especially in the area of responsibility accounting.

This book is nontraditional in three important respects: its user orientation, its organizational focus, and its emphasis on interactive learning.

User Orientation

Although it would be nice if a user orientation could be achieved without working through some of the details of accounting, that is not possible.

EXHIBIT I-1

Learning Objectives

Full Cost Accounting (Chapters 1, 4, and 5)

- The meaning of terms such as cost object, cost center, direct and indirect costs, overhead cost allocation, and cost systems
- The way costs can be allocated to determine the cost of a particular product or service
- The distinction between production (or mission) centers and service centers
- The nature of the managerial choices inherent in a cost accounting system
- Overhead rates and overhead variances, including predetermined overhead rates
- The distinction between absorption costing and variable costing
- The concept of activity-based costing (ABC) and second-stage cost drivers

Differential Cost Accounting (Chapters 2 and 3)

- The rationale for the statement "different costs are used for different purposes"
- The distinction between full costs and differential costs and when each should be used
- The nature of the factors that influence changes in cost, including the distinction among fixed, variable, step-function, and semivariable costs
- The technique of cost-volume-profit analysis, how to prepare such an analysis, and its uses and limitations
- The nature of alternative choice decision making and the types of alternative choice decisions most organizations make
- The concepts of unit contribution margin and total contribution and their roles in alternative choice decision making

Responsibility Accounting (Chapters 6 through 11)

- The definition of a responsibility center, the different types of responsibility centers, and the basis for choosing the most appropriate type
- The definition of a transfer price and its role in a responsibility accounting system
- The phases of the management control process and the characteristics of each
- The formal techniques used to assess the financial viability of a capital investment proposal
- The special considerations faced by nonprofit and public sector organizations in capital budgeting
- The key elements of a good operational budgeting process, including its relationship to responsibility centers
- The distinction among the capital budget, the operating budget, and the cash budget
- The meaning of the term *flexible budget* and its role in a responsibility accounting system
- The technique of variance analysis, its uses and limitations, and its relationship to management reporting
- Some of the issues involved in measuring nonfinancial performance
- The linkages among the responsibility accounting system and other organizational activities, including the organization's strategy formulation process

However, accounting details are discussed only to the extent that they are needed to describe the concepts and techniques used in most organizations. The term *used in most* is key in this regard. In general, the text does not cover exceptions to the rules or some of the possible variations on traditional themes. However, each chapter contains footnotes that allow a reader to pursue particular topics if he or she wishes to do so.

The focus on senior and middle managers as users is based in large measure on the fact that management accounting is one of the most neglected topics in both the popular business literature and management education. Its neglect is partially a result of the fact that in most organizations the design of the needed systems is delegated to the accounting department, but accounting training in most schools and universities gives the topic only a cursory treatment. The goal of most undergraduate accounting programs, for example, is to prepare students to become certified public accountants (CPAs) and enter public accounting, and there are very few questions on the CPA examination concerning management accounting. Given that many chief financial officers (CFOs) began their careers in public accounting, the unfortunate consequence is that they have had little formal education in management accounting principles. What they know they have learned on the job, and as a result, their knowledge frequently is incomplete and sometimes inaccurate. This is especially true in the area of responsibility accounting, where in many schools there are no courses that address the topic in even a minor way.

Despite this lack of formal responsibility accounting training on the part of most organizations' accounting staffs, all organizations, even the tiniest, engage in some form of responsibility accounting. In large organizations the responsibility accounting system tends to be formal; in smaller ones it is often quite informal. Responsibility accounting has been around as long as organizations have been in existence, but it could be more comprehensive and sophisticated if senior and middle managers played an active role in its development and ongoing operation. By having a user orientation, this book aims to help those managers be more effective in carrying out that role.

Organizational Focus

Many texts use manufacturing examples to illustrate management accounting concepts and principles. This book uses both manufacturing and nonmanufacturing examples. Some examples involve service organizations, and some involve nonprofit organizations. Since most management accounting concepts are universal, the type of organization used to illustrate a point is relatively unimportant. Service and nonprofit organizations are used as examples in recognition of their growing importance in the economy and to help readers see the universal applicability of the concepts. Moreover, most of the examples have been chosen with the hope that they will "resonate" with the reader because they involve organizations with which he or she has some familiarity.

Interactive Learning Process

A key philosophical principle of the book is that the development of new skills requires practice. Throughout each chapter readers are given opportunities to practice, using the techniques that are covered. Readers do this by preparing answers to the problems that appear throughout the chapter. The idea behind these interactive materials is to shorten the "feedback loops" in the learning process. Rather than waiting until the end of a chapter to answer questions or analyze problems, the reader is asked to do so immediately after the discussion of a particular topic. Sometimes, if the discussion of a topic is lengthy, there are problems within it.

Some of the chapters may seem rather short. Unlike chapters in many books, however, they are not meant to be read quickly. Because of the interactive nature of the learning process, you should move through each chapter at a relatively slow pace. Depending on your speed in mastering the material, your reading of a chapter may take several hours. Additionally, you may find that you need time to digest the material as you go along, and so you should not try to work through the whole book in a single sitting.

You can best prepare for the problems by having a pencil and a calculator handy while reading a chapter. A problem begins with an icon like the one below:

 PROBLEM   The problem is in a smaller type font like this.

ANSWER   The answer follows and is also set in the smaller type.

You should work out the solution and then compare your associated reasoning with the answer that is given. If you had the right answer, you should continue reading. If not, you should spend as much time as needed to figure out where you went wrong. This may require rereading the section of the chapter immediately preceding the problem. Similarly, if you believe you understand the material in a particular section and therefore do not need to read that section, you might prepare answers to the section's problems to verify your understanding.

Readers who are seeking an overall understanding of management accounting may wish to skip the interactive materials and simply absorb the content of each chapter from their reading of the text. Much depends on your goals, prior knowledge, and available time, among other factors. However, if you are considering skipping the interactive materials you should bear in mind that although management accounting is rather intuitive, a true understanding of its subtleties and intricacies requires working with the concepts and techniques to see how they are developed and applied in practice. This can happen most effectively through the use of the interactive materials.

However you decide to approach the interactive materials, you should work through the chapters in order, since the discussion in each chapter assumes an understanding of the material covered in previous chapters.

Each chapter is discussed briefly below. The Contents shows the major headings in each chapter.

Chapter 1: Essentials of Full Cost Accounting

The question "What did it cost?" is one of the trickiest in accounting for all organizations—manufacturing, service, and nonprofit. Chapter 1 discusses the kinds of managerial decisions that are made in answering this question as well as the managerial utility of full cost information. It also links the cost accounting effort to the economist's three factors of production: land, labor, and capital. Appendix A discusses the reciprocal method of cost allocation.

Chapter 2: Cost Behavior

The notion that different costs are used for different purposes is a basic principle of management accounting. This chapter explains why that notion is important, focusing in particular on cost behavior, including the distinction among fixed, variable, step-function, and semivariable costs. It takes up the subject of cost-volume-profit (CVP) analysis, looking at CVP analysis (sometimes called *breakeven* analysis) in its most basic form and then examining a variety of special considerations that can complicate it.

Chapter 3: Differential Cost Accounting

Chapter 2 identifies a number of instances in which full costs are inappropriate for decision making, such that a manager needs to analyze cost behavior. This chapter takes that idea a step further, showing how full costs are inappropriate for several types of decisions that managers frequently must make. These decisions, called *alternative choice decisions*, occur when a manager must analyze cost behavior under two or more approaches to accomplishing a particular task. The chapter discusses how full cost information can lead managers to make decisions that are financially detrimental to the organization and makes the point that for alternative choice decisions, the appropriate information is differential costs.

Chapter 4: Absorption Costing

Chapter 1 focuses principally on service organizations. Chapter 4 looks at the various types of costs that exist in a manufacturing setting and shows how to compute the cost of goods manufactured and the cost of goods sold with job order and process systems. The chapter also discusses overhead rates, including predetermined overhead rates, flexible overhead budgets, the computation of overhead variances, and the managerial uses of overhead variances.

Chapter 5: Activity-Based Costing and Variable Costing

This chapter first examines the concept of activity-based costing (ABC) and cost drivers, including second-stage cost drivers. Many service and manufacturing organizations are turning to ABC as a way to both measure costs more accurately and exert greater control over them. Thus, this chapter also serves as a bridge to the chapters on responsibility accounting. The chapter then looks at the distinction between absorption costing and variable costing and discusses the advantages and disadvantages of each.

Chapter 6: Responsibility Accounting: An Overview

This chapter emphasizes the distinction between measuring and managing resources, a key principle of responsibility accounting. It begins with an analysis of the relationship between cost accounting and responsibility accounting systems and then moves into the realm of responsibility accounting. To design a good responsibility accounting system, a manager must think about both the *responsibility accounting structure* and the *management control process*. The chapter puts most of its emphasis on structure, discussing the different types of responsibility centers that can exist in an organization, the basis for choosing one type in preference to another, and the relationship between the responsibility accounting structure and the organization's formal authority structure. The chapter also briefly describes the characteristics of the four phases of the management control process: programming, budgeting, measuring, and reporting.

Chapter 7: Key Issues in Designing the Responsibility Accounting Structure

This chapter expands upon the concepts covered in Chapter 6 and discusses the topics of transfer prices, residual income, fairness, and goal congruence. Inadequate attention by senior management to these four topics—either individually or in combination—explains why many responsibility accounting systems fail to achieve the goal of allowing managers to exert control over the resources for which they are held responsible.

The chapter also examines three important issues: (1) the link between the responsibility center structure and the organization's motivation system, (2) some of the informal matters that arise in the context of decentralizing responsibility in large, complex organizations, and (3) the issues that senior managers must consider if they are to make either profit centers or investment centers work to the overall benefit of the organization, including some tricky design matters in matrixlike organizations. It concludes by emphasizing the contingency notion of responsibility accounting systems: that there is no one *right* responsibility accounting system. Instead, a responsibility accounting system must *fit* the organization's strategy and structure.

Chapter 8: Programming

Because money can earn interest, a given sum of money received at some point in the future is worth less than the same sum received today. This concept lies at the heart of capital budgeting, in which an organization invests some money today in order to receive some returns on that investment over a number of years in the future. This chapter discusses some of the techniques for analyzing investments by using the concept of present value. It also looks at the effect of taxes and accelerated depreciation on a capital investment decision and examines the issues involved in choosing a discount rate for assessing a capital project, including how companies deal with risk in assessing a capital investment proposal. The chapter concludes with a discussion of political, behavioral, and other considerations that can influence senior management's choice of a proposal, including ways in which programming links to both an organization's culture and its conflict management processes.

There are two appendixes at the end of the book. The first discusses the concept of the reciprocal method of cost allocation. The second discusses the concept of present value.

Chapter 9: Operational Budgeting

In addition to capital budgets, which flow from the programming phase of the management control process, organizations typically prepare both operating budgets and cash budgets. This chapter focuses on the operating budget. Among the topics addressed are the relationship between the operating budget and responsibility centers, the organizational and strategic contexts in which budgeting takes place, the mechanical aspects of building a budget, and the seven important linkages between the budget and other organizational activities.

Chapter 10: Measuring and Reporting

Two important phases in the management control process are those which measure and report information to managers. This chapter discusses those phases, placing particular emphasis on flexible budgets and variance analysis—techniques that allow managers to see with some clarity the reasons underlying a difference between budgeted and actual revenues and expenses. The chapter also discusses the limitations of variance analysis and some of the criteria for a good reporting process. It concludes by discussing the topic of measuring and reporting *nonfinancial performance*, an issue that is taking on increasing importance in many organizations.

Chapter 11: Management Accounting in Context

This chapter briefly summarizes the material in the first 10 chapters and places it into a broader context. It begins with a discussion of the idea that different costs are used for different purposes and then summarizes the criteria for a good responsibility accounting system. Next, it positions the responsibility accounting system as one of several activities that take place in an organization and that must be integrated if an organization is to be successful. The chapter concludes with a "Managerial Checklist" concerning these interrelationships.

CHAPTER 1

Essentials of Full Cost Accounting

The question "What did it cost?" is an important one for managers in many different organizational settings. Arriving at an answer is much more difficult than it might first appear. Obviously, the question can be answered easily if one is discussing the purchase of inputs (supplies, labor, and so on) for a production or service-delivery process. Even calculating the full cost of a unit produced—whether it is an airplane or a manicure—is relatively easy as long as the organization is producing goods or services that are completely homogeneous. Complications arise, however, when an organization provides multiple goods and/or services, particularly when it uses different kinds and amounts of resources to manufacture the goods or provide the services.

This chapter addresses some of the key decisions that are made in designing a full cost accounting system and discusses how those decisions can influence the answer to the "What did it cost?" question. In this regard, there are three important considerations. First, the chapter is not meant to be an all-inclusive description of cost accounting; instead, its goal is to provide an introduction to the topic. Second, it will use service organizations as examples to illustrate the principles. Because cost accounting can be quite complicated in other kinds of organizations, especially manufacturing companies, the principles are best seen in relatively uncomplicated settings such as service organizations. Cost accounting for manufacturing companies is discussed in Chapter 4.

The third consideration is that there is much disagreement among managers and accountants about the best way to calculate full costs. There even is disagreement about whether *full* cost is the most appropriate calculation. Indeed, many managers and accountants believe that a computation of full costs is inherently distorted and therefore of little value for management's decision-making purposes. Nevertheless, for the purposes of this chapter we will assume that senior management wishes to know the full cost of providing a particular service and will look at the choices it must make to arrive at that figure.

The chapter begins with a discussion of the uses of full cost information, followed by an assessment of the broad set of issues that must be considered in calculating costs. Next, we look conceptually at the factors that influence the use of resources, linking cost accounting to the economist's three factors of production: land, labor, and capital. After this, we turn to an assessment of the basic decisions that must be made in calculating a full cost figure, what often is called the *cost accounting methodology*. The chapter concludes by examining the effect of the cost accounting methodology on an important managerial decision: pricing an organization's products or services.

USES OF FULL COST INFORMATION

Full cost information has three basic uses: pricing, profitability assessments, and comparative analyses.

Pricing

One of the basic functions of cost information is to assist managers in setting prices. Clearly, cost information is not the only relevant information for this purpose, but it is an important ingredient in the decision-making process. Many firms are *price takers:* They must accept whatever price prevails in their market. In these instances, prices are based not on costs but on the market. For other firms, especially market leaders, cost information is much more important to the pricing decision, although even these firms must consider other factors.

One of those factors might be the goal of increasing market share, which may justify setting a price below a product's full cost. (This is quite different from "predatory pricing," in which a large firm sets its price below its full cost in an effort to drive smaller firms out of the industry.) Similarly, a firm may price one product below full cost to increase its sales, and this may lead to the sale of other products at prices set well above full cost. Hewlett-Packard, for example, may sell its printers below their full cost in an effort to maximize printer sales. Once consumers have printers, they purchase paper and toners, where the company may earn much of its profits. Of course, if a firm is to price below full cost, it must have a good understanding of its costs. Thus, cost information remains an important ingredient in price setting.

An important variant of pricing based on full cost is *cost-plus pricing*. With this type of pricing, the purchaser of an organization's products or services agrees to pay the full cost plus an agreed-upon increment, usually a percentage. Many government contracts are written this way, especially in the defense industry, where the argument is made that the activities needed to design and manufacture a product are so uncertain that it is impossible to determine the cost in advance and hence to set a reasonable price.

Similarly, some health-care insurance companies pay hospitals on the basis of cost. Because health policy analysts believe these cost-based payments have contributed to the rising cost of health care, many insurers have shifted or are shifting to fixed-price arrangements in which their price is based on a patient's diagnosis. In these situations, health-care providers become price takers.

Profitability Assessments

Even firms that are price takers must calculate full costs if management is to know whether a product or service is profitable. Management may take a variety of actions if a product is not profitable on a full cost basis, which we will examine in some detail in Chapters 2 and 3. Any product whose price is below its full cost is a "loss leader." Since an organization cannot have all its products be loss leaders, cost accounting serves to highlight areas where cross subsidization is taking place, thus allowing senior management to assess whether that cross subsidization is consistent with the organization's overall strategy.

Comparative Analyses

Many organizations can benefit from comparing their costs with those of similar organizations that manufacture similar goods or deliver similar services. Organizations that have franchises, for example, no doubt find it useful to compare the costs of different franchisees. Full cost information can assist them in this effort. Other organizations may have access to industry norms through common knowledge, trade associations, or other sources. For example, in the restaurant industry there are well-established norms for each cost element as a percentage of revenue. This applies not only to food and beverage costs but to all other items, such as linens and breakage.

Comparative analyses are inherently tricky. For example, an organization undertaking such an analysis would need to know whether the organizations with which it is comparing itself measure their costs in the same way as it does. Typically, this is not a concern for a company with, say, franchised operations, since the cost accounting effort for franchisees can be standardized. In other types of organizations, there can be a variety of complexities, some of which are illustrated in the following problem:[1]

 PROBLEM   Northern College, a small private liberal arts college, is interested in comparing its cost per student with the cost per student in other similar colleges. What are some of the issues it must consider in making this comparison?

ANSWER   The college must consider such issues as average class size; the existence of specialized programs in athletics, art, music, or other subjects; special services such as career counseling; whether it wishes to include room and board and/or library costs in the comparison; the method used to calculate the cost (e.g., whether it amortizes its library collections and, if so, over what time period); and a variety of similar matters.

As this problem suggests, even the definition of what should be included in a "full cost" calculation requires a managerial decision. Indeed, because an organization's cost accounting system embodies such a wide range of choices, managers frequently find it difficult to compare costs between their organization and similar organizations in which the cost accounting choices may have been made differently.

Issues to Consider in Calculating Full Costs

If senior management does not wish to undertake pricing, profitability assessment, or comparative analyses, it does not need to become involved in the effort to calculate full costs. Instead, it can delegate that responsibility to the accounting staff. Generally accepted accounting principles (GAAP) require manufacturing organizations to calculate the full manufacturing cost of the products they produce to determine a cost of goods sold figure that abides by GAAP's matching principle. Therefore, these organizations must undertake a full cost accounting effort if they are to receive a clean opinion on their audited financial statements. Senior management usually does not become involved in this effort in a significant way.

In most merchandising and service organizations, full cost accounting is not required by GAAP. Indeed, in merchandising organizations, the cost of goods sold figure generally includes only the cost of the items the company sold during the relevant accounting period. All other operating items are expensed as incurred. Few, if any, merchandising organizations will make an effort to allocate these expenses to products to obtain the "full cost" of each item sold.

In situations where a "third-party payer" pays on the basis of cost, an organization usually must calculate its full costs in accordance with certain guidelines. The organization then must submit the resulting cost report to the third party before receiving payment.

This kind of requirement by an oversight organization happens in many instances in which the government reimburses an organization's costs. For example, when the government contracts with a university to do research, the university's reimbursement must be in accordance with the principles set forth in the Office of Management and Budget's *Circular A-21, Cost Principles for Educational Institutions*. Those principles provide for direct costs plus "an equitable share" of overhead costs. Overhead costs include a use allowance for depreciation of buildings and equipment, operations and maintenance of plant, general administration, departmental administration, student administration and services, and the library.[2]

However, these are the exceptions. In most merchandising and service organizations, there is no requirement to calculate full costs. Instead, full costs are calculated only if senior management believes the information will assist it in decision making. Because of this, some service organizations do not undertake a full-cost accounting effort, and some manufacturing and merchandising organizations do no more than satisfy the requirements of GAAP. For example, restaurants do not calculate the full cost of a meal. Instead, they compute the cost of the ingredients for each item on the menu and set the price at a certain markup over those costs. The difference between the price and the ingredient cost must cover the costs of kitchen labor, bussers, expediters, the wait staff, management, and all other operating expenses. The accounting staff then computes each expense item (such as kitchen labor) as a percentage of total revenue and uses industry standards to see if it is on target. Senior management makes no effort to determine, for example, the cost of kitchen labor included in each meal. As a result, the cost of goods sold on a restaurant's financial statement typically refers only to ingredients, not to labor.

Role of Senior Management

As the discussion above suggests, if senior management sees a need for cost information, it can compute costs in a variety of ways, many of which can be defended as valid. On the other hand, because the cost accounting effort is inherently complex in any good-sized organization, some approaches to computing full costs can produce misleading results. Moreover, in many organizations, the cost accounting effort is complicated by questions of product or service mix, standby capacity, customers' use of related products and services, seasonal purchase patterns, managerial efficiency, and periodic changes in wages and supply prices. Nevertheless, if senior management has made the decision to calculate full costs, it must work with its accounting staff to select an appropriate methodology.

The use of the words "work with" rather than "delegate to" emphasizes an important distinction. Because the issues are complex, the decisions cannot be delegated completely to the accounting staff. Instead, senior management must be intimately involved in setting the ground rules for the cost accounting effort and in guiding the work of the accounting staff. Otherwise, the information that emerges from the effort may be of little managerial value. Indeed, because there is no single "right" cost figure, managers with differing needs will set different ground rules and request that the cost accounting decisions be made in different ways. Moreover, the decisions may change at different times in the life of an organization as managers' needs change. Consequently, the key question is, "What does management find useful?" It is this question that must drive the cost accounting effort.

Because there are no cost accounting rules similar to GAAP in financial accounting, we now move to a discussion of the conceptual structure that underlies a cost accounting effort, after which we will look at several key cost accounting decisions. These decisions affect the way the accounting staff gathers and presents information for the purpose of calculating the cost of an organization's goods or services.

RESOURCE USAGE: A CONCEPTUAL FRAMEWORK

Fundamentally, cost accounting addresses the *use of resources.* Accordingly, an appropriate question to ask is, "What are these resources, and how can they be defined and measured?"

At the most fundamental level, the resources used in any organization—manufacturing, merchandising, or service—are the classic ones of the economist: land, labor, and capital. These resources are shown schematically in Exhibit 1-1. Take a few minutes now to review this exhibit so that you can relate it to the following discussion.

Land

Land is the simplest of the three resources. Unlike the other two, it has no subclassifications. It can be somewhat complicated for agricultural firms or companies in the extraction industries (oil, coal, etc.), but in general it consists of the properties on which a company's plants and offices are located.

Labor

Labor can be subclassified into mission (sometimes called production) and support. Mission labor includes the individuals who actually manufacture

EXHIBIT 1-1

Resource Usage: A Conceptual Framework

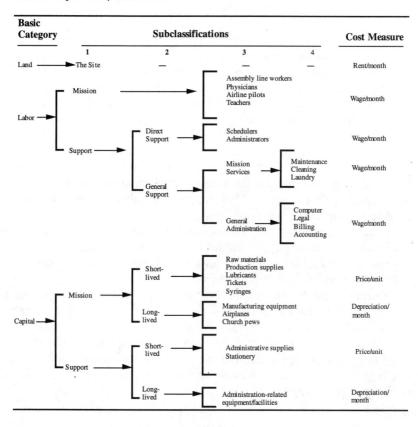

Basic Category	Subclassifications				Cost Measure
	1	2	3	4	
Land ──────►The Site	—		—	—	Rent/month
Labor ── Mission			Assembly line workers Physicians Airline pilots Teachers		Wage/month
Support ──	Direct Support		Schedulers Administrators		Wage/month
	General Support		Mission Services ──	Maintenance Cleaning Laundry	Wage/month
			General Administration ──	Computer Legal Billing Accounting	Wage/month
Capital ── Mission	Short-lived		Raw materials Production supplies Lubricants Tickets Syringes		Price/unit
	Long-lived		Manufacturing equipment Airplanes Church pews		Depreciation/ month
Support ──	Short-lived		Administrative supplies Stationery		Price/unit
	Long-lived		Administration-related equipment/facilities		Depreciation/ month

an organization's products or deliver its services—personnel who are directly associated with the organization's main mission. Support labor includes everyone else in the organization. It can be divided into direct support and general support.

Direct support consists of the activities that take place in any *mission department* (e.g., scheduling production in a factory or providing secretarial support for a research project). General support can be related to mission services or can be part of general administration. In the former case it includes centralized functions that assist the organization's production departments but are organized separately from them, such as central maintenance and cleaning. General administration consists of an organization's central office staff activities, which typically are not directly related to specific production departments. These activities include computer operations, payroll, purchasing, legal work, and billing, among others.

Capital

Capital also can be looked at as either mission or support. Mission capital includes all the capital resources needed to provide direct support to the manufacturing or service-delivery activity. It is divided between *short-lived* (used up in a year or less) and *long-lived* (used up over several years).

Short-lived mission capital consists of *raw materials* (sometimes called *direct* materials) and *production-related supplies*. Raw materials are the items in a manufacturing effort that enter the final product, that is, the items to which a manufacturing organization adds value. Production-related supplies do not enter the final product. Instead, they support the manufacture of that product. They range from lubricants in a factory to tickets in a symphony orchestra.

Long-lived mission capital includes the equipment and facilities used in production or service-related activities. Manufacturing plant and equipment, aircraft, classroom facilities, church pews, and x-ray machines are all examples of long-lived mission capital.

Support capital is also either short-lived or long-lived and consists of those items that provide general support rather than being associated with production or service delivery. Supplies used in the president's office in an oil company or the controller's office in a hospital are examples of short-lived support capital. Similarly, equipment such as centralized photocopying machines, fax machines, and a computing center are considered long-lived support capital.

Units of Measure

The cost of land is usually measured in terms of rent per unit of time (e.g., a month) for a given amount of space (e.g., a square foot). Since land does not depreciate, organizations that own the land used for their facilities have no out-of-pocket cost for rent, although they usually pay property taxes and also have an opportunity cost of the capital tied up in the land. An exception is land that "depletes" over time, such as land from which minerals or oil is being extracted.

The cost of labor is measured by wages—either per unit of time (e.g., an hour) or per unit of activity (e.g., a product, visit, or flight). Short-lived capital—either mission or support—usually is measured in terms of the factor price per unit: or what the organization paid to obtain the item. Long-lived capital typically is measured in terms of depreciation per unit of time.

THE FULL COST ACCOUNTING METHODOLOGY

The conceptual framework in Exhibit 1-1 puts cost accounting into its broader economic context. Specifically, the principal objective of full cost accounting is to measure as accurately as possible the resources consumed in producing a particular good or delivering a particular service. In some instances the measurement process is quite easy. For example, an organization that produces a single good or service usually has little difficulty calculating the cost of each unit. All the costs associated with the organization can be summed and divided by the number of units produced during a particular accounting period to arrive at the cost per unit.

 PROBLEM Lawncare, Inc. (LI), does gardening work. As far as management is concerned, the company produces a single service: an hour of gardening work. Management wishes to calculate its cost per hour of service. Last year the organization had total costs of $175,000 and delivered 15,625 hours of service. What is LI's cost per service unit?

ANSWER As indicated above, this cost accounting process is quite simple: $175,000 ÷ 15,625 hours = $11.20 per hour of service.

Organizations that produce a variety of goods or services each of which requires different amounts of land, labor, and capital, will have a much more difficult time determining the cost for each unit sold. For example, the cost accounting process for Lawncare, Inc. would become somewhat more complex if senior management wished to distinguish between its hourly cost for mowing lawns and its hourly cost for other gardening services.

This more complex process requires management to make several decisions in order to determine the cost of each activity. These decisions include (1) defining a cost object, (2) determining cost centers, (3) distributing indirect costs, (4) choosing bases for allocating service center costs, (5) selecting an allocation method, and (6) attaching costs to cost objects. Taken together, these six decisions constitute the full-cost accounting methodology.

Decision 1: Defining the Cost Object

The cost object is the unit of a good or service for which an organization wants to know the cost. Generally, as the cost object becomes more specific, the methodology to account for the associated costs becomes more complex. In some acute-care hospitals, for example, the cost object is a day of care. Sometimes the day is "all-inclusive"; that is, it includes surgical procedures, laboratory tests, radiology exams, pharmaceutical usage, and so on. When this is the case, calculating the cost of a day of care is as simple as the calculation made above for Lawncare, Inc.

In most hospitals, however, there are several cost objects, each of which is more specific than an all-inclusive day of care. In some instances, for example, it is a day of care for "routine" activities only (e.g., room, dietary, housekeeping, laundry, and nursing), with separate cost objects for other activities, such as laboratory tests. Obviously, various other combinations are possible, and even the routine-nonroutine distinction is not implemented in a uniform way among similar institutions. For example, nursing supplies may be classified as routine in some hospitals and as nonroutine in others.

Hospitals also can use a totally different cost object from a day of care, such as an admission (or discharge). When an admission is the cost object, the hospital includes all the costs associated with the patient's entire stay (i.e., for all days of care rather than just an average single day).

In general, then, depending on the particular cost object chosen, there is a need for either different kinds of cost information or different ways of analyzing and presenting that information. As a result, the choice of a cost object can have a significant effect on the answer to the question "What did it cost?" In effect, the cost object defines the "it" in the question.

 PROBLEM LI's management has decided to become more specific about its activities. It has classified them into lawn mowing and special projects. The second category includes activities such as trimming shrubs, fertilizing, planting, and weeding. What do you think LI's cost object should be? Consider the various possibilities for mowing and special projects and choose one. What criteria did you use in making your choices?

ANSWER In the mowing category the possibilities would seem to be (1) a mown lawn, (2) a mown lawn of a certain size (perhaps distinguishing among large, medium, and small lawns), (3) a mown lawn of a certain complexity (perhaps distinguishing between flat lawns with no trees or complications and lawns with steep slopes, many trees, or many small areas where a mower won't fit, and (4) an hour of lawn mowing.

In the special projects category the company might identify fertilizing, hedge trimming, planting, weeding, and other services as potential cost objects. If it does this, it will have to make some of the same distinctions of size and complexity it made for lawns. Alternatively, LI might use an hour of time.

Final versus Intermediate Cost Objects. For purposes of simplicity, an hour of time would seem to be the best approach. The choice of an hour of time poses a small problem in that customers most likely will want to know the price for an entire job (which usually will be LI's cost plus a markup). LI then would need to look at the customer's project, determine the number of hours needed, and calculate a total estimated cost. In effect, then, a "job" becomes a cost object, and just as no two jobs are alike in an automobile repair garage, a law office, a custom home builder, and many other "job order" organizations, no two LI jobs would be alike. As a result, LI would have to link its cost object (an hour of service) to the customer's cost object (a completed job).

Because of this need, managers tend to distinguish between *final* and *intermediate* cost objects. A final cost object typically is the unit that fits with the price charged to a customer. Intermediate cost objects are smaller units that are summed to produce the final cost object. For example, at Lawncare, Inc., whereas the final cost object in the mowing category is a mown lawn, the intermediate cost object would be an hour. In this regard, an important question is whether the cost of an hour of mowing is the same as the cost of an hour of special projects. To answer this question, LI must consider some of the other cost accounting choices.

Decision 2: Determining Cost Centers

Cost centers can be thought of as categories used to collect costs. To understand how they work, consider again an organization that delivers a single product or service. The organization may wish to treat itself as a single cost center, thus creating a relatively simple cost accounting system. In this case only one category will be used to collect cost information.

Alternatively, the organization may subdivide itself into several cost centers—manufacturing, administration, maintenance, and the like—for the purpose of the cost accounting effort. If this is done, the cost of a particular cost object will be the sum of the costs attributed to it in each cost center.

The criteria for selecting an appropriate cost center arrangement will be discussed later in this chapter. At the moment, we are concerned principally with the *effects* of different choices on the full cost of a cost object. In this regard, the distinction between an intermediate cost object and a cost center can be confusing. On occasion both can be viewed as "purposes" for which costs are collected; indeed, cost centers sometimes are called intermediate cost objects. This distinction will become clearer in the material that follows.

 PROBLEM LI is choosing between two cost center arrangements. The first possibility is to make the entire organization into one cost center; the second is to use three cost centers: mowing, special projects, and administration. Cost data are available for administrative supplies ($14,425), mowing supplies ($13,575), special project supplies ($12,000), administrative salaries ($40,000), mowing salaries

($50,000), special project salaries ($35,000), and the contracted services the company uses for repairing its trucks ($10,000).

As in the previous problem, the company provided 15,625 hours of lawn care services (11,772 hours of mowing and 3,853 hours of special projects). What would LI's cost per hour be for one cost center? For three cost centers?

ANSWER   If we use only one cost center, the computation will look as follows:

Direct and administrative salaries ($40,000 + $50,000 + $35,000)	$125,000
Supplies (administrative and customer-related)	40,000
($14,425 + $13,575 + $12,000)	
Contracted services	10,000
Total costs	$175,000
Hours of service	15,625
Cost per unit	$11.20

If three cost centers are used, the analysis will give the same result, but with a very different structure:

Cost Items	Administration	Mowing	Special Projects	Total
Salaries	$40,000	$50,000	$35,000	$125,000
Supplies	14,425	13,575	12,000	40,000
Contracted services		10,000		10,000
Total	$54,425	$73,575	$47,000	$175,000
Hours of service*	—	11,772	3,853	15,625
Cost per hour of service		$6.25	$12.20	$11.20†

*Hours of service applies only to customers, not administration.
†Cost per hour figures do not sum to $11.20 since the $175,000 includes the cost of administration (for which there is no hourly cost of service).

Note that the total cost per hour remains the same in both situations. This must be the case, since total costs ($175,000) and total hours (15,625) are unchanged. What value, then, derives from the extra effort associated with separating the company into three cost centers?

There are two answers to this question: an accounting-oriented one and a management-oriented one. From an accounting perspective, costs are better understood and more easily computed if they are for relatively homogeneous groupings of activities. For example, if a photocopying company had an extremely sophisticated photocopying machine and an extremely simple one, it most likely would want to create two cost centers: one for each machine. The sophisticated machine no doubt was more costly to purchase (and hence has higher depreciation), is more costly to service and repair, and perhaps requires a more highly skilled (and hence higher-salaried) operator. Calculating the average cost of a photocopy by combining the two machines, their operators, and the other costs would produce a misleading cost figure. The average would over-state the cost of a copy on the simple machine and understate it on the sophisticated one.

For this reason the choice of cost centers ordinarily is based on homogeneity; that is, a cost center ideally includes a collection of com-pletely similar activities. Clearly, *complete* homogeneity rarely is possible, and even if it were, the cost of making the requisite computations would be prohibitive. Thus, compromises frequently are necessary. We will return to this issue later in this chapter, after we have covered the remain-ing cost accounting decisions.

The management-oriented answer to this question is that the choice of cost centers depends largely on senior management's plans for using the information. For example, LI's three-cost-center structure may be helpful to management in pricing its services competitively or in compar-ing its costs with those of other lawn care companies. A comparison between Lawncare, Inc.'s, administrative costs and those of similar orga-nizations, for example, could reveal areas of potential inefficiency and thus assist management in its efforts to streamline the company's admin-istrative operations. Of course, management will have to bear in mind the caveats discussed earlier about the difficulty of making such comparisons.

Production Centers versus Service Centers. In a multi-cost-center structure an organization's cost centers generally are divided into two broad categories: production centers and service centers. Produc-tion centers, as the name implies, produce the organization's products (or deliver its services). They sometimes are called mission centers since they are considered to represent the organization's mission. In some service organizations they are called revenue centers, since they charge for their services and thus earn revenue.

Service centers, by contrast, contain the costs of the activities carried out to support production centers. In the above example, administration would be considered a service center whereas mowing and special proj-ects would be production centers. In larger settings, administration, insti-tutionwide depreciation, personnel services, and plant maintenance are examples of service centers whereas manufacturing departments are pro-duction centers.

The cost for a given cost object, then, depends on (1) the production center or centers in which a product was produced or a customer received services, (2) the number of units of activity a product received in each (such as hours of labor) or the number of units of service a customer received in each, and (3) the cost per unit of activity. The cost per unit of activity in each production center depends in part on that center's "fair share" of the organization's service center costs.

PROBLEM In addition to the cost center decision described in the last example, Lawncare, Inc., decided to establish a machine maintenance department and to treat that department as a separate service center. In so doing, it hired a mechanic at a salary of $20,000. The maintenance supplies totaled $5000. What do the company's costs look like now?

ANSWER There is now an additional service center, giving LI two service centers and two production centers. The total costs now look as follows:

| Cost Items | Service Centers | | Production Centers | | Total |
	Maintenance	Administration	Mowing	Special Projects	
Salaries	$20,000	$40,000	$50,000	$35,000	$145,000
Supplies	5,000	14,425	13,575	12,000	45,000
Contracted services			10,000		10,000
Total	$25,000	$54,425	$73,575	$47,000	$200,000

At this point the cost per hour of service becomes somewhat more difficult to calculate, since it now relies on certain other decisions. We therefore will defer the per-unit calculations until those decisions have been discussed. Note, however, that the total costs have increased to $200,000 as a result of the additional $25,000 for the maintenance department.

Decision 3: Distributing Indirect Costs

A third decision in a cost accounting system involves the requirement to distinguish between direct and indirect costs (sometimes called *traceable* and *nontraceable* costs). *Direct costs* are unambiguously associated with or physically traceable to a specific cost center. *Indirect costs* apply to more than one cost center and thus must be distributed among them.

Again, in the simplest situation, where an organization produced one product in one cost center, there would be no indirect costs, since it would not be possible to have costs that applied to more than one cost center. The creation of multiple cost centers means that some costs become indirect, necessitating their distribution.

Indirect costs can be distributed into the appropriate cost centers in one of two ways: (1) by developing techniques to measure their usage or (2) by establishing formulas.

 PROBLEM The mechanic in the maintenance cost center at Lawncare, Inc., is supervised by someone whose salary at present is included in the administration cost center. What kind of a cost is the supervisor's salary? Why? What should be done with it?

ANSWER   The salary of the supervisor is an indirect cost since it applies to activities in both the maintenance and administration cost centers. This means that it must be distributed to the two cost centers.

There are several possible ways to distribute the supervisor's salary. LI might ask the supervisor to maintain careful time records, which then could be used to distribute it. If this is done, LI effectively will have converted the indirect cost into a direct cost, since it will have made the cost (time) physically traceable to each cost center. Alternatively, LI might establish a distribution formula, using, say, salary dollars or number of personnel in each cost center as the distribution mechanism.

 PROBLEM   Assume LI decides to use number of personnel as the means to distribute the supervisor's salary. Also assume that the supervisor's salary is $15,000 and that other than the supervisor (who does not supervise herself), there are two people working in administration and one person working in maintenance. How would you distribute the salary?

ANSWER   The calculations are as follows:

Salary	$15,000
Number of people supervised	3
Cost per person supervised	$5,000
Distributed to Administration (2 × $5,000)	$10,000
Distributed to Maintenance (1 × $5,000)	5,000
Total distributed	$15,000

The conclusion of this analysis is that $5000 of the supervisor's salary should be distributed to the maintenance department. As a result, the following adjustments must be made to our costs:

Cost Center	Cost	
Maintenance	$30,000	($25,000 + $5,000 for supervisor)
Administration	49,425	($54,425 − $5,000 for supervisor)
Mowing (no adjustment)	73,575	
Special projects (no adjustment)	47,000	
Total	$200,000	

Note that this approach effectively has used a formula to distribute the supervisor's salary between the two relevant cost centers. Of the $15,000 salary, $5,000 is now in the maintenance cost center and $10,000 is in the administration cost center. Note also that although this particular indirect cost has been distributed between two service centers, LI could have an indirect cost that applied to more than two service centers or even conceivably to both service and production centers. The same sort of formula approach could be used in these situations as well.

Decision 4: Choosing Allocation Bases
for Service Center Costs

The hourly cost of mowing relies on more than the direct and distributed indirect costs of that cost center. It also must include the center's *fair share* of the organization's service center costs. The same is true for the hourly cost of special projects. As one might imagine, the notion of what is fair can be highly debatable in cost accounting, just as it is in other aspects of life.

Because of the need to allocate service center (sometimes called "overhead") costs to production centers, the fourth cost accounting decision concerns the *bases of allocation*. Here it is necessary to choose a metric for each service center that measures its use by the remaining cost centers (both other service centers and production centers) as accurately as possible. In this regard, to the extent feasible, we are seeking the *activity* that *causes* the service center's costs.

We then determine each remaining cost center's proportion of the activity. For example, if the "activity" for the plantwide depreciation cost center is square feet, we determine each cost center's proportion of the total square footage in all cost centers (except the one being allocated). We use that proportion to allocate the service center's costs to the remaining service and production centers.

Distribution versus Allocation. It is important to distinguish between distribution and allocation. *Distribution,* which was discussed in Decision 3, precedes allocation and serves to place costs into service and production centers. Costs that are direct for a given cost center do not have to be distributed, whereas indirect costs (i.e., those applying to more than one cost center) must be distributed to the appropriate centers. By contrast, *allocation* places service center costs in production centers to determine the full cost of each production center.

This terminology can be confusing, since the terms *distribution, allocation,* and *apportionment* occasionally are used interchangeably. In addition to these differences in terminology, service center costs that are allocated to revenue centers often are called *indirect costs.* The context usually clarifies the meaning, but because of these terminology differences, it is important to understand the processes being used rather than attempting to memorize the meanings of the terms.

In summary, before we can allocate service center costs, we must (1) determine the direct costs of each cost center, (2) distribute indirect costs to the appropriate cost centers, and (3) choose a basis of allocation for each service center. We then will be ready to allocate service center costs to the production centers.

Determining an Appropriate Basis of Allocation.

In the case of Lawncare, Inc., we already have determined the direct costs of each cost center and distributed the indirect costs to the appropriate cost centers. If we are to determine the full cost for each production center, we now must choose an allocation basis for each service center (maintenance and administration in this case) so that we can allocate its costs. How might we go about doing this?

Let's begin with maintenance. The goal is to find a basis of allocation that measures as accurately as possible the use of the maintenance resource by the other cost centers. Although several allocation bases may be available, one that may be appropriate is the number of machines. That is, the more machines a receiving cost center has, the more it will use the maintenance resource, and therefore the greater will be its share of the maintenance expense.

 PROBLEM The following information is available about the machines in the cost centers to receive an allocation from the maintenance cost center:

Cost Center	No. of Machines
Administration	2
Mowing	17
Special projects	11
Total	30

How much of the cost of the maintenance cost center will be allocated per machine?

ANSWER The allocation rate is $1000 per machine ($30,000 of maintenance ÷ 30 machines).

 PROBLEM Given the above calculation, how much maintenance should be allocated to each cost center?

ANSWER The amount of maintenance allocated to each cost center is calculated as follows:

Cost Center	No. of Machines	×	Rate	=	Allocation
Administration	2	×	$1,000	=	$2,000
Mowing	17	×	$1,000	=	17,000
Special projects	11	×	$1,000	=	11,000
Total	30				$30,000

There are two items of importance here. First, it is possible to allocate maintenance only to production centers, not to other service centers.

Alternatively, maintenance could be allocated to other service centers (as has been done here with the administration cost center) as well as to the production centers. This approach, known as the *sequential* or *stepdown* allocation method, is discussed more fully in the next section. Second, although maintenance is a service center, it has not been allocated to itself; that is, we do not calculate the cost of maintaining any machines in the maintenance department. (Therefore, we do not need to know the number of machines in that department.)

We will defer the allocation of the administration cost center until we have discussed a few other matters concerning the allocation rate and have looked at Decision 5 (selecting an allocation method).

Determining the Allocation Rate.   As the above example suggests, the following formula can be used to determine the allocation rate:

Allocation rate = total costs in the service center to be allocated ÷ total units of allocation basis in *receiving* cost centers

The important point here is that the denominator of the formula does not include the units of the allocation basis in the cost center from which the allocation is taking place. In the stepdown method, it also does not include any units from cost centers that already have been allocated. It includes only the units in *receiving* cost centers. The reason for this will become clear in the next few examples.

Precision of Allocation Bases.   In the context of deciding on allocation bases, it should be noted that increased precision generally requires greater measurement efforts and hence higher accounting costs. For example, rather than using number of machines to allocate maintenance costs, those costs could be allocated on the basis of hours of maintenance provided to the receiving cost centers. Clearly, while hours of service is a more accurate basis and would provide a more accurate cost figure, its use requires an ongoing, and possibly costly, compilation of the necessary data.

A decision to use the more accurate basis depends largely on senior management's planned uses for the information. In some instances, the information can enhance profitability assessments; in others, it may improve pricing decisions; in still others, it may influence the motivation of people responsible for managing the cost centers. These types of considerations will determine whether senior management wishes to use more accurate (and generally more costly) allocation bases.

In summary, the more precise the distribution and allocation processes are, the more accurately one captures true resource consumption.

Exact measurement of resource consumption can be a time-consuming and complicated process, however, and less accurate approaches occasionally are adopted in response to time, staffing, and technical constraints. For example, a typical basis of allocation for some service centers is square feet of floor space. Computation of square footage for all cost centers is a one-time activity. Once it has been completed, a service center's costs can be allocated easily. By contrast, the hours-of-service method generally requires regular measurement of the number of units of the allocation basis. The square footage allocation basis can lead to over- or underrepresentation of the actual use of a service center's services, however, whereas the hours-of-service basis presumably would not have this problem. As with many other full-cost accounting decisions, if senior management is to use the information, it needs to make this choice. It should be informed by the accounting staff of the options and trade-offs, but the decision should not be delegated to the accounting staff.

Decision 5: Selecting an Allocation Method

Three methods of varying complexity and accuracy are available for allocating service center costs to production centers: the *direct allocation, stepdown,* and *reciprocal* methods.

1. *The direct allocation method,* which was mentioned briefly above, allocates service center costs to production centers only, not to other service centers. This is the simplest method of the three and is used by many companies. It is the least precise of the three methods, however, since it does not include the cost effects associated with one service center's use of another service center.

2. *The stepdown method* sequentially "trickles down" service center costs into other service centers and production centers. This stepping-down process begins with the first service center in the sequence and spreads its costs over the remaining service centers and production centers. The distribution is based on each receiving center's use of the service center's resources as determined by the chosen allocation basis. This process is followed for all the remaining service centers.

   Because it allocates service center costs to other service centers as well as to production centers, the stepdown method is more complicated than the direct method, but it is also more precise in that it includes the cost effects associated with one service center's use of another. However, once a service center's costs have been allocated, it cannot receive an allocation; thus, for each service center, the stepdown method includes only the cost effects of its use of the service centers that precede it in the sequence, not their use of its services.

3. *The reciprocal method* is the most complex technique; in it, all service centers both make and receive allocations to and from each other. The allocation amounts are determined by a set of simultaneous equations. Because all service centers can both make and receive allocations, the reciprocal method is the most accurate of the three.

An example of the reciprocal method is contained in Appendix A. As this appendix demonstrates, because of the simultaneous equations, even when only two service centers are used, this method is very complex. When the number of service centers (and hence simultaneous equations) exceeds three, a person has considerable difficulty using the method. It is relatively easy to use, however, when a computer solves the equations. Because of the reciprocal method's precision and the increasing prevalence of computers, the reciprocal method is preferred by the Cost Accounting Standards Board (CASB). Nevertheless, many organizations find that the stepdown method strikes the right balance between accuracy and ease of use. We thus will use it here for illustrative purposes.

Choosing a Service Center Sequence. When the stepdown method is used, the sequence followed in allocating the service centers can have an impact on the costs in each production center. The sequence will not affect total costs, however, which will remain the same under all sequences ($200,000 for Lawncare, Inc.). However, the effect of the sequence decision on a particular production center occasionally is significant, and it therefore should be considered carefully.

In general, the approach to choosing a sequence is to allocate service centers in order of their use by other service centers. That is, the service center that uses other service centers the *least* is allocated *first*, and the service center that uses other service centers the *most* is allocated *last*. Clearly, considerable judgment is required to determine this sequence.

 PROBLEM What judgment has management at LI made through its decision to allocate the maintenance cost center before the administration cost center? Is a similar judgment involved in choosing the sequence of production centers? Why or why not?

ANSWER Management's judgment apparently is that the maintenance department uses the administration department less than the administration department uses the maintenance department. We thus will learn about the cost of maintaining the machines in the administration department but not the cost of administering the activities of the maintenance department. With regard to production centers, since there is no allocation *out of* production centers, their sequence is unimportant.

Allocating Administration Costs at Lawncare, Inc.   We
have not yet allocated the costs of the administration cost center at LI to the remaining cost centers. Doing so will allow us to see how the step-down method works.

As with the maintenance center, the first step in allocating the administration center's costs is to choose an allocation basis. Several alternative bases could be used, such as number of personnel or salary dollars. Assume the company decides to use salary dollars, presumably reasoning that there is a causal relationship between increases in salary dollars in a cost center and increases in the use of the administration resource by that cost center. Also assume that the following information is available:

Cost Center	Initial Salary Costs	With Supervisor Distribution
Maintenance	$20,000	$25,000*
Administration	40,000	35,000†
Mowing	50,000	50,000
Special projects	35,000	35,000
Total	$145,000	$145,000

* $5,000 added for supervisor.
† $5,000 deducted for supervisor.

Allocating administration is somewhat more complicated than it was for maintenance because total costs in administration were increased by the amount allocated to it from maintenance. When we include the maintenance allocation, the total costs in administration become $51,425, calculated as follows:

Direct plus distributed indirect costs ($54,425 − $5,000 for supervisor) $49,425
Maintenance allocation   2,000
Total costs to be allocated $51,425

You may wish to return to the data on previous pages to verify the sources of these figures.

 PROBLEM   Since the administration costs must be allocated to the remaining cost centers (mowing and special projects) and since the basis of allocation is salary dollars, it is necessary to determine the allocation rate, that is, administration dollars per salary dollar. What is the allocation rate? Careful, this is a little tricky.

ANSWER:

Total costs to be allocated =	$51,425
Total salary dollars in receiving cost centers =	$85,000
($50,000 in mowing + $35,000 in Special Projects)	
Allocation rate =	$0.605 per salary $

Note that, as discussed above, the denominator for the rate calculation has used only the salary dollars in the two *receiving* cost centers, that is, the cost centers to which the administration costs are to be allocated. We have not included the salary dollars for either the maintenance or the administration cost centers in the denominator of the computation.

We cannot use salary dollars from the maintenance cost center since maintenance costs already have been allocated, and with the stepdown method, once a cost center's costs have been allocated, that cost center cannot receive allocations from other cost centers. This is why the *sequence* of service center allocations is an important consideration in the stepdown approach. (This problem is avoided with the *reciprocal* approach.)

We cannot use salary dollars from the administration cost center, since doing that would result in an inability to fully allocate all of the administration costs. The reason for this may be unclear at the moment; it will be clarified once we have allocated the costs of the administration cost center.

 PROBLEM   Use the above allocation rate to allocate administrative service costs to the remaining cost centers.

ANSWER   The allocation of the administration service center costs now can be carried out as follows:

Receiving Cost Center	Salary Dollars	×	Rate	=	Allocation
Mowing	$50,000	×	$0.605	=	$30,250
Special projects	35,000	×	$0.605	=	21,175
Total	$85,000				$51,425

Note that the full $51,425 has been allocated to mowing and special projects. Also note that if we had included the salary costs in administration in determining the allocation rate, we would not have allocated the full $51,425 of administration costs.

Final Step.   The final step in this stage of the cost accounting effort is to determine the cost of each production center, as follows:

Production Center	Direct Cost	Allocated Costs		Total Cost
		Maintenance	Administration	
Mowing	73,575	17,000	30,250	$120,825
Special Projects	47,000	11,000	21,175	79,175
Total				$200,000

Note that the *total* costs of $200,000 are unchanged. However, we now have fully allocated the service center costs (maintenance and administration) to the two production centers. We did this by first allocating the maintenance service center costs to the administration service center as well as to the two production centers and then allocating the administration service center costs (with its maintenance allocation included) to the two production centers.

Summary of the Allocation Process.   In summary, the total costs in a production center are the sum of (1) its direct costs, (2) any indirect costs distributed to it, and (3) the costs allocated to it from the service centers. Exhibit 1-2 shows this process schematically, using the service and production centers at Lawncare, Inc. Spend a few minutes reviewing this exhibit and relating it to the discussion that follows so that you can see how it works. The stepdown method is a little tricky, so be sure to spend enough time to make sure you understand all the elements.

The process used to prepare Exhibit 1-2 begins with the total of direct and distributed costs in the maintenance department. This amount of $30,000 is located in the *row* labeled "Maintenance." The *allocated* maintenance costs are shown in the *column* labeled "Maintenance" (a dotted-line box), with the $30,000 total at the bottom. As this column shows, the $30,000 has been allocated to the administration service center and the two production centers.

The use of number of machines as the basis of allocation for maintenance is shown by including the term *machines* in parentheses at the top of the "Maintenance" column.

With the allocation of the maintenance costs, the administration service center now has a total of $51,425 to be allocated, that is, its $49,425 of direct plus distributed costs *plus* the $2000 of maintenance that was allocated to it. These amounts are shown in the heavily outlined box in the "Administration" row (the sum of the two amounts is not shown). Administration costs are allocated by using salary dollars (shown in parentheses at the top of the "Administration" *column*), and the dotted-line box shows the allocation of the $51,425 to the remaining cost centers: the two production centers in this case. The total amount allocated is shown at the bottom of the column.

EXHIBIT 1-2

The Stepdown Procedure

Cost Centers	Direct plus Assigned Costs	Maintenance (Machines)	Administration§ (Salary $)	Total Costs
Service centers				
Maintenance	30,000			
Administration	49,425	2,000*		
Production centers				
Mowing	73,575	17,000†	30,250#	120,825
Special projects	47,000	11,000‡	21,175**	79,175
Total costs	200,000	30,000	51,425	200,000

* $1000 per machine × 2 machines = $2000
† $1000 per machine × 17 machines = $17,000
‡ $1000 per machine × 11 machines = $11,000
§ Administration costs = $51,425 ($49,425 + $2000);
  administration costs per salary dollar = $0.605 ($51,425 ÷ $85,000)
$0.605 per salary dollar × $50,000 salary dollars = $30,250
** $0.605 per salary dollar × $35,000 salary dollars = $21,175

In summary, the total costs in an organization's production centers are determined by a combination of their direct and distributed costs, plus the costs allocated to them from the service centers. The stepdown method shown in Exhibit 1-2 is the formal technique used to carry out this process.

Key Aspects of the Stepdown Method There are several important points to keep in mind in carrying out an allocation effort using the stepdown method:

1. Only service center costs are allocated. Production centers receive costs from service centers, but once a cost has been allocated to a production center, it stays there.

2. With the stepdown process, a *basis of allocation* is chosen for each service center that attempts to measure its use by the other cost centers—both service and production. For example, an organization that has a laundry (such as a hospital or a hotel) frequently

uses "pounds of laundry" as the basis for allocating the laundry service center. Each cost center thus receives a portion of the laundry costs in accordance with its proportion of the total pounds of laundry processed. If a particular cost center used no pounds of laundry, it would not receive any allocation from the laundry service center.

3. The amount of a service center's costs allocated to a specific production center depends in part on whether that service center is allocated early or late in the sequence. If it is allocated late in the sequence, it will be "loaded" with some costs from service cost centers above it. If it is allocated early, it will not.

4. Total costs do not change. All that changes with different allocation bases and stepdown sequences is the distribution of total costs among the production centers.

Decision 6: Attaching Costs to Cost Objects

A final decision in a full-cost accounting system concerns the way production center costs are "attached" to an organization's cost objects. Although there is a range of choices, we will look only at the two ends of the spectrum. At one end is the *process system*, which typically is used when all units of output are roughly identical. The production of chairs, plastic cups, gallons of gasoline, and so on—activities often performed by a production line—usually calls for a process system of cost accounting. All production-related costs for a particular accounting period are calculated and then divided by the total number of units produced to give an average cost per unit.

At the other end of the spectrum is the *job order system*, which typically is used when there are heterogeneous units of output. In an automobile repair garage, for example, adding the costs for a day and dividing by the number of cars repaired would give an average cost per repaired car. However, this procedure would provide very misleading cost information. Instead, the cost accounting system uses a job ticket to record the time and parts associated with each car repaired and then computes the cost per repaired car by means of hourly wage rates, unit prices, and so on.

Job order and process systems are discussed in greater detail in Chapter 4 and are treated at length in most cost accounting textbooks. In both systems there is a need for one or more *overhead rates*, which can be quite tricky to compute and use but are needed to attach overhead costs to each product passing through the center.

EFFECT OF THE METHODOLOGY ON PRICING DECISIONS

Since the cost accounting decisions discussed in the previous section have an impact on costs, they frequently affect pricing decisions as well. This is especially true in situations where prices are based almost exclusively on full costs.

Of all the decisions discussed in the previous section, the two that typically require the most judgment from senior management are the definition of a cost object and the determination of cost centers. The distribution of indirect costs is largely a matter for the accounting staff. The choice of allocation bases and the selection of an allocation method require some involvement by senior management, but largely with regard to the balance between the precision a particular basis or method provides and the cost of using it. This is an important decision since some bases require a costly compilation of data and some methods are more costly to operate than others are.

Defining an organization's cost object requires senior management's judgment about how a given cost object fits with its pricing policies. In LI's case, the *final* cost object probably is a job, since this is how most customers think about LI's work. However, senior management also will be interested in the cost per hour: its intermediate cost object. This amount depends to a great extent on senior management's choice of cost centers

 PROBLEM LI currently bills its customers on the basis of the number of hours spent on a job. How would its hourly rate differ between the one-cost-center and multi-cost-center approaches? (Recall that LI spent 11,772 hours in mowing and 3,853 hours in special projects.)

ANSWER If the company used one cost center, it would calculate its hourly cost as follows:

Total costs	$200,000
Total hours	15,625
Average cost per hour	12.80 ($200,000 ÷ 15,625)

If, however, the company decided to use multiple cost centers, it would have different rates for mowing and special projects. Its cost per hour for each would look as follows:

Activity	Total Cost	Number of Hours	Cost per Hour
Mowing	$120,825	11,772	$10.26
Special projects	$79,175	3,853	$20.55

Cost Homogeneity as a Goal in Choosing Cost Centers.

The potential use of the multiple-cost-center approach raises the issue of the most appropriate number and kind of cost centers. So far we have focused most of our attention on the *impact* of one versus several cost centers and have addressed only briefly the criteria for choosing the most appropriate cost center structure.

As was discussed earlier, the main objective in choosing cost centers is to organize costs into homogeneous collections of activities. When this happens in a service center and when an appropriate allocation basis has been chosen, we can be fairly certain that the portion of the service center's costs that is allocated to each other cost center is a fair measure of the use of the service center.

Similarly, with homogeneous activities in a production center, the production center costs that are attached to a product passing through that center depend completely on the *amount of time* the product spent in the cost center, not on *what happened* to the product while it was in the cost center. That is, if the cost center consists of homogeneous activities, the same activities will take place for every product; the only difference will be the length of time during which they take place.

As an example, consider the photocopying company discussed earlier in this chapter, where there were two photocopying machines: a simple one and a sophisticated one. If senior management sets up each machine as a separate cost center, the cost of a job will depend on (1) the rate for the machine that is used and (2) the amount of time the machine is used. The cost thus will come close to the true consumption of resources. If, in contrast, senior management uses one cost center, the cost will be based on an average rate for the two machines. It will overstate the true cost of using the simple machine and understate the true cost of using the sophisticated one.

Unfortunately, resource and time constraints sometimes make it necessary to group heterogeneous activities into a cost center. When this happens, the costs that are allocated to a receiving cost center or attached to a product will not be solely a function of the allocation basis or the time that product spends in a particular cost center. They also will depend on the nature of the activities that take place while the product is in the cost center.

 PROBLEM What additional information would you like to have about the maintenance cost center at LI to determine whether it is appropriately structured as a single cost center or if it should be divided into two or more cost centers?

ANSWER We would like to know what sorts of activities take place in the Maintenance cost center and whether there are different kinds of maintenance that would influence the costs allocated to Administration, Mowing, and Special Projects. For example, we would like to know if mowing machines require special equipment for maintenance that is not used for maintaining equipment in administration or special projects. If this is the case, we probably need two cost centers: one for special equipment maintenance and one for general maintenance.

 PROBLEM Assume we create the two maintenance cost centers suggested above. What might we use as the allocation bases? What additional information would have to be collected as a result?

ANSWER We probably still could use the number of pieces of equipment in a receiving cost center, but we now would want to determine which equipment used which maintenance cost center. Thus, the costs of the special equipment maintenance center would be allocated on the basis of the number of machines in the receiving cost centers that require special maintenance. The costs of the general maintenance center would be allocated on the basis of all the other machines in a receiving cost center. Of course, there would be complications if certain pieces of equipment required both general and special maintenance.

Impact on Customer Prices. Information structured into multiple cost centers can be extremely useful for pricing purposes. If we assume for the moment that LI's management wants a 10 percent markup over costs when pricing its services, the multi-cost-center approach will give a very different pricing structure than will the single-cost-center approach.

 PROBLEM A customer has asked Lawncare, Inc., for a bid on mowing his lawn, which the manager estimates will require 3 hours. Another customer has asked the company for a bid on fertilizing and weeding her lawn, which the manager estimates also will require 3 hours. LI uses a 10 percent markup over cost as its price. How would the prices LI proposes to these customers differ between the one-cost-center and multi-cost-center approaches?

ANSWER Under the one-cost-center approach, the price per hour for either mowing or special projects would be the cost plus 10 percent, or $14.08 ($12.80 + $1.28). Under the multi-cost-center approach, the price per hour would differ for mowing and special projects. Mowing's price would be $11.29 ($10.26 + $1.03), and the price for special projects would be $22.61 ($20.55 + $2.06). Thus, the cost-based prices proposed to the customers for the two jobs would be as follows:

One Cost Center

Lawn mowing	3 hours @ $14.08 = $42.24
Fertilizing and weeding	3 hours @ $14.08 = $42.24

Multiple Cost Centers

Lawn mowing	3 hours @ $11.29 = $33.87
Fertilizing and weeding	3 hours @ $20.55 = $67.81

Note that with the one-cost-center approach, the prices are identical for a 3-hour job, whereas with multiple cost centers, the fertilizing and weeding price is some 60 percent above the one-cost-center price and the lawn mowing job is about 20 percent below that price. If we assume that the multi-cost-center approach provides a more homogeneous collection of activities in each cost center, the cost on which the price is based comes closer to the true consumption of resources needed for each job. As a result, the multi-cost-center approach helps eliminate the cross subsidization that takes place in the one-cost-center approach.

SUMMARY

As the discussion in this chapter has indicated, the managerial choices involved in developing a cost accounting system can be difficult. Moreover, they are highly interdependent. The choice of cost centers will influence the distinction between direct and indirect costs. The choice of a particular final cost object frequently will require the use of certain intermediate cost objects or call for certain kinds of cost centers. Allocation of service center costs will be determined in part by the choice of the service centers themselves and by the allocation method used, and so on.

In this context, it is important to emphasize that any change to the cost of one cost center always is accompanied by changes in another direction to other cost centers. That is, once total costs have been incurred, they do not change. Hence, they will be the same on any cost report. The effect of any change in methodology is solely a matter of making shifts among cost centers. Sometimes these cost shifts can be quite significant, however, as we saw in the Lawncare, Inc., situation.

In addition, it is important to note that this chapter has focused on direct and indirect costs and on the allocation of service center costs into production centers. This way of viewing costs has some limitations. Specifically, whether a cost is direct or indirect says little about its actual behavior as the volume of activity in a production center increases or decreases. For this reason, full cost information is not especially useful for making certain kinds of decisions called "alternative choice decisions." The costs appropriate for these decisions are discussed in the next two chapters.

In addition, this chapter has covered only what is called "the first stage" of the cost accounting effort. In this stage one defines cost centers and allocates service center costs into production centers. In the "second stage" of the cost accounting effort production center costs must be attached to the products passing through those centers so that each product's full cost is known. We did this in a minor way with Lawncare, Inc.

However, in a manufacturing setting this activity becomes considerably more tricky, as will be shown in Chapters 4 and 5.

NOTES

1. For a discussion of the sorts of issues that an organization must consider, see David W. Young, "Cost Accounting and Cost Comparisons: Methodological Issues and Their Policy and Management Implications," *Accounting Horizons,* Volume 2, Number 1 (March 1988).

2. Robert N. Anthony and David W. Young, *Management Control in Nonprofit Organizations,* 7th ed. Burr Ridge, IL, Irwin/McGraw Hill, 2003.

CHAPTER 2

Cost Behavior

One of the most significant aspects of cost accounting is the notion that *different costs are used for different purposes.* Although the full-cost accounting principles discussed in Chapter 1 are potentially valuable for activities such as pricing, profitability analysis, and cost comparisons, they have some important limitations. Specifically, they do not address how costs vary with changes in volume or changes in other factors, such as time. However, information on cost behavior is an important ingredient in several types of decisions that managers make on a regular basis. As this chapter explains, using full cost information as a basis for deciding how costs will change under different decision-making scenarios can lead managers to make decisions that are financially detrimental to their organizations. Cost behavior must be assessed in a very different way.

This chapter first addresses the nature of costs. Once these terms and concepts have been defined, we take up the subject of cost-volume-profit (CVP) analysis. We look at CVP analysis (sometimes called *breakeven* analysis) in its most basic form and then examine a variety of special considerations that can complicate it. The chapter concludes with a discussion of the concept of contribution.

THE NATURE OF COSTS

Chapter 1 identified the distinction between direct and indirect costs and between production and service center costs, but costs also can be assessed in terms of whether they are fixed or variable. In general, the fixed/variable distinction shows more clearly how a change in the volume of activity of a cost center will affect its costs. To understand this idea fully, we also need to include the refinements of semivariable and step-function costs. The four types of costs are shown in Exhibit 2-1. A discussion of each one follows.

1. *Fixed costs* are independent of the number of units produced. Although no cost is fixed if the time period is long enough, the *relevant range* for fixed costs (i.e., the span of units over which they remain unchanged) or the time period within which they are considered generally is large, and so they can be viewed graphically as shown in Exhibit 2-1*a*.

    A good example of a fixed cost is rent. Regardless of the number of units produced or other volume of activity, the amount of rent a company pays will remain the same. Of course, when the relevant range is exceeded because the company has grown so large that it needs to rent new facilities, even this cost will increase.

2. *Step-function costs* are similar to fixed costs except that they have a much narrower relevant range. Therefore, they do not change in a smooth fashion but are added in "lumps," or "steps." The result is that graphically they take the form shown in Exhibit 2-1*b*, where the broken lines represent discontinuous jumps.

EXHIBIT 2-1

Types of Cost Behavior

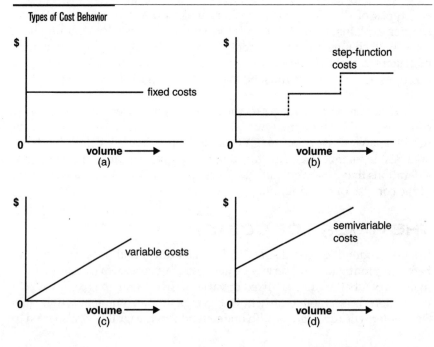

A good example of a step-function cost is supervision. As the number of workers increases, supervisory personnel must be added. Since it is difficult for most organizations to add part-time supervisory help, supervisory costs tend to behave in a step-function fashion.

3. Variable costs, which are shown in Exhibit 2-1c, behave in a roughly linear fashion in accordance with changes in volume such that as volume increases, total variable costs increase in a constant proportion. The line's slope (height of vertical rise per horizontal unit) is determined by the amount of variable costs associated with each unit of output.

An example of variable costs in many manufacturing organizations is raw materials, which increase in almost direct proportion to increases in manufacturing output. Some organizations have relatively high variable costs per unit, resulting in a line that slopes upward quite steeply; other organizations have variable costs that are relatively low for each unit of output, resulting in a more gradual slope.

4. *Semivariable costs* (sometimes called *mixed* or *semifixed* costs) share features of both fixed and variable costs. There is a minimum level of costs that is fixed, but the cost line then rises with increases in volume. The result, as shown in Exhibit 2-1d, is a line that begins at some level above zero and slopes upward.

An example of a semivariable cost is electricity. Typically, an organization incurs a base cost for electricity even if it uses no electricity at all. Costs then increase in a linear fashion in accordance with the level of usage. Similar cost patterns exist for other utilities as well, such as telephone service.

Estimating Cost-Volume Relationships

In working with cost information, it sometimes is difficult to separate fixed costs from variable costs, especially when a cost is semivariable in nature. To make the separation, one needs at least two historical or projected data points, preferably more. With these two points, it is possible to draw a straight line and determine where it intersects the vertical axis. One then can use algebra to determine both the line's slope and its fixed-cost component.

As an example, suppose a company used 10,000 kilowatt-hours of electricity in June and 12,000 kilowatt-hours in July. The June electric bill was $1500; the July bill was $1700. To compute the fixed and variable components of the cost line, take the following steps:

1. Begin with the total cost formula: total cost = fixed costs + variable costs/unit × volume, or $TC = a + bx$, where a is the fixed cost component and b is variable costs per unit.

2. Apply the formula to June as follows: $\$1,500 = a + b \ (10,000)$; $a = \$1,500 - 10,000b$.

3. Then apply the formula to July as follows: $\$1,700 = a + b \ (12,000)$.

4. Substitute from the June equation as follows: $\$1,700 = (\$1,500 - 10,000b) + 12,000b$.

5. This permits us to solve for b as follows: $\$200 = 2,000b$; $b = \$0.10$.

6. We then can solve for a: $a = \$1,500 - 10,000 \ (\$0.10) = \$500$.

7. The total cost formula therefore is $TC = \$500 + \$0.10 \times$ kilowatt-hours.

8. We can test this with July: $TC = \$500 + \$0.10 \ (12,000) = \$1,700$.

Other Techniques.   When there are more than two data points, one can plot them on a graph, fit a straight line to them, and determine where the line intersects the vertical axis (its fixed cost component). It then is possible to compute its slope as we did above. Alternatively, one can use a statistical technique called *least squares* to fit the points to a line rather than doing this manually.

When the least squares method is used, it is important to eliminate outliers so that the fit will reflect the general experience. This, of course, raises the question of what constitutes an outlier. Because of this complexity, many analysts prefer the manual method, reasoning that when outliers are introduced, the precision of the least squares technique is compromised.

 PROBLEM   The cafeteria at First National Bank has the following information for the last 3 months.

	December	January	February
Number of meals served	3,000	5,000	8,000
Cost of food sold	$18,000	$30,000	$48,000
Staff salaries and fringe benefits	14,500	16,500	19,500
Rent and depreciation	4,000	4,000	4,000
Utilities and other	2,100	3,300	5,100
Total	$38,600	$53,800	$76,600

In March the cafeteria expects to serve 10,000 meals.

Develop a cost equation for the cafeteria's monthly costs and use it to predict costs for March.

ANSWER   A cost equation requires us to analyze each cost for its fixed and/or variable components. The results are shown below, followed by the calculations for each item.

Cost of food sold	Variable	$6 per meal
Salaries and fringe benefits	Semi-variable	$11,500 + $1 per meal
Rent and depreciation	Fixed	$4,000 per month
Utilities and other	Semi-variable	$300 + $.60 per meal

1. *Cost of food sold:* This calculation is relatively easy. For each month it is the total divided by the number of meals. For example, in December it is $18,000 ÷ 3,000 = $6.00 per meal.

2. *Salaries and fringe benefits:* This calculation requires two equations and two unknowns:

   - Begin with the total cost formula: $TC = a + bx$.
   - Apply it to December as follows: $14,500 = a + b$ (3,000); $a = 14,500 - 3,000b$.
   - Then apply it to January as follows: $16,500 = a + b$ (5,000).
   - Substitute from the December equation as follows: $16,500 = (14,500 - 3,000b) + 5,000b$.
   - This permits us to solve for b as follows: $2,000 = 2,000b$; $b = 1.
   - We can then solve for a: $a = 14,500 - 3,000 (1) = $11,500$.

3. *Rent and depreciation:* This is a flat $4000 per month.

4. *Utilities and Other:* This requires following the same approach used for salaries and fringe benefits:

$$TC = a + bx; 2,100 = a + b (3,000); a = 2,100 - 3,000b$$
$$3,300 = a + b (5,000); 3,300 = (2,100 - 3,000b) + 5,000b$$
$$1,200 = 2,000b; b = $0.60$$
$$a = 2,100 - 3,000(0.60) \, a = $300$$

The cost equation is the sum of all the individual elements, or

$$TC = (11,500 + 4,000 + 300) + (6.00 + 1.00 + 0.60)x$$
$$TC = 15,800 + 7.60x$$

Costs in March would be predicted as 15,800 + 7.60 (10,000), or $91,800.

Relation of Cost Behavior to Full Cost Accounting

The analysis of differential costs would be simplified if, as is assumed occasionally, all service center costs were fixed and all production center costs were variable. Unfortunately, this is almost never the case. Exhibit 2-2 shows four different cost types and their fixed versus variable and production center versus service center distinctions. The example refers to the costs of Lawncare, Inc., from Chapter 1.

EXHIBIT 2-2

Fixed and Variable Costs versus Production and Service

	Fixed	Variable
Production Center Costs	Supervisor's salary in the mowing production center	Gasoline costs for operating the lawn mowers in the mowing production center
Service Center Costs	Portion of chief executive officer's salary (which is a cost of administration that is allocated to the mowing production center)	Lubricant costs for maintaining the lawn mowers (which are costs of maintenance that are allocated to the mowing production center)

In reviewing this exhibit, keep in mind that terms can vary. As was discussed in Chapter 1, "service center costs" sometimes are called "indirect" or "overhead" costs. In general, the context will make the meaning clear.

Cost Behavior in Organizations

Generally, an organization's costs can be classified as fixed, step-function, variable, or semivariable. Doing this requires an analysis of the actual or expected behavior of each cost item in the organization and a prediction of how it will change with changes in the volume of activity.

 PROBLEM   The Hawthorne Hair Salon currently provides 2000 haircuts each month. At this level of activity it incurs, among others, the following costs:

Barbers	$11,000
Hair supplies (e.g., shampoo)	4,000
Other supplies (e.g., aprons)	2,000
Utilities	1,000
Rent	3,000
Total	$21,000

Classify each cost into one of the four categories shown in Exhibit 2-1.

ANSWER   Barbers are probably step-function costs: They will remain fixed until the number of haircuts increases by a fairly sizable number. Hair supplies, by contrast, are variable costs: They will change in direct proportion to a change in the number of haircuts. Other supplies are a little tricky, but since they probably vary with the number of personnel, they could be thought of as step-function costs.

Utilities most likely are semivariable costs; the center probably pays a fixed amount each month with a variable component based on usage. Usage probably is proportional to the number of hours the salon is open, which is related somewhat to the number of haircuts.

Rent probably is fixed (although with some ceiling on the number of haircuts; once they reach a certain level, the salon will need to rent a larger facility).

Cost Behavior as an Organization Grows

One reason for undertaking the type of cost analysis discussed above is that it helps managers assess what will happen to costs as the organization grows and be better able to manage growth as a result. Once managers have determined that certain costs are variable, for example, they can assume that the costs will grow in a linear fashion as volume grows. In contrast, both fixed and step-function costs will not grow linearly. Since revenue tends to grow in a linear fashion and to increase more steeply (one hopes) than do variable costs, growth should allow the company to increase its profits.

 PROBLEM   Hawthorne Hair Salon incurred the costs shown above in delivering 2000 haircuts. Management also has determined the following: (1) There currently are five barbers, each of whom can provide 20 haircuts a day, or 400 haircuts a month (the salon hires only full-time barbers, and each one works a 20-day month), (2) hair supplies are variable costs, (3) other supplies will increase to $3000 when the number of haircuts reaches 5000 and to $4000 when the number of haircuts reaches 10,000, (4) utilities are semivariable costs with a fixed component of $600 a month regardless of the number of haircuts, and (5) rent remains at $3000 as long as the number of haircuts does not exceed 10,000.

What will the salon's costs be for these five items at 5000 haircuts? At 10,000 haircuts?

ANALYSIS   Let us look at each cost item separately.

- *Barbers:* At the moment there are five barbers (2000 haircuts ÷ 400), who have a total cost of $11,000. Therefore, the cost per barber averages $2200 per month ($11,000 ÷ 5 barbers). A barber can deliver 400 haircuts a month. That means that every time we increase the number of haircuts by 400, we must add a barber. Therefore, at 5000 haircuts per month, we will need 12.5 barbers (5000 ÷ 400), but since we cannot add a half barber, we must have 13 barbers for 5000 haircuts. You may have decided to "stretch" your 12 barbers or to use a part-time barber and not hire the thirteenth barber until total haircuts reach 5200 (13 × 400). That's a very reasonable approach. If you take the "stretch" approach, the barber cost for 5000 haircuts will be $26,400 (12 × $2,200). That is the nature of a step-function cost. By using similar reasoning, we can conclude that for 10,000 haircuts we will need 25 barbers; this time there are no fractions of a barber. Thus, at 5000 haircuts (with 13 barbers), the barber cost will be $28,600 (13 × $2200), and at 10,000 haircuts (25 barbers) that cost will be $55,000 (25 × $2200).

■ *Hair supplies:* Using the baseline information, we can see that hair supplies must increase at a rate of $2.00 per haircut. That is, since we incurred $4000 in costs with 2000 haircuts and since the cost is variable, the variable cost rate must be $4000 ÷ 2000 haircuts. This means that at 5000 haircuts the cost will be $10,000 (5,000 × $2.00) and that at 10,000 haircuts the cost will be $20,000 (10,000 × $2.00).

■ *Other supplies:* These were given as $3000 and $4000, respectively.

■ *Utility costs:* Since utility costs are semivariable, they have both a fixed component and a variable component. We were told that the fixed component is $600. Since utility costs totaled $1000 at 2000 haircuts, the variable component must be $400 ($1000 − $600). Therefore, these costs must increase at a rate of $0.20 per haircut ($400 ÷ 2000 haircuts). Alternatively, we could use the following formula: [(total costs at volume x − fixed component) ÷ x]. In this case: [($1000 − $600) ÷ 2000] = $0.20. Given this, the utility costs at 5000 haircuts will be $1600 ($600 + [5000 × 0.20]). At 10,000 haircuts, they will be $2600 ($600 + [10,000 × 0.20]).

■ *Rent:* This was given as $3000 as long as we do not exceed 10,000 haircuts (although it's hard to imagine increasing the number of barbers from 5 to 25 without needing more space!).

To summarize, the cost figures at all three levels are as follows:

	2,000 Haircuts	5,000 Haircuts	10,000 Haircuts
Barbers	$11,000	$28,600	$55,000
Hair supplies	4,000	10,000	20,000
Other supplies	2,000	3,000	4,000
Utilities	1,000	1,600	2,600
Rent	3,000	3,000	3,000
Total	$21,000	$46,200	$84,600
Average cost per haircut	$10.50	$9.24	$8.46

The fact that the per-haircut cost declines as the number of haircuts increases is indicative that all costs do not increase in proportion to volume. As we have seen, several costs are fixed, have fixed components, or are step-function in nature.

COST-VOLUME-PROFIT ANALYSIS

The purpose of CVP analysis is to determine (1) the volume of activity needed for an organization to achieve its profit goal, (2) the price an organization needs to charge to achieve its profit goal, or (3) the cost limits (fixed and/or variable) to which an organization needs to adhere to achieve its profit goal.

CVP analyses usually are done for a particular activity within an organization, such as a product line or a program. A CVP analysis thus begins with the basic equation for profit:

$$\text{Profit} = \text{total revenue (TR)} - \text{total costs (TC)}$$

Total revenue for many activities is easy to calculate. If we assume that price is represented by the letter p and volume by the letter x, total revenue is price times volume, or

$$TR = px$$

Total costs are somewhat more complicated. CVP analysis requires recognition of the different types of cost behavior in an organization: fixed, step-function, variable, and semivariable. Let us begin with the simplest case, in which there are no step-function or semivariable costs. In this instance the formula would be quite simple:

$$\text{Total costs} = \text{fixed costs} + \text{variable costs}$$

As before, fixed costs are represented by the letter a and variable costs per unit are represented by the letter b. Thus, total variable costs is bx, where, as before, x represents volume. The resulting cost equation is the one given above:

$$TC = a + bx$$

This means that the fundamental profit equation can be shown as

$$\text{Profit} = px - (a + bx)$$

Graphically, we can represent the formula as shown in Exhibit 2-3.

Point $x1$, where $px = a + bx$, is the *breakeven volume;* it is the point at which total revenue, px, equals total costs, $a + bx$. With volume in excess of $x1$, the organization earns a profit; below $x1$, it incurs a loss.

To illustrate how this formula can be used, assume an organization wishes to determine its breakeven volume. If we know price, fixed costs, and variable costs per unit, we can solve the formula algebraically for x,

EXHIBIT 2-3

Profit $= px - (a + x)$.

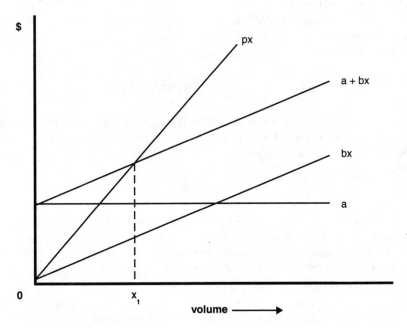

which would be the breakeven volume. Similarly, if we know any three of the four items in the equation, we can solve for the fourth.

PROBLEM Littleton News, Inc., publishes a monthly magazine for the town of Littleton. The company has fixed costs of $100,000 a month and variable costs per magazine of $0.80. It charges $1.80 per magazine. What is its breakeven volume (number of magazines per month)?

ANSWER We begin with the CVP formula and substitute the known elements. We then solve for the unknown, which in this case is volume, or x.

$$\text{Profit} = px - (a + bx)$$

At breakeven, profit $= 0$; therefore, $px = a + bx$, or

$$1.80x = 100,000 + 0.80x$$
$$1.00x = 100,000$$
$$x = 100,000$$

Breakeven is 100,000 magazines. To confirm:

Revenue: $1.80 × 100,000 =	$180,000
Less: costs:	
Variable: $0.80 × 100,000 =	80,000
Fixed:	100,000
Total	180,000
Profit	$ 0

Unit Contribution Margin

An important aspect of CVP analysis is the idea of the unit contribution margin: the contribution to fixed costs that comes about as a result of each additional unit sold. In effect, the unit contribution margin is the difference between price and unit variable cost. By rearranging the terms of the CVP formula, we can arrive at the conclusion that breakeven volume is simply fixed costs divided by the unit contribution margin, as follows:

$$px = a + bx$$
$$px - bx = a$$
$$x(p - b) = a$$
$$x = a \div (p - b)$$

In effect, price minus unit variable cost indicates how much each unit sold contributes to the recovery of fixed costs. Dividing this amount into fixed costs gives the volume needed to recover all the fixed costs: the breakeven volume.

To illustrate, Littleton News, Inc., has a unit contribution margin of $1.00 ($1.80 − $0.80). When this amount is divided into its fixed costs of $100,000, we arrive at its breakeven volume of 100,000 magazines.

Incorporating Other Variables into a CVP Analysis

Thus far we have been using CVP analysis to solve only for the breakeven volume. Clearly, if we knew how many units of the product we were likely to sell, fixed costs, and unit variable costs, we could determine the price needed to break even. Similarly, if we were in an environment where price was market-driven and we knew about how many units could be sold at that price, we could set up either fixed costs or unit variable costs as the unknown and solve for it.

Profit Considerations. We can incorporate the need for a profit into CVP analysis simply by adding the amount of desired profit to the fixed costs and then calculating a breakeven point with that new level of "fixed costs." Similarly, if we were planning to pay dividends or needed a margin of safety, we could incorporate those amounts into the so-called fixed cost figure.

SPECIAL CONSIDERATIONS IN COST-VOLUME-PROFIT ANALYSIS

There are a number of special considerations that can complicate a CVP analysis: the presence of semivariable costs, the behavior of step-function costs, and the existence of more than one product. Let's look at each of these separately.

CVP Analysis with Semivariable Costs

Incorporating semivariable costs into a CVP analysis is relatively easy. Since semivariable costs have fixed and variable components, one simply needs to add the fixed component to the fixed cost total and add the variable component to the existing unit variable cost.

 PROBLEM In addition to its other costs, Littleton News, Inc., has electricity costs that are $2000 a month regardless of usage, plus an additional amount per kilowatt-hour of use. Electricity usage is tied directly to the number of magazines produced. The company's accountants have determined that the rate is about $0.04 per magazine. What is the monthly breakeven volume (number of magazines)?

ANSWER Again, we begin with the basic formula, insert the known elements, and solve for the unknown:

$$px = a + bx$$
$$1.80x = (100,000 + 2,000) + (0.80x + 0.04x)$$
$$96x = 102,000$$
$$x = 106,250$$

Breakeven is 106,250 magazines.

CVP Analysis with Step-Function Costs

The introduction of step-function costs is a little tricky. Ideally, for any given relevant range, we would simply add the designated step-function costs to the fixed costs to yield the total applicable fixed costs for that range. We then could use the formula. Unfortunately, the process is not that simple, as the following problem illustrates.

PROBLEM Return to the first problem for Littleton News, Inc. (i.e., ignore the electricity costs). In addition to the $100,000 in fixed costs stipulated in that problem, Littleton has supervisory costs. These costs behave as follows:

Volume	Costs
0–50,000	$10,000
50,001–100,000	20,000
100,001–150,000	30,000
150,001–200,000	40,000

What is Littleton's breakeven volume?

ANSWER To solve the breakeven problem at the first level of fixed costs, use the following equation:

$$1.80x = (100,000 + 10,000) + 0.80x$$
$$1.00x = 110,000$$
$$x = 110,000$$

Unfortunately, while the breakeven volume is 110,000 magazines, the relevant range for the step-function costs was only 0 to 50,000 magazines. Thus, a breakeven greater than 50,000 magazines is invalid, and we must move to the next step on the step function, which yields the following result:

$$1.80x = (100,000 + 20,000) + 0.80x$$
$$1.00x = 120,000$$
$$x = 120,000$$

This solution is also invalid. Only when we get to the third level do we encounter a valid solution, as follows:

$$1.80x = (100,000 + 30,000) + 0.80x$$
$$1.00x = 130,000$$
$$x = 130,000$$

The conclusion that can be drawn from this analysis is that incorporating step-function costs into the CVP formula requires a trial-and-error process to arrive at the breakeven volume.

CVP Analysis with Multiple Products or Services

Thus far, we have made all the CVP calculations by using situations where there was only one product. When there are two or more products, the analysis becomes more complicated. Consider the following situation.

PROBLEM Quicky Legal Services, a firm of lawyers offering one-stop resolution of legal problems, has three types of cases: regular, hard, and extra hard. Annual fixed costs are $2,565,000. Other information is as follows:

	Regular	Hard	Extra Hard
Fee per case	$3,000	$4,000	$5,000
Variable costs	1,800	2,200	2,500
Unit contribution margin	$1,200	$1,800	$2,500
Cases served per year	1,000	400	600

What is the breakeven point for the law firm? Use your intuition to do the calculations.

ANSWER To determine breakeven under these circumstances, we must calculate a weighted average unit contribution margin and then divide it into fixed costs. The easiest way to calculate a weighted average unit contribution margin is to begin by calculating total contribution margin for all case types, as follows:

	Regular	Hard	Extra Hard	Total
Unit contribution margin	$1,200	$1,800	$2,500	
Cases per month	1,000	400	600	2,000
Total contribution	$1,200,000	$720,000	$1,500,000	$3,420,000

The weighted average unit contribution margin is calculated by dividing total contribution by total cases, as follows:

$$\$3,420,000 \div 2,000 = \$1,710$$

We now can calculate the breakeven point by dividing fixed costs by the weighted average unit contribution margin: $2,565,000 ÷ 1,710 = 1,500. Thus, we must have 1500 cases a year to break even.

The Impact of a Changing Product Mix.

One problem with the weighted average approach is that changing the product mix (case types in the example above) will change the breakeven point. It is relatively easy to observe this problem in the above example since changing the mix of cases (but keeping the total number of cases at 2000) will change the total contribution. This in turn will change the weighted average unit contribution margin. The result is that fixed costs will be divided by a different number than was the case before, resulting in a different breakeven figure.

To illustrate, assume the agency served 2000 cases during a year, but with the following mix:

Regular   500
Hard   200
Extra hard   1300

All the other cost and fee figures given above remained the same.

 PROBLEM   What is the breakeven point now? If the cost and price figures have remained the same, why has the breakeven point changed?

ANSWER   The computations are as follows:

	Regular	Hard	Extra Hard	Total
Contribution margin	$1200	$1800	$2500	
Cases per month	500	200	1,300	2,000
Total contribution	$600,000	$360,000	$3,250,000	$4,210,000

The weighted average unit contribution margin now is $2105, calculated as follows:

$$\$4,210,000 \div 2,000 = \$2,105$$

Breakeven now is $2,565,000 ÷ $2,105 = 1,219 cases (rounded).

The breakeven number of cases has changed because the mix of cases has changed. This will happen any time an organization's products have different individual unit contribution margins. In this case, the mix of products has changed to more higher unit contribution margin cases. Other things being equal, a higher unit contribution margin means a lower breakeven point. That is why the breakeven point has fallen (from 1500 cases to 1219 cases) with the change in the mix of cases.

An important conclusion to be drawn here is that a breakeven figure with multiple products or services can be very unstable: As the mix changes, so will the breakeven figure. It is important to bear in mind, however, that an unstable breakeven figure comes about only when the individual contribution margins diverge. If they are roughly similar, changes in mix, even if they are large, will have a relatively small impact on breakeven.

Because of this instability, CVP analysis tends to be used relatively rarely on an ongoing basis in companies with multiple products. It is used frequently, however, in conjunction with an analysis of the possible introduction of a new product. Indeed, it is an essential aspect of a good marketing analysis for a new product.

TOTAL CONTRIBUTION

On an ongoing basis, managers tend to be much more interested in each product's *total contribution* to the company's overhead costs, that is, the unit contribution margin multiplied by the product's actual or anticipated volume.

To understand how this works, consider the situation in a hypothetical company, Clearwater Taxi Service. Clearwater operates just one taxi. It charges 50 cents a mile for each passenger mile driven. Last year the taxi drove 60,000 passenger miles. The variable cost per mile (gasoline, tires, wear and tear) was 20 cents. The driver was paid a salary of $5000 per year (the remainder of the driver's income was earned in tips). Rent and administration were fixed costs totaling $15,000. Clearwater lost money, as the following analysis shows:

Item	Amount
Revenue 0.50 × 60,000 =	$30,000
Expenses:	
Variable costs 0.20 × 60,000 = 12,000	
Driver 5,000	
Overhead costs	
(rent and administration) <u>15,000</u>	32,000
Profit (loss)	$(2,000)

In thinking about how to address this problem, management has decided that one possibility is to add a second taxi.

 PROBLEM Assuming the second taxi will charge the same amount per mile and have the same variable cost per mile as taxi 1 but will require no additional overhead costs, how many miles must it drive to eliminate the loss that Clearwater currently incurs?

ANALYSIS To answer this question, we can follow the format suggested earlier in which we compute a unit contribution margin and divide it into fixed costs plus the desired profit. Unit contribution margin is price minus variable costs, or $0.50 − $0.20 = $0.30. Fixed costs are $5000, and we need $2000 in profit to cover the loss from taxi 1. Therefore, we divide $0.30 into $7000. The conclusion is that taxi 2 must drive $23,333 miles to cover its costs and earn a $2000 profit.

Now assume that management believes that taxi 2 actually will drive 30,000 miles during the upcoming year and that overhead costs will remain at $15,000. It has asked the accountants to prepare an analysis of the profitability of taxi 2.

They allocate overhead on the basis of the number of miles driven, and taxi 2 is expected to drive one-third of the miles (30,000 out of a total of 90,000 miles).

 PROBLEM   What would the accountant's profitability analysis look like for taxi 2?

ANSWER   Under the above circumstances, the accountant's profitability analysis quite likely would look as follows:

Revenue 0.50 × 30,000 =	$15,000
Expenses	
Variable costs 0.20 × 30,000 = 6,000	
Driver 5,000	
Overhead costs (⅓ of $15,000) 5,000	16,000
Profit (loss)	$(1,000)

This analysis raises a perplexing problem for management. When overhead costs are included, taxi 2, which was projected to operate considerably above breakeven (30,000 miles versus a breakeven of 23,333 miles), is being presented as a money-losing proposition.

The problem, of course, lies in the allocation of overhead. Because of situations such as this, many managers prefer to think in terms of the total contribution of each product to the organization's overhead costs. *Total contribution* refers to the amount of money that remains after a product's specific costs have been deducted from its revenue. Product-specific costs include variable, semivariable, fixed, and step-function costs. The amount left after deducting these costs *contributes* to the recovery of overhead costs. More specifically, a product (a taxi in this case) provides some revenues and incurs some direct costs. The difference between revenue and direct costs (both fixed and variable) is the contribution of that product or service to the organization's overhead costs.

Contribution Income Statement

A contribution income statement is an income statement with a different format from that of a more traditional income statement. It can be constructed in several different ways, one of which is as follows:

Total revenue (net)

Less: total variable costs

Equals: margin (for fixed and overhead costs)

Less: the product's fixed costs

Equals: product's contribution to the organization's overhead costs

Less: allocated overhead costs

Equals: profit (loss) on a full cost basis

PROBLEM Prepare a contribution income statement for Clearwater.

ANSWER The contribution income statement would look as follows:

Item	Taxi 1	Taxi 2	Total
Revenue	$30,000	$15,000	$45,000
Less: variable costs	12,000	6,000	18,000
Margin (for fixed and overhead costs)	$18,000	$9,000	$27,000
Less: production center fixed costs (drivers)	5,000	5,000	10,000
Contribution (to overhead costs)	$13,000	$4,000	$17,000
Less: overhead costs			15,000
Profit (loss) on a full cost basis			$2,000

The key figures here are the contribution amounts, which show that each taxi is making a positive total contribution such that not using it or, worse, discontinuing it would leave the organization worse off than keeping it would. In fact, it is taxi 2's $4000 contribution that led to the change from a $2000 loss to a $2000 profit.

 PROBLEM Quicky Legal Services's lawyers work in three departments. Each department is responsible for one of the case types: easy, hard, and extra hard. Each department also has some direct fixed costs. The firm's total fixed costs are as shown below, along with some other basic information:

	Fixed Costs	Fee per Case	Variable Cost per Case	Cases Served per Year
Regular department	$500,000	$3,000	$1,800	1,000
Hard department	700,000	4,000	2,200	400
Extra hard department	1,000,000	5,000	2,500	600
General (firm wide)	365,000			
Total	$2,565,000			2,000

Using this mix of cases, structure Quicky's revenues and costs into a contribution income statement format.

ANALYSIS Using these data, a contribution income statement would look as follows:

	Regular	Hard	Extra Hard	Total
Revenue	$3,000,000	$1,600,000	$3,000,000	
Less: variable costs	1,800,000	880,000	1,500,000	
Margin	$1,200,000	$720,000	$1,500,000	$3,420,000
Less: fixed costs	500,000	700,000	1,000,000	2,200,000
Contribution	$700,000	$20,000	$500,000	$1,220,000
Less: overhead costs				365,000
Profit				$855,000

Note that we did not allocate overhead costs to case types. We could have done that by using a reasonable allocation basis, but that is not really necessary in an analysis of this sort.

 PROBLEM How would the contribution income statement look under the second mix of cases (regular = 500; hard = 200; extra hard = 1300)? As a member of the senior management team at Quicky, how might you respond to this change in the mix of cases?

ANALYSIS The revised contribution income statement would look as follows:

	Regular	Hard	Extra Hard	Total
Cases served per year	500	200	1,300	2,000
Revenue	$1,500,000	$800,000	$6,500,000	
Less: variable costs	900,000	440,000	3,250,000	
Margin	$600,000	$360,000	$3,250,000	$4,210,000
Less: fixed costs	500,000	700,000	1,000,000	2,200,000
Contribution	$100,000	$(340,000)	$2,250,000	$2,010,000
Less: overhead costs				365,000
Profit				$1,645,000

The firm's senior management presumably would be pleased with the change in the mix of cases, since it has increased profits from $855,000 to $1,645,000. It might wish to look at the hard cases, however, to see if eliminating them would result in the loss of cases of the other two types. If that were not the case, profits could be improved by $340,000 by eliminating the hard cases. Moreover, if some of the overhead costs could be reduced through elimination of the hard category, profits could be improved even further. A key issue, of course, is that the firm no longer would be able to offer a "full line" of legal services, and this might lead to a decline in cases of the other two types.

With this knowledge of cost behavior, and an understanding of the concept of contribution, you are now ready to look at the broader topic of differential cost accounting. In addition, you now can begin to examine the role that differential costs play in alternative choice decision making. These topics are taken up in Chapter 3.

CHAPTER 3

Differential Cost Accounting

Chapter 2 made the point that a significant aspect of cost accounting is the notion that *different costs are used for different purposes.* That chapter discussed a number of instances in which full costs were inappropriate and managers had to understand cost behavior. This chapter takes that idea a step further, showing how full costs are inappropriate for several types of decisions that managers frequently make. These *alternative choice decisions* include (1) keep versus discontinue an unprofitable product or service, (2) make versus buy (e.g., make a subassembly in house or contract out with another company to have it made), (3) accept versus reject a special request (e.g., to sell a product below full cost in order to use a certain amount of otherwise unused capacity), and (4) sell obsolete supplies or equipment. In making alternative choice decisions, the appropriate information again is differential costs.

A key question asked in the context of an alternative choice decision is, "How will costs (and sometimes revenues) change under the alternative arrangements?" If a product line or service is discontinued, for example, some costs will be eliminated, but so will some revenues. In a make-versus-buy decision, by contrast, certain costs will be eliminated but other costs will be incurred. In special request and obsolete asset situations, certain revenues will be received but costs will not change in accordance with the indications of a full cost analysis.

As this chapter explains, the use of full cost information as a basis for deciding how costs will change under these sorts of alternative choices can lead managers to make decisions that are financially detrimental to their organizations. A different analytical approach is needed.

The chapter builds on the concept of contribution that was discussed toward the end of Chapter 2 but takes the analysis to a greater depth than was done in that chapter. It begins with a discussion of the differential cost concept and some of its key principles. It then addresses the concept of sunk costs, the question of nonquantitative considerations, and the role of overhead in differential cost decisions. As we will see in this chapter, dealing with overhead is not as simple as one might have concluded from reading Chapter 2. Indeed, overhead cannot always be ignored in a differential cost analysis, and the chapter addresses those areas where at least some overhead costs may be relevant to the decision under consideration.

THE DIFFERENTIAL COST CONCEPT

With an understanding of costs according to the fixed, step-function, variable, or semivariable nature of their behavior discussed in Chapter 2, we are in a position to undertake a differential cost analysis. Effectively, differential cost analysis attempts to identify the behavior of an organization's costs under one or more alternative scenarios. Those scenarios are related to the type of decision under consideration. Let us begin with the problem that was discussed at the end of Chapter 2, but put into a slightly different decision-making context.

 PROBLEM   Clearwater Taxi Service operates two taxis. It charges 50 cents a mile for each passenger mile driven. Last year, taxi 1 drove 60,000 passenger miles and taxi 2 drove 30,000 passenger miles. The variable cost per mile (gasoline, tires, wear and tear) for each taxi was 20 cents. Each driver was paid a salary of $5000 per year (the remainder of each driver's income was earned in tips). Rent and administration are fixed costs totaling $15,000; they are allocated to each taxi on the basis of the number of miles driven. Prepare an analysis of the profit earned by each taxi on a full-cost basis.

ANSWER   Total revenues and expenses for the year were as follows:

Item	Taxi 1	Taxi 2	Total
Revenue	0.50 × 60,000 = $30,000	0.50 × 30,000 = $15,000	$45,000
Expenses			
Variable costs	0.20 × 60,000 = 12,000	0.20 × 30,000 = 6,000	18,000
Drivers	5,000	5,000	10,000
Overhead costs (rent and administration)	10,000	5,000	15,000
Total expenses	$27,000	$16,000	$43,000
Profit (loss)	$3,000	$(1,000)	$2,000

 PROBLEM   Would the profitability of Clearwater Taxi Service have been improved if taxi 2, which lost money, had been discontinued at the beginning of the year? By how much would the company's profit have improved or worsened? Be clear about any assumptions you need to make. If you have difficulty with this problem, return to the discussion at the end of Chapter 2.

ANSWER   The analysis is best structured in terms of differential costs. The question is not whether taxi 2 lost money on a *full cost* basis (as it did) but instead the nature of its differential costs and revenues, that is, how Clearwater's revenues and costs would have changed if taxi 2 had been discontinued.

Although the data are not as good as we might like, we can see that discontinuing taxi 2 would have eliminated its revenue and variable costs as well as the fixed cost of the driver. From all indications, however, the overhead costs (rent and administration) would have continued (i.e., they were not differential). The result would have been a shift from a profit of $2000 to a loss of $2000, as the analysis below indicates:

Item	Taxi 1
Revenue 0.50 × 60,000 =	$30,000
Expenses:	
Variable costs 0.20 × 60,000 =	12,000
Driver	5,000
Overhead costs	
(rent and administration)	15,000
Total expenses	32,000
Profit (loss)	$(2,000)

This, of course, is the situation Clearwater faced before it added taxi 2 at the end of Chapter 2.

Key Principles

This situation illustrates six important principles.

1. *Principle 1. Full cost information can be misleading.* Full-cost accounting information can be misleading if it is used for alternative choice decisions, in this instance a "keep or discontinue" decision. In the Clearwater example the full cost data seem to indicate that the company could increase profits by dropping taxi 2, but this clearly is not the case.

2. *Principle 2. Differential costs can include both fixed and variable costs.* Although this may be counterintuitive, differential costs can include *both* fixed and variable costs. In the example above, the driver was a fixed cost of taxi 2, yet the elimination of taxi 2 eliminated that fixed cost. The key point is that as long as we operate the taxi, we have the driver's salary; it does not fluctuate in accordance with the number of miles driven (within the relevant range). However, when we eliminate the taxi, we also eliminate this cost in its entirety; thus, it is differential in terms of the alternative choice decision we are making. (In effect, we have

moved outside the relevant range when we reduce the number of miles to zero; at that point the fixed cost also falls to zero.)

3. *Principle 3. Assumptions are needed.* Differential cost analysis invariably requires assumptions. Although the analysis of the Clearwater situation focused on what would have happened in the prior year, the real intent of the analysis is to assist management in making a decision concerning the future. One assumption that underlay our analysis, therefore, was that next year's prices, costs, volume, and so on, would be the same as last year's.

Of course, it is not true that next year will be just like last year. Inflation will affect the company's costs, and it may be possible to raise prices. The general state of the economy, along with a wide variety of other factors, will affect the company's volume next year such that it quite likely will be different from last year's. This raises some important concerns about the reliability of the analysis.

Despite those concerns, however, since we do not have perfect knowledge of the future, we must speculate about how costs will behave. In the Clearwater example we made two important assumptions that went beyond the general ones mentioned above: (1) The number of miles driven by taxi 1 will not increase with the elimination of taxi 2, and (2) we will not be able to reduce or eliminate any rent or administrative costs by eliminating taxi 2. Changes in either of these assumptions clearly would have an impact on the new profit (or loss) figure and might in fact make it financially beneficial to eliminate taxi 2.

4. *Principle 4. Sensitivity analysis is essential.* Because assumptions play such a crucial role in a differential analysis, it is important to identify and document them as completely as possible. It also is important to explore how changes in the assumptions would affect the conclusions of the analysis—an activity called *sensitivity analysis.* If we were doing a sensitivity analysis for the Clearwater Taxi situation, we might try to determine how many more miles taxi 1 would have to be driven for the organization to maintain its $2000 profit. Or, if we thought we might be able to reduce rent and administrative costs through the elimination of taxi 2, we might ask by how much those costs would need to fall to maintain the $2000 profit. We then could assess whether managerial action could be taken that would allow those assumptions to become reality.

PROBLEM   Assuming no increase in the number of miles driven by taxi 1, by how much would rent and administrative costs have to fall to maintain the $2000 profit? How could this information be incorporated into a sensitivity analysis?

ANSWER   Since profit fell by $4000 with the elimination of taxi 2 (from a positive $2000 to a negative $2000), it would be necessary to reduce rent and administrative costs by $4000 to maintain the $2000 profit.

With this information in hand, we now can ask if the elimination of taxi 2 will allow us to reduce our administrative costs by *more* than $4000. If so, the reduction is a differential item that is associated directly with the elimination of taxi 2 and should be included in a sensitivity analysis. Doing that would lead to the conclusion that if we could reduce these costs by more than $4000, it would be financially beneficial to eliminate taxi 2.

1. *Principle 5. Causality must be present.* A key aspect of differential analysis is causality. Specifically, for an item to be included in a differential analysis, it must be *caused* by the alternative under consideration. For example, if we assume that there will be an increase in the miles driven by taxi 1, that increase has to be *caused* by the elimination of taxi 2. If taxi 1 would have driven more miles anyway, the increased mileage is irrelevant for the differential analysis. If, however, we assume that the elimination of taxi 2 means that some passengers who would have used taxi 2 now will use taxi 1, the increased mileage is relevant for the differential analysis. We would have to include that additional mileage in computing taxi 1's revenue and variable expenses under the alternative scenario.

   The same principle applies to cost items such as rent and administration. If we were planning to decrease administrative costs with or without taxi 2, the change is irrelevant for the differential analysis. If, however, the elimination of taxi 2 will *allow us to decrease* administrative costs, we would include this decrease in our analysis.

2. *Principle 6. Information must be structured appropriately.* The Clearwater Taxi situation illustrates the importance of structuring information appropriately for decision making. For example, one way to structure the Clearwater information is in the form of a contribution analysis, as was illustrated in Chapter 2. However, even a contribution income statement does not deal with the underlying assumptions. Specifically, in the Clearwater case a key assumption was that the company's overhead costs (rent and administration) would not be reduced by eliminating taxi 2. As was indicated above and as will be discussed in greater detail later in this chapter, an assumption of this sort is not necessarily

valid. Nevertheless, in most instances an analysis of differential costs can be performed most easily when the direct fixed and variable costs of the particular activity itself are analyzed separately from the overhead costs of the organization, much as we did with the contribution income statement in Chapter 2.

SUNK COSTS

One of the most difficult aspects of differential cost analysis concerns the matter of *sunk costs*. As was mentioned above, an alternative choice decision always looks toward the future rather than the past. This is one reason why full cost analyses, which typically rely on historical data, are inappropriate for these kinds of decisions. Nevertheless, even when we focus our analytical efforts on the future, we frequently are plagued by history, particularly when it presents itself in the form of sunk costs.

The term *sunk cost* refers to an expenditure that was made in the past and that results in an item on a full cost report, but because the expenditure already has been incurred and the decision cannot be changed, the item is inappropriate for future considerations. Consequently, the item should be excluded from a differential cost analysis, which is concerned only with the future.

Sunk Costs and Intuition

For most people the notion of sunk costs is very difficult to accept intuitively. Since sunk costs are present in many alternative choice decisions, however, it is important to be comfortable in dealing with them. Let us use a personal finance example to illustrate their counterintuitive nature.

 PROBLEM Assume that you hold 100 shares of ABC Company stock that you purchased 1 year ago for $30 a share (a total of $3000). Since that time the market has declined, and your stock now is worth only $10 a share (a total of $1000). You have the opportunity to purchase 50 shares of XYZ Company stock at $20 a share. Your stockbroker, whom you trust, informs you that the prospects for XYZ Company's stock are extremely good, while those for ABC Company are quite poor. Do you (1) sell your ABC stock and use the proceeds to purchase XYZ stock or (2) turn down the opportunity to purchase XYZ stock, reasoning that you need to hold on to your ABC stock until you recover your losses or it returns to a price closer to $30 a share?

ANSWER If you answered (2), you, like most people, have difficulty accepting the idea of sunk costs. The $3000 you spent to purchase the ABC stock is gone, and there is nothing you can do about it. Your choice now concerns the best place to have your $1000: In ABC or in XYZ. The only relevant cost to consider is that $1000. The $3000 is sunk.

Sunk Costs in Organizational Settings

The classic example of a sunk cost in organizations is depreciation, which is the financial accounting technique used to spread the cost of an asset over its useful life. Although depreciation appears on a full cost report, it traditionally has been considered by accountants to be inappropriate for differential cost analysis since it does not change regardless of the alternative chosen. That is, it is a sunk cost. To examine this idea, let us look first at the accounting view of sunk costs in organizational settings and then examine sunk costs in a more strategic context.

Accountants typically consider sunk costs from a relatively nonstrategic perspective, meaning that they look at the remaining economic life of any assets that are involved in an alternative choice decision and do not consider the longer-term, strategic consequences of that decision. Because of this, the accounting view ordinarily excludes consideration of any decision to replace the assets. The idea can be illustrated most easily from the perspective of a contract-out decision.

 PROBLEM   Newton Electric Company (NEC) has a machine with a book value of $40,000 that it is depreciating at a rate of $10,000 per year. The machine is a highly specialized one that is used only to make the coil in the motors used in its vacuum cleaners. Because of technological changes, the machine has a market value of zero; it cannot be sold (a junkyard dealer has offered to remove it at no charge, however).

Assume that NEC's profit before depreciation is $100,000 and that another company has offered to make the same number of coils for NEC for a total price (delivered) of $15,000 a year. Is the book value of the machine a relevant cost to consider in deciding whether to accept that offer?

ANSWER   The answer is no, since the cost is the same regardless of whether NEC subcontracts the work. Leave aside for the moment the additional cost of the subcontract. If we scrapped the machine (i.e., received nothing for it), we would no longer have any depreciation on it, and our income statements for the next four years would look something like the following:

Year	1	2	3	4	Total
Profit before depreciation	$100,000	$100,000	$100,000	$100,000	$400,000
Less: depreciation	0	0	0	0	0
Profit before disposal of assets	$100,000	$100,000	$100,000	$100,000	$400,000
Less: loss on sale of machine	40,000	0	0	0	40,000
Net profit	$60,000	$100,000	$100,000	$100,000	$360,000

If we continued with the existing situation (i.e., did not subcontract the work), we would have an entry such as the following for each of the 4 years of the remaining life of the machine:

Year	1	2	3	4	Total
Profit before depreciation	$100,000	$100,000	$100,000	$100,000	$400,000
Less: depreciation	10,000	10,000	10,000	10,000	40,000
Profit before disposal of assets	$90,000	$90,000	$90,000	$90,000	$360,000
Less: loss on sale of machine	0	0	0	0	0
Net profit	$90,000	$90,000	$90,000	$90,000	$360,000

In either case, net profit for the 4-year period is $360,000 and the machine expense is $40,000. The only difference is that in the first alternative NEC incurs the expense in a single year, whereas in the second alternative the expense is spread over 4 years.

To be completely accurate, we would consider the time value of the cash generated from an earlier reduction in income taxes in the first alternative as a differential item. For the purpose of simplicity, this calculation has been excluded from the example. Similarly, if we can sell the machine today for, say, $12,000, that $12,000 "salvage value" is a differential item: It is cash we will receive if we subcontract that we would not have received otherwise.

The fact that NEC could receive something for the machine changes the impact of the transaction on its profit but does not change the fact that the *book value* of the machine was reduced by $40,000. This $40,000 is the sunk cost, and we do not include it in the differential cost analysis. Instead, the analysis looks only at the out-of-pocket expenses that would be eliminated as a result of subcontracting compared with the cost of the subcontract. These items would affect the "profit before depreciation" figure shown above. In this case, if NEC could reduce its *out-of-pocket* expenses associated with the coils for the motors by more than $15,000 (the price of the subcontract), other things equal, subcontracting would be financially beneficial.

Implications of Sunk Costs for Differential Cost Analysis. The example above has some important implications for the accounting approach to a differential cost analysis. Specifically, from a pure accounting perspective, an alternative choice decision (whether to subcontract in this case) excludes consideration of the book value of any equipment that is involved ($40,000 in this case). The book value is not relevant since it will be the same whatever we do. The amount we could receive from selling the equipment ($12,000 in this case) is a relevant item, since it is differential; that is, it occurs only if we accept the subcontractor's offer. (This assumes, of course, that we would not dispose of the machine unless we accepted the offer; if we were going to dispose of the machine anyway, the receipts from its disposal would be nondifferential.)

Clearly, however, the $12,000 is relevant only in the first year of the contract. Therefore, if the contract is for more than 1 year, we need to exclude it from the analysis in years 2 and beyond. This same principle can be applied to any other asset we would dispose of if we accepted a subcontractor's offer, such as inventory that would become obsolete if we subcontracted for some work that historically we did ourselves. In all cases, the book value of the asset is a sunk cost and is irrelevant, but the scrap value (i.e., the revenue from the asset's sale) is a differential item and is relevant. Ordinarily, however, any scrap value is a one-time cash inflow, in contrast to most other items in a differential analysis, which are ongoing.

In summary, in assessing the subcontracting possibility, we look at both the costs that would be eliminated and those that would be incurred if we subcontracted the work, as well as any revenue received as a result of an action such as selling the machine. In the category of eliminated costs, we would use all existing variable costs, including such items as variable labor and supplies associated with the manufacture of the coils. We also would include any fixed costs that would be eliminated if we subcontracted the work (such as the cost of a machine operator).

The Strategic View of Sunk Costs. Although depreciation is a sunk cost and therefore a nondifferential item in any alternative choice decision, an important question is how we should treat depreciation if our perspective is more strategic, that is, if it extends beyond the remaining years of a machine's economic life. This "strategic view" asks a slightly different question from the one asked in the accounting view. With the strategic view, the question is what the relevant costs and revenues will be over an *indefinite* time period. When this is the case, depreciation is a relevant item to include.

Stated somewhat differently, when the time horizon is short, the financial perspective generally is a cash-maximizing one. When the time horizon is long (i.e., extends beyond the economic life of the asset), the decision becomes more strategic in nature. Under these circumstances, depreciation is a relevant consideration, even though it is a noncash expense and a sunk cost.

The strategic perspective occurs in contract-out decisions and in decisions concerning the elimination of a product or product line. Let us look first at the analysis we might do in a contract-out situation and then consider a decision to keep or drop a product line.

A *contract-out decision* typically is not concerned with revenue. Instead, senior management needs to compare costs under two scenarios: (1) manufacture the item or provide the service ourselves or (2) contract out with another company to manufacture the item or provide the service.

 PROBLEM   The Arctic Ice Refrigerator Company manufactures a line of refrigerators that contain automatic ice dispensers. The ice dispensers are made in a separate department that uses some highly specialized equipment. The annual full costs of the Ice Dispenser Department look as follows:

Direct labor	$150,000
Materials	70,000
Department manager	50,000
Depreciation	30,000
Allocated overhead	20,000
Total	$320,000

Arctic Ice has received an offer to manufacture the same annual volume of ice dispensers at an annual cost of $280,000. The contract is for 5 years. If Arctic Ice accepts this offer, it will be able to eliminate the Ice Dispenser Department totally. In considering the offer, management has determined the following:

1. Although the machines in the department have 5 years of depreciation remaining, they are technologically obsolete and have no market value (they can be removed at no charge, but that is all). However, they can last for another 5 years before they have to be replaced.

2. No inflation is expected.

3. The department manager is willing to accept early retirement (at no additional cost to the company) if the department closes. That is, her salary will be eliminated, and she will draw her retirement income from the company's pension fund, which is a separate entity.

4. None of the allocated overhead is differential; that is, it will be reallocated to other departments if the Ice Dispenser Department is eliminated.

5. The expected number of ice dispensers needed for each of the 5 years of the contract is well known and will be the same as it was during the year in which these figures were computed.

6. The local firm making the offer has an excellent reputation for quality and delivery.

Identify the costs to consider as the relevant savings if Arctic Ice accepts the offer.

ANSWER   If we adopt the traditional approach to this analysis, we would use the following costs as the relevant savings if we subcontract:

Direct labor	$150,000
Materials	70,000
Department manager	50,000
Depreciation (sunk)	0
Allocated overhead (nondifferential)	0
Total	$270,000
Less: cost of contract	280,000
Net financial benefit	($10,000)

If we adopt a more strategic perspective and include depreciation in the analysis (even though it is a sunk cost), we would use the following costs as the relevant savings if we subcontract:

Direct labor	$150,000
Materials	70,000
Department manager	50,000
Depreciation	30,000
Allocated overhead (nondifferential)	0
Total	$300,000
Less: cost of contract	280,000
Net financial benefit	$20,000

 PROBLEM   Thus, all other things being equal, under the first cost analysis we would *not* accept the offer, whereas under the second analysis we would accept it. What should management do?

ANSWER   A short-term, cash-maximizing perspective would lead us to reject the offer. We would save only $270,000 in expenses and spend $280,000 for the contract. The traditional approach, which excludes sunk costs, certainly would lead us to this conclusion.

From a longer-term, strategic perspective, however, the focus shifts to what might be called "steady state" operations. This more strategic focus recognizes that at some point we will have to replace the equipment and thus includes depreciation in the analysis. In these circumstances we would accept the offer since, in the long term, it improves our financial performance. In fact, if technology were changing, we might include depreciation on the *replacement* equipment, which would be either higher or lower than the current depreciation, depending on the type of technological change taking place.

Ideally, of course, we would wait for 5 years to accept the contract. Much could change in the interim, however, that would affect our decision. More important, this option is not available to us.

In the decision to keep or drop a product line, senior management must carefully assess the behavior of *both revenue and costs* under the two options. Again, sunk costs present some analytical difficulties.

 PROBLEM 1   Sunshine Pen Company manufactures a line of felt-tipped pens. The annual revenue and full costs of the Felt-Tipped Pen Department look as follows:

Sales revenue (net)			$600,000
Less:	Direct labor	$200,000	
	Materials	260,000	
	Departmental administration	120,000	
	Depreciation	80,000	
	Allocated overhead	110,000	770,000
Profit (loss)			($170,000)

The accountants have recommended that the line be discontinued since it is losing money. The manager of the department has decided to prepare a contribution income statement to demonstrate that the department is financially beneficial to the company. He has asked his staff assistant to prepare such a statement by using the data given above. Prepare that statement, assuming that direct labor is a fixed cost.

ANSWER A contribution income statement would look as follows:

Sales revenue (net)	$600,000	
Less variable costs (materials)	260,000	
Margin (for fixed and o/h costs)		$340,000
Less department fixed costs:		
Direct labor	200,000	
Departmental administration	120,000	
Depreciation	80,000	400,000
Contribution to overhead costs		($60,000)
Less allocated overhead costs		110,000
Profit (loss)		($170,000)

 PROBLEM 2 As the department manager, how would you react to this statement? Can you prepare an argument to senior management that the department is financially beneficial to the company despite its negative contribution? Organize your financial analysis and reasoning before reading the answer.

ANSWER If we make the argument that the depreciation expense is a sunk cost and choose a short-term perspective for the analysis (i.e., one short enough that the machines do not have to be replaced), the contribution income statement would look as follows:

Sales revenue (net)	$600,000	
Less variable costs (materials)	260,000	
Margin (for fixed and o/h costs)		$340,000
Less department fixed costs:		
Direct labor	200,000	
Departmental administration	120,000	320,000
Contribution to overhead costs		$20,000
Less allocated overhead costs		110,000
Profit (loss)		($90,000)

The argument we then could make is that at least in the short run the department is making a contribution to the recovery of overhead costs. Therefore, it makes sense to keep it.

 PROBLEM 3   As senior management, how would you react to this argument? Organize your thoughts before reading the analysis that follows.

ANSWER   Senior management probably would focus on the following issues:

1. In the very short run (the next 6 months or so) it makes sense to keep the department since it indeed is contributing $20,000 in cash to help cover overhead costs.

2. In the medium run (the next year or so) we need to ask two questions:

    ■ Could we, by discontinuing the Felt-Tipped Pen Department, eliminate more than $20,000 of overhead? For example, suppose there was an employee benefits clerk in the administrative service center who worked full time on behalf of the employees of the felt-tipped department. That clerk's salary plus fringe benefits totals $28,000. It might be possible to eliminate this person and save the $28,000. This savings would more than offset the $20,000 contribution, making it financially beneficial to discontinue the department.

    ■ Assuming that we are capacity-constrained, can we find another product line to pursue that would generate more than $20,000 in contribution? The difference between the contribution from this new product line and the $20,000 becomes the *opportunity cost* of keeping the Felt-Tipped Pen Department.

3. In the long run can we find another product line to pursue that would cover all of its costs, *including* depreciation and allocated overhead?

Increasingly, as companies develop strategic alliances with their suppliers and as their manufacturing operations become more automated (i.e., as the number of assets increases), the strategic view takes on greater significance in alternative choice decision making. As a result, some companies are beginning to move away from the more traditional approach that excludes depreciation (and other sunk costs). In this regard, a key question is whether the decision is a short-term one or one that will have longer-term strategic implications. If the decision is short-term in nature, excluding sunk costs such as depreciation (and the book value of other assets involved in the decision) is appropriate. Otherwise, the inclusion of depreciation (and other relevant sunk costs) is appropriate.

Traditionally, the *strategic perspective* was used only when a company was deciding whether to purchase replacement equipment. At that time, management would analyze the annual cash flows associated with the proposed investment and compare their "present value" with the amount of the proposed investment (a technique for doing this is discussed in

Appendix B). The problem with this approach is that it typically did not consider alternatives such as contracting out. Instead, the decision usually was made in relative isolation.

Moreover, treating depreciation as a sunk cost (and thus excluding it from an analysis of differential costs) suggests that senior management will wait until one of the assets involved in the associated product line must be replaced before it undertakes a strategic analysis. Even when this happens, however, the analysis will not be complete if the product line uses more than one asset. That is, if a particular product line uses several assets, it is unlikely that they all will require replacement simultaneously. Using a strategic perspective for the replacement of a single asset when a product line uses several assets will result in a partial analysis. Instead, senior management must include either a current or a simulated depreciation amount for all the assets associated with the product line if it is to do a full analysis of the situation under consideration.

To correct for these sorts of incremental approaches to decision making, senior management must ask the strategic question whenever an opportunity to contract out presents itself. To do this, many managers will include depreciation in the cost analysis since its inclusion provides a good approximation of the company's costs from a steady state perspective. Clearly, depreciation is not a precise measure, since inflation and technological advances will change the cost of a replacement asset, but it provides a rough approximation of steady state operations. Doing a rough approximation is better than completely excluding the cost of the associated assets.

NONQUANTITATIVE CONSIDERATIONS

The strategic perspective also must include nonquantitative considerations. That is, in any alternative choice decision there are a variety of factors that cannot be quantified easily, if at all, but that can tip the balance in one direction or another, frequently overriding the financial analysis. This is especially true if the financial analysis indicates that the two approaches have roughly similar cost and revenue implications.

In the decision to keep or drop a product or product line, nonquantitative considerations usually include product interdependencies, that is, the extent to which sales of some of the company's products are dependent on sales of the product being considered for elimination. A company that manufactures both cameras and film probably would find it unwise to eliminate the cameras as a product line, since film sales are highly dependent on consumers having cameras. Indeed, as was suggested in Chapter 1, some companies treat certain products as "loss leaders," suggesting that they lose money on those products deliberately in order to maximize consumer purchases of their more profitable product lines. The idea is that if the consumer has the loss-leading product in hand, he or she then will purchase some of the company's other products that are used in conjunction with the loss leader. Those products usually are quite profitable.

In a contract-out decision, nonquantitative considerations typically include factors such as quality, service, delivery, and the reputation of the vendor. They also may include market considerations such as the difficulty and cost of switching from one vendor to another if a particular relationship does not work out to management's satisfaction. A company that contracts for snow plowing services for its parking lot, for example, typically has an easy time switching from one vendor to another. There are many individuals with pickup trucks and snow plowing blades who can provide the service. In contrast, a company that contracts for the manufacture of specialized packing materials for its products may have a difficult time switching vendors because the market for such vendors may be quite small.

Another nonquantitative consideration in contracting out is the cost of switching back to internal manufacture. Once a company contracts out, it may eliminate its facilities, equipment, and trained personnel. Leasing or purchasing new facilities and equipment and training new personnel may be very costly. In this regard, the nature of the market for vendors is quite important. In a highly competitive market, a company that is dissatisfied with one vendor can simply switch to another. If the market is more oligopolistic, however, it may be difficult to find a replacement vendor. Moreover, if the company has eliminated its capacity for internal manufacture, it may be at the mercy of its vendor.

THE ROLE OF ALLOCATED OVERHEAD

Additional complexities are introduced into the differential cost analysis when overhead costs are associated with a particular effort for which the differential analysis is to be made. There are two such complexities, each of which relates to one of the full-cost accounting issues discussed in Chapter 1: Allocation Bases and the Stepdown Sequence.

Misleading Allocation Bases

Although a company may be attempting to measure the use of service center resources as precisely as possible, there can be many instances in which a service center's bases of allocation do not reflect the *actual* use of its services by receiving cost centers. This becomes an important consideration in alternative choice decisions.

PROBLEM Lawncare, Inc. (LI), is considering the possibility of dropping its special projects product line. If it drops that product line, it will be able to eliminate all the direct costs of the special projects production center. Because special projects has 11 machines, it is allocated 11/30ths of the maintenance costs, or $11,000. What do you think will happen to these costs if the special projects product line is eliminated? How does the allocation basis for maintenance help us understand cost behavior?

ANSWER It is likely that some of the costs in the maintenance service center are differential with respect to the number of machines. It is highly unlikely, however, that exactly 11/30ths of the costs in the maintenance service center will be eliminated if LI eliminates the special projects product line. That would mean that all maintenance costs were variable with respect to the number of machines in the company. Thus, the allocation basis for the costs of the maintenance service center does not provide an accurate picture of the *behavior* of the service center's costs.

To analyze the behavior of the maintenance service center's costs, we must determine which costs are variable, semivariable, step-function, or fixed. With this information, we can assess with reasonable accuracy what will happen to the costs in the service center.

In essence, then, if a company contracts out for some services or discontinues the production of a particular product line, it is quite likely that some of the service center costs *allocated* to the production center in question will fall. In most instances, however, few of those service center costs actually will be eliminated. Only the variable, semivariable, and perhaps some step-function costs in the service center will be eliminated. The rest will be allocated to other cost centers.

For example, consider an administration and general (A&G) service center. A reduction in staff in a given *production* center will lead to a reduction in total salaries in that production center. If A&G costs are allocated on the basis of salary dollars, there will be a reduction in the amount of A&G *allocated* to the production center. It is highly unlikely, however, that there will be any reduction in the staff costs or other costs associated with the A&G service cost center. Thus, rather than being reduced, A&G costs simply will be reallocated to other cost centers.

The reverse may happen as well; that is, although the costs *allocated* to a production center from a given service center may not fall, it is possible that some of the service center's costs themselves actually will be eliminated. An example of this might be a cleaning service center. Assume that the center's costs are allocated on the basis of square feet. A reduction in the level of, or a change in, the nature of the activities in a given production center may reduce the center's need for cleaning services. This may permit the manager of the cleaning service center to reduce the service center's costs. However, unless the space utilized by the production center is reduced, the cost report (which allocates cleaning on a square-footage basis) will not show a corresponding reduction in the cleaning costs allocated to the production center. Instead, the costs allocated to the production center will fall slightly as a result of the lower amount of cleaning costs *overall*, but the decline will be much less than the actual cost reduction that took place in the cleaning service center. The rest of the savings will be realized by other receiving cost centers that continue to receive the same amount of cleaning as they did before.

Effects of the Stepdown Sequence

As was discussed in Chapter 1, the costs in each service center are allocated to all the remaining cost centers (service centers and production centers) as one moves down the steps in the stepdown sequence. Therefore, the total costs of those service centers farthest down in the stepdown sequence will include portions of the costs of the service centers above them. That is, the total cost allocated from each service center includes both its direct and distributed indirect costs *and* the costs that have been allocated to it from previous service centers (or "steps") in the stepdown sequence.

In a hospital, for example, if social work is a service center that is far down in the stepdown sequence, the total social service costs allocated to a particular production center will include a significant allocated component (administration, housekeeping, laundry and linen, and so on). It may be possible to reduce the use of social workers in a production center by reducing the number of patients treated or changing the nature of the treatment plans, but the full impact of that reduction on the costs in the social services cost center will be overstated if one uses the fully allocated social service totals (including both direct and previously allocated service center costs). This is the case because the costs being allocated from the social services cost center contain costs from a variety of other cost centers that may not be affected by the reduction in the production center's volume of activity or that center's use of social workers.

 PROBLEM Lakeside Trucking sells new and used trucks. It also has a service department that repairs and maintains trucks. One unit in the service department is the tune-up unit, which does tune-ups on large trucks. That unit has 12 workstations, each of which contains highly sophisticated electronic equipment. Total depreciation on the equipment is $120,000 per year. At present, the unit performs 10,000 tune-ups a year at a price of $140 each. Fixed costs, excluding depreciation, are $500,000 per year. Variable costs are $80 per tune-up. Service center costs allocated to the unit total $330,000 a year. The company's accountants have suggested that the unit should be discontinued since it is losing $350,000 a year, calculated as follows:

Revenues (10,000 × $140)		$1,400,000
Less:		
Variable costs (10,000 × $80)	800,000	
Depreciation	120,000	
Other fixed costs	500,000	1,420,000
Contribution		($20,000)
Less allocated service center costs		330,000
Profit (loss)		($350,000)

Do you agree with the accountants' suggestion? Prepare an analysis, including your reasoning.

ANALYSIS If the time perspective is a relatively long one and if the "other fixed costs" are all associated with the Tune-up Unit, the accountants are correct that the unit is losing money. Unless strategic reasons dictate its continuation (e.g., senior management believes that it is important to be able to service the trucks it sells), it should at least be evaluated against other activities that might either lose less or produce a profit for the company.

If, however, the time perspective is a short one—in this case, one in which the current machines can continue to be used without the need for replacement—the tune-up unit is making a positive contribution to the company, as follows:

Revenues	$1,400,000
Less: variable costs	800,000
Contribution margin	$600,000
Less: fixed costs (other than depreciation)	500,000
Contribution to company overhead	$100,000

This situation arises because, as was discussed above, depreciation is a sunk cost: It already has been incurred, and there is nothing we can do to change that fact. Hence, it is irrelevant for the decision to discontinue the tune-up unit in the short run. Unless a substitute activity with a higher contribution can be found, the company is financially better off with the unit than without it.

Before reaching a final conclusion, however, we need to examine the allocation of service center costs. If, by eliminating the tune-up unit, we can eliminate more than $100,000 of these costs, we are financially better off without it. Assume, for example, that by discontinuing the unit we can save $150,000 of the $330,000 of allocated service center costs. In that case, by discontinuing the unit, we lose $100,000 in contribution but are able to eliminate $150,000 in overhead. We thus are $50,000 better off financially by eliminating the unit.

The Analytical Effort

Recognizing these complexities and incorporating them into analytical efforts is one of the most challenging aspects of differential cost accounting. Determining which costs are indeed differential and how they behave is extremely difficult, particularly when a full cost report is the principal source of information. There are no easy answers to this dilemma.

CHAPTER 4

Absorption Costing

Chapter 1 described some of the basic decisions that are made in a cost accounting system: defining a cost object, determining cost centers, distinguishing between direct costs and indirect costs, choosing allocation bases for service center costs, selecting an allocation method, and choosing between process and job order cost systems. The examples in that chapter involved companies that deliver services rather than manufacturing products. In a service-delivery organization the cost accounting effort, although occasionally difficult, is not complicated by the presence of manufacturing inventories.

The discussion in Chapter 1 took us to the point where costs had been allocated from service centers to production centers. That chapter touched only briefly on the process for attaching costs to the products (or services) that are worked on (or provided by) a production center. In many organizations, especially manufacturing ones, attaching costs to products—the "second stage" of full cost accounting—can be very tricky. Indeed, some organizations make a considerable effort to determine precise allocation bases to allocate service center costs to production centers but then use an overly simplistic approach to attach production center costs to products. As a result, they may be deceived about the accuracy of their products' costs.

This chapter moves to the next level of thinking about cost accounting systems. In particular, it focuses on some complexities in cost accounting that arise in manufacturing companies and discusses the second stage of the cost accounting effort. It also introduces some new concepts that are useful in both manufacturing and service organizations, such as standard costs and overhead variance analysis. Both are relatively old but powerful ideas.

The chapter begins by introducing terminology that is especially important in manufacturing operations and then shows the financial statements that report the results of manufacturing activities. Next, the chapter turns to the computation of costs in a manufacturing context. This requires understanding the various manufacturing inventories and bringing them into the cost accounting effort. We look at these ideas in terms of the job order and process systems of accounting that were discussed very briefly in Chapter 1.

The chapter next addresses the question of manufacturing overhead, relating it to the discussion of allocation bases in Chapter 1. This leads to the idea of *standard costs,* an important aspect of both cost measurement and cost control. Next, we take up *absorption costing* (sometimes called *full costing*), a technique used by manufacturing organizations to account for costs as raw materials move through the production effort to become finished goods.

In most situations absorption costing requires the use of standard costs, and this creates the need to look at the *variances* between those costs and actual production costs. We examine three important variances in overhead costs: volume, efficiency, and spending.

A FUNCTIONAL CLASSIFICATION OF MANUFACTURING COSTS

In a manufacturing environment, there are several elements that make up the cost of the product. Those elements are shown in Exhibit 4-1 and discussed below.

Direct Manufacturing Costs

Direct manufacturing costs consist of direct labor and direct materials. They are the costs that are traceable to the product. *Direct materials* (sometimes called *raw materials*) actually become part of the product; examples are steel, wires, upholstery, and plastic in an automobile. *Direct labor* includes the individuals in the work force who actually lay hands on the product or on the machines that produce the product. These people mix the ingredients in an ice cream factory, pour the molds in an extruding plant, tighten the bolts in an automobile assembly plant, operate the robots in an electric motor manufacturing plant, and so forth.

Indirect Manufacturing Costs

Indirect manufacturing costs (sometimes called manufacturing overhead) include both labor and materials as well as all manufacturing costs other

EXHIBIT 4-1

Manufacturing Cost Terminology

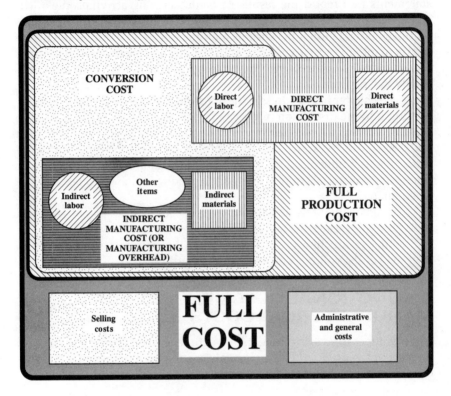

than direct costs. *Indirect labor* includes a variety of people who are needed for the operation of a factory but who ordinarily do not actually produce the product, such as supervisors, schedulers, material handlers, and janitors.

Indirect materials include two kinds of items: (1) materials that are needed for the smooth operation of the factory but that do not go into the product, such as cleaning solvents, rags, and paper supplies, and (2) items that go into the finished product but are so small that it is not worth keeping track of them separately, such as grease on ball bearings and glue in toys. The decision to include some of the latter items as direct materials is a matter of judgment, and different companies producing similar products may treat the same items differently.

In addition to labor and materials, indirect manufacturing costs typically include equipment depreciation as well as the cost of a variety of items needed to operate the factory, such as heat, electricity, maintenance, insurance, and rent. In general, indirect manufacturing costs include both the service center costs that are allocated to the plant as part of the full cost allocation effort discussed in Chapter 1 and a variety of costs that are *direct* costs of the factory but are *indirect* with respect to any given product manufactured in it.

This latter point can be tricky. To understand it, consider the case of a plant that manufactures textbooks. The plant is a production center. The textbooks are manufactured in batches of 5000 to 10,000. With respect to a batch of textbooks, there are two general categories of indirect costs:

- *Category 1: Direct costs of the plant but indirect costs with respect to any batch of product manufactured in the plant.* These are costs that are unambiguously associated with the plant; that is, they were not allocated to the plant from a service center. However, they cannot be directly attributable to any particular batch of books. The salary of a supervisor is an example. Because this person supervises several batches of books being manufactured at any given time, his or her salary is an *indirect manufacturing cost* with respect to any particular batch of books. Yet the company must find a way to attach a portion of this salary to each batch of books produced.

- *Category 2: Service center costs that have been allocated to the plant as part of the cost allocation process discussed in Chapter 1.* These costs frequently are called indirect (or overhead) costs of the plant. The maintenance service center is an example. Maintenance services may be provided to all production cost centers, and the plant is allocated its "fair share" of those costs. Once maintenance costs have been allocated to the plant, a portion of them also must be attached to each batch of books produced. Thus, they too are *indirect manufacturing costs.*

Conversion Costs

Accountants and managers sometimes use the term *conversion cost*. This is the cost of transforming raw materials into a finished product. Conversion costs do not include the cost of the raw materials; rather, they include direct labor and all the indirect manufacturing costs needed to "convert" raw materials into a finished product.

Full Production Cost

When conversion costs are added to direct materials, the result is the *full production cost* of a product. Alternatively, full production cost may be thought of as the sum of all direct and indirect costs in the factory. The two totals are the same.

Selling Costs and Administrative and General Costs

In general, selling costs and administrative and general costs are not added to the full production cost. Instead, they are expensed each accounting period regardless of the level of production during the period. However, to obtain the *full cost* of each product, some accountants add them to the full production cost, especially in service organizations.

Selling costs, as the name suggests, include the costs that an organization incurs to sell its products, such as advertising, salaries and commissions of the sales force, travel costs of the sales force, market research activities, and rent and utilities in sales offices. Less obviously, they also include the activities (logistical and otherwise) that are used to get a product to the customer. These activities include the cost of holding the product in a warehouse until it is shipped (which includes rent for the warehouse, shipping and handling clerks, and so forth), as well as the costs of order processing, shipping, and customer service.

Everything else is included in *administrative and general* (A&G) costs. Even if there is an interest expense associated with a loan to finance a specific piece of equipment in the factory, that expense ordinarily is included in A&G costs. A&G also includes the costs of personnel and accounting, legal, and staff analysts and the salaries of the company's senior managers.

Period and Product Costs

The distinction between period costs and product costs is important because product costs are "attached" to a product and held in inventory until the product is sold, whereas period costs are expenses of each accounting period; that is, they are not attached to products. The accounting process deals with this distinction as follows:

- The work in process inventory is used to add value to raw materials. Using the terminology discussed above, it is here that conversion costs are added to the cost of direct materials to obtain the full production cost. In the accounting system this is done by (1) increasing the work in process inventory by the cost of the direct materials introduced into the manufacturing process and (2) increasing work in process, rather than an expense account, for all conversion costs.

- When a product has been completed, it moves to the finished goods inventory. At this time, the work in process inventory decreases and the finished goods inventory increases by the product's full production cost.

- When a product is sold, the finished goods inventory decreases and the cost of goods sold increases by the product's full production cost.

- Cost of goods sold is an expense account. In accordance with the matching principle, an item's product cost becomes part of cost of goods sold when that item is sold, not before. These matters are discussed in most financial accounting textbooks as part of the process of accounting for inventories and cost of goods sold.

Some Terminology Cautions

As was discussed in Chapter 1, terminology in cost accounting can be tricky. Throughout this chapter, for example, the terms *overhead* and *indirect manufacturing costs* are used synonymously. Accountants frequently use other terms in similar ways, such as *apply, allocate,* and *assign.* Many terms such as these tend to be used somewhat interchangeably in manufacturing organizations, and one frequently must ascertain the precise meaning from the context or by asking.

COMPUTING COST OF GOODS SOLD

A question that arises in the context of preparing an organization's financial statements is, "How do the accountants obtain the cost of goods sold amount?" One of the principal tasks of the cost accounting effort is to compute this amount. To do this, we must know both the number of units of products that were sold and the cost of each unit. Let us look at these questions under two cost accounting scenarios: a job order system and a process system.

Job Order System

Chapter 1 stated that a job order system is used when each product is unique or when products are manufactured in batches and each batch is unique. Let us look at this system in Buzzard Woodworks (BW), a hypothetical company that produces custom-made furniture. Each time BW begins a job, it sets up a job ticket. The job ticket might look like the one shown in Exhibit 4-2. As materials are requisitioned for jobs and as employees work on jobs, the employees record the information, and the accounting staff enters the appropriate cost information on the job ticket. When the job is complete, the job ticket shows the cost.

E X H I B I T   4 - 2

Job Ticket for Buzzard Woodworks

\	\	\	\	\	\
BUZZARD WOODWORKS JOB TICKET					
Job No. __3226__ Date Begun __3 Aug 99__ Date Completed __24 Aug 99__					
Description of Work __Desk and bookcase for Sanford residence__					
Week	**Materials**	**Direct Labor**	**Overhead**	**Total**	
3 Aug	$550.00	$275.00	$137.50	$ 962.50	
10 Aug		350.00	175.00	525.00	
17 Aug	100.00	200.00	100.00	400.00	
24 Aug		125.00	62.50	187.50	
TOTAL	$650.00	$950.00	$475.00	$2,075.00	

The direct material and direct labor costs on the job ticket are pretty clear, but the overhead may be less clear.

 PROBLEM   Spend a few minutes now looking at the job ticket shown in Exhibit 4-2. How was overhead calculated?

ANSWER   Overhead is 50 percent of the direct labor amount charged.

Although it is relatively easy in situations such as this to figure out *how* overhead was calculated, it is much more difficult to determine *why* it was calculated in this way. There are several aspects to the answer to the "why" question. We will return to them later in the chapter.

Process System

A process system typically is used when there is a continuous production activity or when all the units produced are identical so that it is not necessary to identify the costs associated with any specific product or batch of products. Oil refineries are perhaps the classic example of a process system, but most factories with assembly lines also use a process system. A company that produces only one product in a particular plant would use a process system.

The dividing line between a process system and a job order system sometimes is fuzzy, and there are companies with systems that contain elements of both. In most instances the choice between the two depends on the size of the batch. When production runs are long, as in a bottling plant, it does not matter that different runs produce different types of bottles. Each run is a separate process.

One also can imagine a company that manufactures, say, circuit boards. It would be foolish to attach a job ticket to each circuit board since the actions of each worker in the manufacturing process are the same for any given board. If the batch of boards was small, say, 100 or so, and if different batches had different characteristics that affected the labor and materials needed to produce them, we might attach a ticket to the batch and use a job order system. However, if the batch consisted of several thousand boards, requiring several days of production, we would simply keep track of the time spent during the period when the units were manufactured.

Unit Costs

With either a job order system or a process system, the computation of unit costs is relatively easy. We add up the total costs and the number of units and then divide the two. In a job order system such as the one shown above for Buzzard Woodworks, where only one unit (the desk and bookcase) is involved, we do not even have to divide. If a job order system is being used for batches of products, such as a batch of 5000 textbooks, and the job ticket shows that the batch cost $125,000, it is a relatively simple matter to divide the two items and determine that each textbook cost $25 to manufacture.

Equivalent Units.   A complexity in calculating unit costs arises in a process system when several (or several hundred) units are still in process at the end of an accounting period. When a production line is shut down at the end of a day, for example, some units may be 50 percent complete, others only 10 percent complete, and others 90 percent complete. To calculate a unit cost, the accountants need to know how many units were involved in the production effort that generated a certain level of costs.

To make this determination, they employ the concept of *equivalent units.* The details of this method are covered in cost accounting textbooks and essentially consist of adding the percentages of completion. Thus, if 10 units are in a stage of production in which they are approximately 50 percent complete, this is equivalent to having 5 units fully completed. Of course, the accountants also must *deduct* the equivalent unit amount as of the *beginning* of the accounting period, since some of the units that were completed during that period were partially completed when the period began.

In this manner, the accountants are able to determine how many equivalent units were produced during the accounting period. The process becomes somewhat more complicated when several different departments work on a single product, when raw material and other inventory costs are changing because of changing prices, or when there are other complexities. However, this is the essence of the approach.

Inventory Cost and Cost of Goods Sold

Once we know the unit cost of an item that has been produced, or the average cost of each item in a batch, that amount stays with the unit until it is sold. Thus, if we want to know the cost of our inventory, we simply need to count the number of units in it and multiply by the unit cost. Sometimes this requires the specific identification of items in the inventory so that each unit has its own unit cost. This would happen if the units were large and unique, such as the desk and bookcase at Buzzard Woodworks. Sometimes the unit cost is an average for a batch. In a process system it would be an average per unit, such as the cost per gallon in a paint manufacturing factory.

When items are sold, the accounting staff determines which ones were removed from inventory. It multiplies that total by the price to determine revenue and by the unit cost to calculate cost of goods sold.

Financial Statements

An expanded version of the income statement frequently is used in manufacturing organizations. The principal characteristic of this statement is that it incorporates a computation of the *cost of goods manufactured* as well as the cost of goods sold. As the term suggests, the cost of goods manufactured is the cost of all the items *manufactured* during the accounting period regardless of whether they were sold.

Exhibit 4-3 contains a sample statement of the cost of goods manufactured. Exhibit 4-4 shows how the cost of goods manufactured would be included on an income statement using a "functional classification."

 PROBLEM   In an economy with stable prices, do you think cost of goods manufactured is bigger or smaller than cost of goods sold? Careful: this is a little tricky.

ANSWER   It could be either, depending on whether the company is building or reducing inventories. If the company is building inventories, more will be manufactured than sold; therefore, the cost of goods manufactured will be bigger. If the company is reducing inventories, more will be sold than manufactured; therefore, the cost of goods manufactured will be smaller. Of course, if production and sales are more or less equal, the two cost amounts will be about the same.

Now let us look at a somewhat more complex situation that pulls all the pieces together to obtain the full cost of some products.

 PROBLEM   Curtainworks produces custom-made curtains and drapes. Its direct materials consist of fabric that it purchases by the yard. Unless a special order is received, the company always uses the same quality fabric, which costs $5.00 per yard. Curtainworks had the following items in its inventories at the beginning of April:

EXHIBIT 4-3

Statement of Cost of Goods Manufactured

For the Quarter Ended March 31, 2002

Direct materials

Beginning balance of raw materials inventory	$ 700,000	
Plus: Purchases	1,200,000	
Equals: Raw materials available	$1,900,000	
Less: Ending balance of raw materials inventory	500,000	
Equals: Direct materials used		$1,400,000
Direct labor		2,300,000
Manufacturing Overhead		
Indirect labor	300,000	
Depreciation	800,000	
Supplies and materials	100,000	
Rent and utilities	200,000	
Maintenance and repair	400,000	
Taxes	50,000	1,850,000
Total Manufacturing Costs This Period		$5,550,000
Plus: Beginning balance of work in process inventory		850,000
Equals: Total manufacturing costs this plus prior periods		$6,400,000
Less: Ending balance of work in process inventory		650,000
Cost of Goods Manufactured		$5,750,000

EXHIBIT 4-4

Income Statement: Functional Classification

For the Quarter Ended March 31, 2002

Sales revenue		$8,900,000
Less: Cost of goods sold		
Beginning balance of finished goods inventory	$ 200,000	
Plus: Cost of goods manufactured	5,750,000	
Equals: Goods available for sale	$5,950,000	
Less: Ending balance of finished goods inventory	300,000	
Equals: Cost of goods sold		5,650,000
Gross margin		$3,250,000
Less: Nonmanufacturing expenses		
Selling expenses	1,200,000	
Administration and general	900,000	2,100,000
Operating income		$1,150,000

Inventory	No. of Units	Unit Cost	Total Cost
Direct Materials	1,000	$5	$5,000
Work in Process	0		0
Finished Goods	1	$2,000	2,000
Total			$7,000

During April the company (1) purchased an additional 2000 yards of fabric at $5 per yard, (2) sold for $3000 the item that was in finished goods inventory, and (3) worked on the following three jobs:

Job	Direct Material	Direct Labor	Over- head	Total	Sales Price*
1	$500	$1,200	$500	$2,200	$3,300
2	800	1,500	800	3,100	4,650
3	1,000	2,000	1,000	4,000	6,000

*Or, with Job #3, the price *quoted* to the customer.

Jobs 1 and 2 were sold. Job 3 remained in finished goods inventory at the end of April.

Prepare a statement of cost of goods manufactured and an income statement (functional classification) through the gross margin line for the month of April. What kind of a cost system do you think Curtainworks uses? How does it attach overhead to jobs?

ANALYSIS   The statements for Curtainworks would look as follows (with information sources shown in parentheses):

Curtainworks. Statement of Cost of Goods Manufactured

Direct materials		
Beginning balance of raw materials inventory (Given)	$5,000	
Plus: Purchases (2000 yards @ $5)	10,000	
Equals: Raw materials available	$15,000	
Less: Ending balance of raw materials inventory*	12,700	
Equals: Direct materials used		$2,300
Direct labor		4,700
Manufacturing Overhead:		2,300
Total Manufacturing Costs this Period		$9,300
Plus: Beginning balance of work in process inventory		0
Equals: Total manufacturing costs this plus prior periods		$9,300
Less: Ending balance of work in process inventory		0
Cost of Goods Manufactured		$9,300

*Since we keep track of each job individually, we can make the following computation: BB + Purchases − Uses = EB, or $5,000 + $10,000 − ($500 + $800 + $1,000) = $12,700. A physical count of the inventory might help to ascertain whether there had been any shrinkage.

Curtainworks. Income Statement: Functional Classification

Sales revenue ($3,000 + $3,300 + $4,650)		$10,950
Less: Cost of goods sold:		
Beginning balance of finished goods inventory (given)	$2,000	
Plus: Cost of goods manufactured (from above)	9,300	
Equals: Goods available for sale	$11,300	
Less: Ending balance of finished goods inventory*	4,000	
Equals: Cost of goods sold (i.e., $2,000 + $2,200 + $3,100)		7,300
Gross margin		$3,650

*Reconciles to $4,000 unsold order.

- *Cost system.* Since it treats each job separately, Curtainworks appears to use a job order system.
- *Assignment of overhead.* Curtainworks assigns $1 of overhead to a job for every $1 of direct materials used on that job.

THE OVERHEAD RATE

In the Buzzard Woodworks example overhead was attached to jobs at a rate of $0.50 for every $1.00 of direct labor. At Curtainworks the rate was $1.00 per $1.00 of raw materials. Although it may appear that these are simplistic approaches to overhead attachment, the determination of these rates is anything but simple.

To understand the complications associated with determining an overhead rate, recall that in Chapter 1 we spent considerable time discussing allocation bases, which are ways to distribute service center costs to production centers. Recall also that the cost accounting effort does not stop once service center costs have been allocated to production centers. At that point we begin the second stage of the cost accounting effort, during which manufacturing overhead costs must be attached (or assigned) to products (or jobs) that pass through each production center. To do this, we need a rate. As we will see in Chapter 5, we could use several rates, but in this chapter we will illustrate the concept with only one rate.

To understand the difficulty of determining the overhead rate, assume that Curtainworks is one department (a production center) in a much larger company and that $10,000 of the company's service center costs have been allocated to it. Curtainworks also has $20,000 in indirect manufacturing costs, that is, costs that although direct for the department are indirect for the jobs it works on. Together, these two categories of costs constitute its manufacturing overhead.

Curtainworks now must find a way to attach a portion of this manufacturing overhead to individual jobs, such as job 2. In the example above, the company chose to do this by using the rate of $1 of overhead for every

$1 of raw materials. This gives rise to two questions: (1) Why did it choose raw materials as the basis? and (2) How did it make the computation?

The Basis

With regard to the first question, just as it was important to select appropriate bases to allocate service center costs to production centers, it also is important to use an appropriate basis to attach a production center's manufacturing overhead to its products. Here, as with the allocation of service center costs, we are seeking a good cause-and-effect relationship. That is, we are attempting to answer the question, "What activity in the department *drives* the use of the department's manufacturing overhead?

In most instances this is a difficult question to answer. Buzzard Woodworks said it was direct labor; Curtainworks said it was raw materials. Other departments, particularly ones that are capital-intensive, might use machine hours. Still others might use direct labor *hours* (as opposed to direct labor *dollars*). If management decides to use only one basis per production center for attaching overhead to products, it must exercise considerable judgment in selecting the one that measures cause and effect most accurately.

Although we will look at multiple bases in Chapter 5, it is worth noting here that the number of bases could be expanded by dividing the department into several cost centers, each of which would have its own basis. As with service centers in Chapter 1, the goal is to have the activities in each cost center be as homogeneous as possible. When this is the case, the assignment basis usually is a better indicator of the use of overhead than it is when the cost center's activities are heterogeneous.

The Computation

Once we have selected the basis and have the total amount of overhead to be attached, we must determine the amount in the denominator of the ratio. That is, in the Curtainworks example, we know the numerator is $30,000 and know the basis is dollars of raw materials used. Thus, to compute the rate we need to know how many total dollars of raw materials were used during the year. Since the rate Curtainworks used was $1 of overhead for every $1 of raw materials, the company must have used $30,000 of raw materials during the year.

 PROBLEM Assume that the machining department in a company is highly capital-intensive and that it has $100,000 in manufacturing overhead. The department has had 10,000 direct labor hours for a total cost of $80,000, $5000 of raw material costs, and 20,000 machine hours. How would you attach the $100,000 of manufacturing overhead to the products worked on by the department? Specify the basis you would use and compute the rate.

ANSWER Since the department is highly capital-intensive, it probably makes sense to attach manufacturing overhead on the basis of machine hours. With $100,000 in manufacturing overhead and 20,000 machine hours, the overhead rate is $5.00 ($100,000 ÷ 20,000) per machine hour. Thus, for every hour a product spends on a machine, it receives $5 of manufacturing overhead.

Predetermined Overhead Rates

The process described above works when we can wait until the end of the accounting period to calculate overhead rates and attach overhead to products. There are two reasons why we ordinarily do not want to do this. First, we would have to compute overhead rates every time we wanted to prepare a set of financial statements. Although spreadsheet and other software packages have simplified this task greatly compared with the situation, say, 10 or 15 years ago, the effort is time-consuming and costly in many organizations.

Second, when overhead rates are computed on a monthly or quarterly basis, they tend to have seasonal variations embedded in them. When products are manufactured in the winter, for example, they have the cost of heating included in the computation; those manufactured in the summer have the cost of air-conditioning; and those manufactured in the spring and fall have little of either. Ideally, of course, each product will bear its *fair share* of the overhead incurred at the time of its manufacture. However, when managers are attempting to analyze the relative profitability of certain products or product lines, the inclusion of overhead costs that vary because of seasonality can make the analysis unnecessarily complicated.

The problem of seasonal changes in overhead rates can be especially troublesome for a company that uses a process system. In a company that manufactures, say, disks for microcomputers, there no doubt would be some reluctance among managers to accept the idea that disks manufactured in the summer or the winter cost more than do those manufactured in the spring or the fall even though this technically is true. Some managers faced with cost-cutting mandates might be tempted to adjust production so that it peaked in the spring and fall and was minimal in the summer and winter. This could create a variety of problems with the costs of finished goods inventory storage, delivery schedules, and customer satisfaction.

For reasons of time, cost, and comparability, therefore, many companies do not use actual overhead rates to attach overhead costs to products.

Instead, they use *predetermined overhead rates,* which are overhead rates set as part of a budget. Although predetermined overhead rates have some problems, most companies feel that their advantages outweigh their disadvantages.

Advantages of Predetermined Overhead Rates.

The main advantage of a predetermined overhead rate is ease of use. Overhead can be attached to products without the need to undertake repeated cost allocations. Financial statements showing cost of goods manufactured and gross margin can be prepared relatively quickly, which is important if managers are to use financial information as a basis for exercising cost control. Finally, companies that use a cost-plus basis for pricing (such as specialty machine shops, made-to-order manufacturers, and building contractors) need a way to include overhead costs in a bid; predetermined overhead rates serve this purpose.

Disadvantages of Predetermined Overhead Rates.

The main disadvantage of a predetermined overhead rate is its possible lack of accuracy. Because the numerator (a department's manufacturing overhead) and the denominator (the actual number of, say, machine hours) can vary from predetermined levels, the rate will not provide management with a completely accurate measure of the amount of manufacturing overhead actually used by a product. To understand why this is true, consider the following problem.

 PROBLEM Computex, a division of a large company, manufactures wristwatches that feature small computers. Computex's expected and actual production plans, as well as its expected and actual overhead costs for a year, are shown below. Which number is the predetermined overhead rate? Determine the rationale for your choice.

	No. of Units Produced	Machine Hours per Watch	Total Machine Hours	Manufacturing Overhead	Overhead per Machine Hour	Overhead per Watch Produced
Column No. (*)	1	2	3 = 1 * 2	4	5 = 4 ÷ 3	6 = 5 * 2
Expected	5,000	2.0	10,000	$50,000	$5.00	$10.00
Actual	3,000	2.5	7,500	$41,250	$5.50	$13.75

*For reference purposes. For example, column 3 is column 1 multiplied by column 2.

ANSWER The predetermined overhead rate is the $5.00 in column 5. It is based on the expected overhead amount in column 4 and the expected number of machine hours in column 3. Note that the predetermined overhead rate is per machine hour, not per unit of production (a watch in this instance).

This approach is usually the case. That is, the overhead rate is based on *inputs* to the production process rather than on *outputs*. The reason for this is that the inputs, not the outputs, drive the costs. The tricky part, of course, is determining which inputs drive which costs.

 PROBLEM Given the predetermined overhead of $5.00, how much overhead do you think was attached to products? Careful: this is a little tricky.

ANSWER The amount of manufacturing overhead attached to products was $30,000: 3,000 watches × 2 machine hours per watch (i.e., the standard number of machine hours per watch) × $5.00 per machine hour. This compares with actual manufacturing overhead of $41,250.

 PROBLEM Why was attached manufacturing overhead not equal to actual manufacturing overhead?

ANSWER Attached manufacturing overhead (or *applied* or *absorbed* manufacturing overhead; the terms are used interchangeably) is not equal to actual manufacturing overhead because two numbers differed from what was expected: (1) the number of machine hours per watch and (2) the actual overhead amount. Note that the number of machine hours we used in the computation was based on the standard of 2 hours per watch. Thus, the *attached* overhead was based on the number of machine hours per watch *at standard* for the *actual* number of watches manufactured. We will see later how to deal with the different number of machine hours used per watch manufactured.

Some people consider the difference between attached overhead and actual overhead a disadvantage of predetermined overhead rates. They reason that this type of difference does not exist in a system without predetermined rates. It thus adds an unnecessary complication to the accounting effort. However, as we will see below, a predetermined overhead rate, coupled with some additional analytical techniques, can produce useful information for management.

OVERHEAD VARIANCES

The $11,250 difference discussed above between actual manufacturing overhead and the manufacturing overhead attached to products is an important figure for Computex's managers, especially if they are concerned about controlling manufacturing costs. Analyzing the causes of this difference can be difficult. The analysis rests on two new concepts: a flexible overhead budget and variance analysis. Let us look at each one briefly.

Flexible Overhead Budgets

As we saw in Chapter 1, the allocation of service center costs to production centers can be a relatively complicated process, especially when management wants homogeneous cost centers and causal bases of allocation. Once that effort has been completed, all costs reside in production centers. They then must be attached to products. It is relatively easy to do this with direct costs, but indirect costs (or manufacturing overhead) present some complications.

As was discussed earlier, many companies use a single basis of allocation to attach a production center's manufacturing overhead to products. Let us look at such a process. Imagine that Computex expected its $50,000 in annual manufacturing overhead costs to be classified as follows:

Service center	Basis of Allocation	Amount	
Cleaning	Square feet	$2,000	
Utilities	Machine hours	1,000	
Property taxes	Square feet	500	
Insurance	Book value of assets	200	
Rent	Square feet	_1,500_	$5,200
Department indirect costs			
Indirect materials		3,000	
Indirect labor (part-time employees)		14,000	
Supervision		20,000	
Maintenance and repairs		1,600	
Equipment depreciation		_6,200_	_44,800_
Total			$50,000

Note that the second category in this list (department indirect costs) actually consists of costs that are *direct* for the department as a whole but *indirect* with regard to a watch that is produced in the department.

As we saw above, to attach these costs to watches, Computex divided the $50,000 total by the estimated number of machine hours to obtain a predetermined overhead rate. Also, as we saw above, actual overhead for the year was $41,250.

 PROBLEM What are some of the possible reasons why actual overhead fell to $41,250?

ANSWER There are four broad reasons why these costs may have fallen: (1) Service centers spent less, and so the amount allocated to the production center was lower. (2) Although the cost of utilities did not fall, the production center received a lower allocation from the utilities service center because its number of machine hours (the basis of allocation) fell during the year. (3) The production center may have had lower costs for items such as indirect materials and indirect labor as a result of having fewer machine hours. (4) The production center could have saved costs in maintenance and repair, indirect labor, supervision, and so forth, not as a result of fewer machine hours but simply because of increased efficiency.

If they are to control overhead costs, Computex's managers need to be able to identify the costs that are associated with changes in volume of activity (here the number of watches produced) in contrast to changes in spending or efficiency. The flexible overhead budget helps in this effort. It works as follows.

Identify Fixed/Variable Cost Splits. For each line we identify the fixed and variable components, resulting in a cost formula of the type discussed in Chapter 2. For the above costs, the formulas might look as follows:

Cost Item	Basis of Allocation	Fixed Cost	Variable Cost (per Machine Hour)	Total Expected Cost for 10,000 Machine Hours
Service center allocations				
Cleaning	Square feet	$2,000	—	$2,000
Utilities	Machine hours	300	$0.07	1,000
Property taxes	Square feet	500	—	500
Insurance	Book value of assets	200	—	200
Rent	Square feet	1,500	—	1,500
Department direct costs that are indirect to products				
Nonproduct materials (e.g. cleaning solvents)		0	0.30	3,000
Nonproduct labor (part-time employees)		5,000	0.90	14,000
Supervision		20,000	—	20,000
Maintenance and repairs		1,000	0.06	1,600
Equipment depreciation		6,200	—	6,200
Total		$36,700	1.33	$50,000

We can now say that manufacturing overhead is computed according to the following formula:

$$\$36,700 + 1.33x$$
where x is the number of machine hours

Flex the Budget with Actual Production Levels. When
actual production is known, we adjust the original budget by using the
cost formula. Thus, if actual production is 3000 watches, as it was above,
total overhead should be

$$\$36,700 + [1.33 \times (3,000 \times 2)] = \$44,680$$

Note that since each watch should use 2 machine hours, we multiplied the
3000 watches by two to obtain the standard (or expected) number of
machine hours.

Compute the Overhead Volume Variance. The overhead
volume variance can be determined by subtracting the flexed budget from
the amount of overhead attached to products by using the predetermined
overhead rate. This amount usually is called *absorbed* or *applied* manufacturing overhead.

The computation for applied manufacturing overhead is straightforward. We did this earlier by multiplying 6000 standard machine hours
(3000 watches × 2 hours per watch) by the predetermined overhead rate,
as follows:

$$6,000 \times \$5.00 = \$30,000$$

The budget based on standard hours is $44,680, as was calculated above.
The difference between the two is the *overhead volume variance*, or

$$\$30,000 - \$44,680 = (\$14,680)$$

It is caused by the change in volume (expected to actual), holding everything else constant (variable costs per machine hour, machine hours per
watch, and fixed costs).

In this situation, all else being equal, the decline in volume had a
negative effect on profit of $14,680. In general, we will use parentheses to
indicate a situation in which the impact on profit is negative. This sometimes is called a *negative* or *unfavorable* variance.

Distinguish between Volume and Budget Variances.
The flexed budget indicates how much overhead we *should have had* given
the *actual* volume of production. The difference between this number and
actual overhead is the *overhead budget* (or the *controllable*) *variance*. It consists of two parts: (1) an *efficiency variance*, which is based on the actual
number versus expected number of machine hours used per watch, and
(2) a *spending variance*, which is the actual cost versus the expected cost per

machine hour. Let us look at these differences in light of the situation described above.

- *Overhead efficiency variance.* The overhead efficiency variance isolates the effect of using more (or fewer) machine hours per unit of output than was budgeted. It is a result of the difference between the budget based on standard machine hours and the budget based on actual machine hours.

The budget based on actual hours is

$$\$36,700 + [1.33 \times (7,500)] = \$46,675$$

The difference is

$$\$44,680 - \$46,675 = (\$1,995)$$

- *Overhead spending variance:* The overhead spending variance is calculated by subtracting the actual amount spent from the budget based on *actual* hours, as follows:

$$\$46,675 - \$41,250 = \$5,425$$

That is, at the actual number of machine hours, overhead should have been $46,675, but we spent only $41,250. The result was a positive effect on profits.

The sum of these three variances is the total variance, as follows:

$$\$(14,680) + (\$1,995) + \$5,425 = (\$11,250)$$

That is, actual overhead was $11,250 higher than the amount that was attached to products. These computations are shown schematically in Exhibit 4-5.

Spend a few minutes reviewing Exhibit 4-5. Note that all the variance computations begin with the number on the right (the budget) and subtract the number on the left (where actual experience is introduced) from it. For example, the total variance (shown at the bottom of the exhibit) is the applied manufacturing overhead (MOH) minus the actual MOH. In particular, note the following:

- *Volume variance:* If the volume of output is below expectations, as is the case here, less MOH will be applied through the predetermined overhead rate than the budget based on standard hours calls for. That is, the budget based on standard hours is greater

EXHIBIT 4-5

Summary of Manufacturing Overhead (MOH) Variance Computations for Computex Company

Actual MOH	Budgeted MOH Based on Actual Hours	Budgeted MOH Based on Standard Hours	Applied (or Absorbed) MOH
	$36,700 + ($1.33 × 7,500)	$36,700 + ($1.33 × 6,000)	$5.00 × 6,000
$41,250	**$46,675**	**$44,680**	**$30,000**

Spending Variance		Efficiency Variance		Volume Variance
$46,675 − $41,250		$44,680 − $46,675		$30,000 − $44,680
$5,425		**($1,995)**		**($14,680)**

Budget Variance
$5,425 + ($1,995)
$3,430

or

Budget Variance
$44,680 − $41,250
$3,430

Total Variance
$3,430 + ($14,680)
($11,250)

or

Total Variance
$30,000 − $41,250
($11,250)

than the manufacturing overhead that was applied to products (applied MOH). Mathematically, the negative volume variance arises because when actual volume is below budgeted volume, some of the fixed costs ($36,700 in this example) do not get applied to products through the overhead rate. We will return to this point later in this chapter.

- *Efficiency variance:* If the budget based on actual hours is greater than the budget based on standard hours, as is the case here, there is a negative *efficiency variance*. That is, the production effort was less efficient (used more machine hours per unit of output) than anticipated.

- *Spending variance:* If the manufacturing manager spends less on manufacturing overhead than the flexible budget based on *actual hours* calls for, as is the case here, the result is a positive *spending variance*. That is, actual manufacturing overhead (actual MOH) is less than budgeted MOH based on actual hours.

Calculation Steps

Understanding the various parts at work in these computations is tricky. For some people the computations are aided by thinking of them as a sequence of steps. The entire process of developing a predetermined overhead rate, applying it to production, computing the flexible budget, and calculating the variances is in the following 11 steps:

1. Using fixed and variable breakdowns, calculate total expected MOH based on the expected volume of output and specify the standard input units (e.g., machine hours or direct labor dollars) per unit of output.

2. Divide total expected MOH by total expected input units at standard to obtain the predetermined MOH rate.

3. Once the actual volume of output (or production) is known, multiply it by the standard input units per unit of output to obtain the *total* standard input units at *actual* volume. Multiply this figure by the predetermined MOH rate to obtain applied MOH.

4. Use total standard input units at actual volume in conjunction with the initial fixed and variable cost breakdowns to calculate total expected costs based on the *actual* volume of output. This is the budgeted MOH based on standard input units.

5. Subtract the budgeted MOH based on standard input units from applied MOH to determine the *volume variance.* (This will be negative if actual volume is below expected volume.)

6. Using *actual* input units, calculate the budgeted MOH.

7. Subtract the budgeted MOH based on actual input units from the budgeted MOH based on standard input units to determine the *efficiency variance.* This will be negative if more input units per unit of output were used than was budgeted.

8. Obtain actual MOH from the accounting system.

9. Subtract *actual* MOH from the budgeted MOH based on actual input units to determine the *spending variance.* (This will be negative if actual MOH is greater than the amount the budget says should be spent.)

10. Add the efficiency variance and the spending variance to determine the *budget (or controllable) variance.*

11. Add the volume variance and the budget variance to determine the *total variance.* This also can be computed by subtracting actual

MOH from applied MOH (which also provides verification of the volume, efficiency, and spending variance computations).

Using the Techniques

These techniques—the 11 steps shown above and the format shown in Exhibit 4-5—can be difficult to understand. One of the best ways to grasp them is to work through the entire process. The following problem provides an opportunity to do that. Try to work through it by using either the 11 steps or the format in Exhibit 4-5. Either technique should yield the same answer. Your choice of an approach depends on how you best learn; people who are more visual in their learning might try using Exhibit 4-5, for example.

 PROBLEM   Silverado, Inc., manufactures silver belt buckles for Western-style outfits. Each belt buckle is supposed to require 1 machine hour to manufacture. The company's expected costs for the upcoming year are as follows:

Cost Item	Basis of Allocation	Fixed Cost	Variable Cost (per Machine Hour)
Service center allocations			
Cleaning	Square feet	$5,000	—
Utilities	Machine hours	800	$0.50
Property taxes	Square feet	700	—
Insurance	Book value of assets	400	—
Rent .	Square feet	2,500	—
Department indirect costs			
Indirect materials .		1,300	1.50
Indirect labor		10,000	7.50
Supervision		40,000	—
Maintenance and repairs		5,000	.70
Equipment depreciation		10,500	=
Total for year		$76,200	$10.20
Total for a typical month (1/12 of a year)		$6,350	$10.20

Silverado expected to manufacture 12,000 buckles for the year, spaced evenly over the entire 12 months. In March, however, it produced only 800 buckles and used 900 machine hours. In April it more than made up for that decline by producing 1500 buckles, using 1400 machine hours.

Actual overhead in March was $16,000. In April actual overhead was $22,000. Prepare an overhead variance analysis for each of the two months. Explain in your own words what happened.

ANALYSIS   If you followed the 11-step process, your analysis should look as follows:

1. Using fixed and variable breakdowns, calculate total expected costs based on expected volume:

$76,200 + ($10.20/hour × 12,000 units × 1 hour/unit) = $198,600

2. Divide total expected costs by expected volume of inputs to obtain the predetermined overhead rate:

$198,600 ÷ 12,000 hours = $16.55

3. Multiply the predetermined overhead rate by actual volume to obtain applied MOH:

March = 800 units × 1 hour/unit × $16.55/hour = $13,240
April = 1,500 units × 1 hour/unit × $16.55/hour = $24,825

4. Using the original fixed and variable breakdowns, calculate total expected costs based on *actual* volume. This is the budgeted MOH based on standard hours.

   Since this is by month, we need to use *monthly* fixed costs of $6350. The budgeted MOH based on standard hours for each month therefore can be computed as follows:

March = $6,350 + ($10.20 × 800 hours) = $14,510
April = $6,350 + ($10.20 × 1,500 hours) = $21,650

5. Subtract the budgeted MOH at standard hours from applied MOH to determine the volume variance. This will be negative if actual volume is below expected volume:

March = $13,240 − $14,510 = ($1,270)
April = $24,825 − $21,650 = $3,175

6. Using actual machine hours, calculate the budgeted MOH:

March = $6,350 + ($10.20 × 900 hours) = $15,530
April = $6,350 + ($10.20 × 1,400 hours) = $20,630

7. Subtract budgeted MOH at actual hours from budgeted MOH at standard hours to determine the efficiency variance:

March = $14,510 − $15,530 = ($1,020)
April = $21,650 − $20,630 = $1,020

8. Obtain actual MOH from the accounting system. This was given as follows:

March = $16,000
April = $22,000

9. Subtract *actual* MOH from the budgeted MOH at actual hours to determine the spending variance. (This will be negative if actual MOH is greater than the amount the budget says should be spent.)

March = $15,530 − $16,000 = ($470)
April = $20,630 − $22,000 = ($1,370)

10. Add the efficiency variance and the spending variance to determine the budget variance:

March = ($1,020) + ($470) = ($1,490)
April = $1,020 + ($1,370) = ($350)

11. Add the volume variance and the budget variance to determine the total variance.

Month	Volume Variance	Budget Variance	Total Variance
March	($1,270)	($1,490)	($2,760)
April	$3,175	($350)	$2,825

ANALYSIS   If you used the technique shown in Exhibit 4–5, your analysis should look as follows for March (the computations have been excluded, as they are shown in the steps above):

Actual MOH	Budgeted MOH Based on Actual Hours	Budgeted MOH Based on Standard Hours	Applied (or Absorbed) MOH
$16,000	$15,530	$14,510	$13,240

Spending Variance	Efficiency Variance	Volume Variance
($470)	($1,020)	($1,270)

Budget Variance
($1,490)

Total Variance
($2,760)

EXPLANATION   In March, volume that was below expectations led to a negative $1270 volume variance. This was exacerbated by a negative efficiency variance ($1020) caused by the use of more machine hours than expected (900 versus 800) and a negative spending variance ($470), indicating that the company spent more on MOH than the number of machine hours would suggest was appropriate. Schematically, your analysis for April should look as follows:

Actual MOH	Budgeted MOH Based on Actual Hours	Budgeted MOH Based on Standard Hours	Applied (or Absorbed) MOH
$22,000	$20,630	$21,650	$24,825

Spending Variance	Efficiency Variance	Volume Variance
($1,370)	$1,020	$3,175

Budget Variance
($350)

Total Variance
$2,825

EXPLANATION   In April, volume was up, giving the company a $3175 favorable volume variance. Efficiency also was up (it took only 1400 machine hours to produce 1500 buckles), but spending was still a problem: Silverado spent $1370 more than the number of machine hours indicated was appropriate. Overall, April's total positive variance more than compensated for March's negative one.

Terminology Issues

Apart from some of the terminology differences discussed previously, there are two terms that are important in the context of overhead variances: *standard costs* and *overapplied (underapplied) overhead*. Both terms appear frequently in the cost accounting information that managers and others see in many organizations, not just manufacturing companies.

Standard Costs.   Occasionally one sees the term *standard cost* used in conjunction with an overhead variance analysis. In general, a standard cost is the same as an expected cost: It is what senior management believes the cost will be on the basis of the discussions that take place as part of a planning and budgeting effort. Sometimes standards are set using ideal or optimum conditions and thus are not "expected" as such. Instead, they are the *goal* for the involved managers. When this is the case, senior management needs to make its performance expectations clear; otherwise, production managers may become frustrated.

In a manufacturing environment, standard costs are established not only for overhead but also for many of the elements that make up a product's cost as defined in Exhibit 4-1. The result is that there can be several different types of variances between standard costs and actual results, as in the use of direct materials or labor and in the rates paid for those two factors of production.

Overapplied and Underapplied Overhead. When a predetermined overhead rate is used, the overhead that is attached to products can be either *underapplied* (sometimes called *underabsorbed* or *unabsorbed*), or *overapplied* (sometimes called *overabsorbed*). Overhead is underapplied when applied MOH is less than budgeted MOH based on standard units. That is, not enough of the overhead that was incurred at standard was attached to (or absorbed into) the products. Overhead is overapplied when applied MOH exceeds budgeted MOH based on standard units. That is, more overhead was attached to the products than actually was incurred at standard. This is not a new concept; it was at work in the Computex and Silverado problems. It is just new terminology and is illustrated in Exhibit 4-6.

Accounting Implications of an Overhead Variance

From an accounting perspective, the total MOH variance is the difference between actual MOH and applied MOH. The cause of this difference may lie in the underlying conditions that give rise to overhead, such as changes in the volume of output, or the variance may be due to unexpected ineffi-

EXHIBIT 4-6

Overapplied and Underapplied Overhead (or Overabsorbed and Underabsorbed Overhead)

Applied versus Budgeted MOH at Standard	Overapplied	Underapplied
	Applied MOH is greater than budgeted MOH at standard	Applied MOH is less than budgeted MOH at standard
Computation	Applied MOH minus budgeted MOH at standard	Applied MOH minus budgeted MOH at standard
OH volume variance is	Positive	Negative

ciencies in the use of indirect items or changes in factor prices for indirect labor and materials.

The exact reasons for this overhead budget variance usually are difficult to discern from the accounting system. Nevertheless, most manufacturing managers have a feel for the causes. Thus, senior management needs to discuss the variances with the manufacturing manager to determine possible corrective actions. The separation of the variance into its three causes—volume, efficiency, and spending—can facilitate that discussion.

From an accounting perspective, the overhead variance account in the accounting system must be closed out. Usually this is done in one of two ways: (1) making a transaction that closes the account to cost of goods sold or (2) making a transaction that closes the account to a combination of cost of goods sold, work in process inventory, and finished goods inventory.

Technically, the second method is more accurate (and abides by GAAP's matching principle), since portions of the variance are represented in all three accounts. From a practical perspective, the first approach frequently is used since it is easier, and the overhead variances generally are not sufficiently large to have a material effect on the overall results reported on the financial statements. Thus, *materiality* is used as the justification for a technical violation of the matching principle.

MANAGERIAL USES OF OVERHEAD VARIANCES

Few managers have either the time or the inclination to calculate manufacturing variances as has been done here. Instead, they receive reports from their accounting staffs with these computations already made. Thus, the real question from a managerial perspective is, "What is the value of the variances?"

The main value of the variances lies in the information they provide for cost control. In particular, we can see that the overhead variances are the result of two very different forces:

- The *volume variance* arises because production volume was not as anticipated. Although there probably is little that the manufacturing manager can do about this, it nevertheless is a concern of senior management. If, for example, the entire overhead variance was due to volume effects, senior management probably would wish to have some discussions with the marketing and sales forces rather than the manufacturing manager. Of course, there is always the possibility that delays and breakdowns in the plant prevented the manufacturing manager from delivering the orders placed by the sales staff, and this possibility also would have to be investigated.

■ The *efficiency and spending variances* arise because actual overhead differed from what overhead should have been at the actual level of volume produced. If the variances are negative, they suggest that the individuals responsible for the various activities that make up overhead costs spent more than they should have, at least vis-à-vis the budget. While there may be good reasons for this, a large negative efficiency or spending variance provides an indication to senior management that some discussions with the manufacturing manager have to take place.

Because of the complications associated with volume variances and absorbed overhead, senior management in some organizations chooses not to use an *absorption costing system*, as the system we have been discussing is called, for management reporting purposes. Instead, it uses an absorption costing system to value inventory and compute the cost of goods sold for the financial statements but uses another system, called *variable costing*, for internal reporting purposes. The reasons for this are discussed in Chapter 5.

CHAPTER 5

Activity-Based Costing
and Variable Costing

Chapter 1 described what frequently is called the "first stage" of the cost accounting process. In this stage a company (1) defines cost centers, distinguishing between production centers and service centers, (2) assigns all costs to cost centers, and (3) allocates service center costs to production centers. The result is that all costs are contained in production centers.

Chapter 4 described the "second stage" of the process: attaching production center costs to the products that pass through those centers. This ordinarily is called absorption costing because manufacturing overhead (MOH) is *absorbed* into the products. With this approach, MOH remains with the product until the product is sold, at which point it becomes part of the cost of goods sold.

As was indicated in Chapter 4, the absorption process can be tricky and can give misleading results. When only one overhead rate is used to do the absorption, as was the case in Chapter 4, the implicit assumption is that the unit used in that rate (e.g., machine hours or direct labor dollars) is the activity that drives the use of all MOH. However, MOH generally is affected by a somewhat more complex array of forces, and so absorption costing systems that use a single overhead rate can give management incorrect information.

Two techniques frequently are used to correct for this deficiency, both of which are discussed in this chapter: activity-based costing and variable costing. Activity-based costing (ABC) corrects for the deficiency by using multiple overhead rates with multiple "overhead cost pools." To do this, it tries to make the resources in each cost pool as homogeneous as possible and then identifies an activity that drives the use of those resources. For example, one cost pool in a factory might be the labor and supervisory time needed to set up the machines for a production run. In this case, the appropriate cost pool would be everything associated with setting up the machines (such as cleaning and adjusting tolerances) and the appropriate allocation base for overhead would be a setup. Each unit of product in a small production run thus would get a higher share of the setup MOH than would each unit in a large production run.[1]

Variable costing removes fixed MOH from the absorption process, treating it as a period cost rather than a product cost. Although it is not permitted by generally accepted accounting principles (GAAP) for external reporting purposes, this technique frequently is used internally by managers to help them better understand how manufacturing costs are being incurred.

Absorption costing is used by almost all manufacturing organizations, whereas merchandising and service organizations do not have this type of activity. In general, the cost of goods sold for a merchandising organization, such as a book retailer, is only the cost to the retailer of the items that were sold (e.g., the books). Labor, depreciation, and other similar items are treated as period costs rather than being absorbed into the product. They appear as expenses on each income statement for the period covered by that statement.

As will be shown in this chapter, many merchandising organizations and some service organizations can make use of activity-based costing (ABC) for both pricing and control activities. When they do this, they do not absorb MOH into products, as a manufacturing organization does, but instead compute the amount of overhead activities—purchasing, logistics, and the like—associated with different types of goods or services. This allows them to determine whether they are pricing their goods and/or services above full cost and assists them in giving their managers responsibility for controlling the level of some overhead costs.

The chapter begins with activity-based costing, introducing the idea that there is an important link between the *measurement* of costs in a full-cost accounting system, and the *control* of costs in a responsibility accounting system. This sets the stage for the discussion of responsibility accounting systems in the remaining chapters of the book.

The chapter then compares absorption costing with variable costing. Variable costing relies on the distinction between fixed costs and variable costs that was discussed in Chapter 2. The differences between the approaches and the advantages and disadvantages of each then are discussed.

ACTIVITY-BASED COSTING

An important theme that emerges from the discussion of manufacturing overhead variances in Chapter 4 is the distinction between cost *measurement* and *cost control*. Good cost measurement clearly is important and generally is a prerequisite for cost control. Nevertheless, senior and middle managers in many organizations increasingly are demanding that their cost systems play a more active role in helping them control costs.

The field of management accounting has made considerable strides in developing linkages between measurement and control. In manufacturing companies this linkage has been attained in a variety of ways, one of which is activity-based costing.

ABC focuses on two matters of importance to managers: homogeneity of overhead cost pools and the activity that drives the use of each pool. To understand this, we need to return to some of the matters discussed in Chapter 4.

First, recall that in Chapter 4 we were dealing with MOH only, not with direct manufacturing costs. Ordinarily, it is relatively easy to attach direct manufacturing costs to products: One simply records and costs out the amount of labor and raw materials that went into a product, using either a job order system or a process system. Manufacturing overhead presents a difficult problem, however.

The examples in Chapter 4 involved organizations that use a single activity (or cost driver), such as machine hours, to attach MOH to products during the second stage of the cost accounting activity. Although there are situations in which a single rate is adequate, there are many in which it is not.[2]

In general, the presence of one of three factors indicates a need for multiple second-stage cost drivers: (1) product diversity, (2) relative costs, and (3) volume diversity.

Product diversity exists when different products use overhead-related services in different proportions. If one product requires considerably more inspection time than does another, for example, there is product diversity. However, product diversity is important only when the costs of the different overhead activities are significantly different; this is the *relative cost* factor. Finally, since some overhead activities are affected by the size of the batch being produced and others are not, *volume diversity* exists if the products are manufactured in batches of different sizes.[3]

Stated somewhat differently, a company probably could use a single rate to assign its MOH if it produced a single product or several similar products and had production batches that were all about the same size. It also could use a single rate if it had diverse products or varying batch sizes in its production runs but engaged in similar activities regardless of the type of product or the batch size. By contrast, it quite likely has a need for multiple cost drivers if it has either high product or high batch size (volume) diversity and engages in different activities with different products or batch sizes.

An organization that has decided to use multiple second-stage cost drivers usually begins its analysis with the activities in the plant that cause the costs for one batch of products to differ from those for another batch. Each activity then is given its own cost driver. If, for example, different products require different setup times, the appropriate cost driver will be something associated with setups. If a considerable amount of supervision is needed for one type of product but not for another, the appropriate cost driver might be supervisory hours. In this way, each cost driver measures a product's use of the manufacturing overhead resources that are needed to produce it.

Simply having multiple overhead cost drivers is not sufficient, however. Each cost driver must be linked to specific kinds of costs, and it must be the activity that *drives* the use of those costs.

Getting this alignment can be tricky. In one of several *Harvard Business Review* articles on ABC, Robin Cooper and Robert Kaplan, ABC's two architects, give the example of a machining shop that had shifted to ABC and was using three overhead cost drivers: direct labor dollars, direct material dollars, and machine hours. Unfortunately, all three were linked to the number of units of production, whereas more than 40 percent of the shop's overhead was not being used to produce units. The shop's managers found that cost accuracy improved considerably when they began to use new drivers of overhead such as setup time, production runs, and material movements.[4]

Establishing Multiple Second-Stage Cost Drivers

The process for establishing multiple second-stage cost drivers is discussed in many cost accounting textbooks and is beyond the scope of this chapter.[5] There are, however, several important concepts that are important to a manager's understanding of an ABC system. Some of those concepts were discussed in Chapter 1, which emphasized the idea that different products use different kinds and amounts of resources. This is why we used different allocation bases for different service centers. Similarly, at the production center (or department level) in a manufacturing organization, four general categories of activities influence the use of manufacturing overhead.[6]

- *Facility-sustaining activities.* This is the highest-set of activities and includes work such as plant management, building repair and maintenance, security, and grounds maintenance.
- *Product-sustaining activities.* These activities are needed to assure that products are produced according to specifications. They include process engineering, product specifications, engineering change notices, and product enhancements.
- *Batch-related activities.* These are activities that are performed each time a batch of products is manufactured, such as machine setups, material movements, and inspections.
- *Unit activities.* These are activities that are tied directly to the number of units produced, such as utility usage and machine hours.

(Unit-level activities also include direct manufacturing costs; the three other categories include only manufacturing overhead.)

These four categories are the building blocks for multiple second-stage cost drivers. Once they have been defined, we need to identify and measure the unit that causes a product to use them. Conceptually, the search is for a unit—a cost driver—that reflects a product's demand for each activity. For some activities, this is relatively easy; for others, it can be a difficult task.

 PROBLEM   Classify each of the following manufacturing overhead costs into one of the four categories discussed above: *indirect labor*—engineering (to adjust machine tolerances), supervision (for all jobs, relative to size of run), material handling (based on requisitions), maintenance (based on breakdowns), general cleaning, inspectors and quality control; *indirect materials*—solvents (to clean machines after each run) and lubricants (to keep machines running smoothly); *other*—equipment depreciation, property taxes, utilities, insurance. Identify a good cost driver for each one.

ANSWER   There is, of course, room for some disagreement about this classification. Here is one possible list:

	Category	Cost Driver
Indirect labor		
Engineering (to adjust machine tolerances)	product-sustaining	adjustments
Supervision (for all jobs, relative to size of run)	unit-level	units
Material handling (based on requisitions)	batch-related	requisitions
Maintenance (based on breakdowns)	product-sustaining	maintenance hours
General cleaning	facility-sustaining	hours or square feet
Inspectors and quality control	batch-related	units

Indirect materials		
Solvents (to clean machines		
after each run)	batch-related	batches
Lubricants (to keep machines		
running smoothly)	unit-related	machine hours
Other		
Equipment depreciation	unit-level	machine hours
Property taxes	facility-sustaining	square feet
Utilities	unit-related	machine hours
Insurance	facility-sustaining	book value of assets

The key point here is not the "correct" classification of costs or the "correct" identification of cost drivers. In general, this is a task for the accounting staff. Nevertheless, it is important for managers to be involved in the decision-making process since classification of activities in this way permits them to assess more thoroughly the way products consume overhead resources.

The Real Value of ABC

Although it is difficult to implement and clearly is not a precise science, ABC frequently is worth the effort. 3M Company provides an interesting example. 3M initiated ABC by redesigning the structure of its U.S. income statement. Operating units received statements that separated direct production activities from activities devoted to production support. The company applied ABC to the analysis of corporate logistics costs, particularly the processing of customer orders and the making of credit adjustment decisions. It discovered that the cost of *processing* small credit claims was almost as high as the cost of *settling* them. As a result, it established a new policy that allowed sales representatives to approve on-site credit adjustments for small complaints.[7]

In effect, ABC moved 3M beyond cost measurement per se to a system that assisted managers with cost control.

Similarly, Chrysler Corporation estimated that its ABC system generated hundreds of millions of dollars in benefits by helping simplify product designs and eliminating unproductive, inefficient, or redundant activities. The benefits were 10 to 20 times greater than the company's investment in ABC. At some sites the savings were 50 to 100 times the implementation cost.[8] When these sorts of benefits accrue to an organization, the additional complexity and cost of using an ABC system seem small by comparison.

This link between cost measurement and cost control illustrates why senior management should be highly involved in the decision to implement ABC. Given the considerable time and energy needed both to implement an ABC system and then to operate it on an ongoing basis, the implementation decision should not be made exclusively by an organization's accountants. In particular, senior managers must assure themselves that product diversity, relative cost, or volume diversity is present and that it is significant enough to affect the assignment of overhead costs in a material way. Senior management also has to be convinced that improved cost information will result in improved decision making by line managers.

By having this sort of analysis, management not only can be assured that the accounting system is measuring costs accurately, but it also can concentrate on controlling costs by controlling the cost drivers; that is, it can begin to focus on *managing activities rather than costs*. This shift in thinking—from measurement to control—is one of the most powerful benefits of an ABC system and, in particular, of second-stage cost drivers.

Of course, ABC also can be helpful for other cost-accounting-related activities that were discussed in Chapter 1, such as pricing and profitability analysis. Indeed, the use of ABC has led managers in many organizations to reverse their thinking on which of their products are the most profitable.[9]

At Siemens Corporation, for example, when the company's strategy shifted from the production of large batches of standard motors to the production of small batches (sometimes only one) of specialized motors, ABC helped the company understand its "true costs" of producing each batch. When it attached setup costs and other batch-related activities to an order, Siemens discovered that it was pricing its large batches too high and its small batches too low.

A General Approach

The four categories used above—facility-sustaining, product-sustaining, batch-related, and unit-level—provide a useful way to classify costs in a manufacturing setting and to begin thinking about cost drivers. In a more general sense, the analytical effort consists of moving away from the traditional way of thinking about costs, which was based largely on a line-by-line listing of items such as personnel, depreciation, and supplies, and toward the activities that *drive* costs. In a manufacturing setting these activities include factors such as requisitions, setups, maintenance hours, and machine hours, among others.

 PROBLEM Espresso Dopio, Inc. (EDI), is a distributor and processor of two different blends of coffee that it offers to gourmet shops in 1-pound bags. One coffee, Spanish Blend, is very popular and sells in large volumes. The other, French Roast, sells in much smaller quantities. To assure freshness, EDI must purchase French Roast in small quantities and produce it in small batches.

EDI buys roasted coffee beans, which it packages for resale. It has a single facility where it conducts all of its production activities. Its major cost is raw materials (coffee beans). However, there is a substantial amount of MOH in the purchasing, handling, and packaging activities. Most of these activities are highly automated, and the company uses very little direct labor. The expected direct manufacturing cost for a 1-pound bag of each kind of coffee is shown below:

	Spanish Blend	French Roast
Direct material	$3.00	$4.00
Direct labor	0.50	0.50

EDI's annual budget includes MOH of $1.58 million, which currently is allocated on the basis of machine hours. However, EDI's controller believes that this product-costing system may be providing misleading information. She has developed the following analysis of the annual budgeted MOH costs:

Activity	Cost Driver	Budgeted Activity Units	Budgeted Cost
Purchasing	purchase orders	1,200	$600,000
Material handling	batches	1,800	720,000
Packaging	packaging hours	26,000	260,000
Total manufacturing overhead costs			$1,580,000

Budget data for the annual production of the two coffees are shown below:

	Spanish Blend	French Roast
Pounds produced (and sold)	800,000	200,000
Machine hours	400,000	100,000
Purchase orders	400	800
Batches	500	1,300
Packaging hours	17,000	9,000

Based on the annual budget data, determine the cost of a pound of each kind of coffee, first using the traditional approach of absorbing overhead on the basis of machine hours and then using an ABC approach.

ANALYSIS Under the *traditional approach,* manufacturing overhead is calculated as follows:

$1,580,000 ÷ 500,000 machine hours = $3.16 per machine hour.

Spanish Blend uses 400,000 machine hours for a total of $1,264,000. French Roast uses 100,000 machine hours for a total of $316,000.
    To check,

$1,264,000 + $316,000 = $1,580,000

With 800,000 pounds produced, the MOH cost per pound for Spanish Blend is $1.58 ($1,264,000 ÷ 800,000 pounds), the same as for French Roast ($316,000 ÷ 200,000 pounds).

Under the *activity-based approach,* manufacturing overhead is calculated as follows:

Activity	Cost Driver	Budgeted Activity Units	Cost	Cost per unit
Purchasing	purchase orders	1,200	$600,000	$500
Material handling	batches	1,800	720,000	400
Packaging	packaging hours	26,000	260,000	10

	Production Data		Cost per Pound	
	Spanish Blend	French Roast	Spanish Blend	French Roast
Pounds produced (and sold)	800,000	200,000		
Purchase orders	400	800	$0.25*	$2.00†
Batches	500	1,300	0.25‡	2.60§
Packaging hours	17,000	9,000	0.2125#	0.45**
Total			$0.7125	$5.05

* $500 per purchase order × 400 purchase orders = $200,000; $200,000 ÷ 800,000 pounds = $0.25 per pound

† $500 per purchase order × 800 purchase orders = $400,000; $400,000 ÷ 200,000 pounds = $2.00 per pound

‡ $400 per batch × 500 batches = $200,000; $200,000 ÷ 800,000 pounds = $0.25 per pound

§ $400 per batch × 1,300 batches = $520,000; $520,000 ÷ 200,000 pounds = $2.60 per pound

$10 per packaging hour × 17,000 hours = $170,000; $170,000 ÷ 800,000 pounds = $0.2125 per pound

** $10 per packaging hour × 9,000 hours = $90,000; $90,000 ÷ 200,000 pounds = $0.45 per pound

To check,

$$\$.7125 \times 800,000 \text{ pounds} = \$570,000; \$5.05 \times 200,000 \text{ pounds} = \$1,010,000;$$
$$\$570,000 + \$1,010,000 = \$1,580,000 \text{ of total overhead}$$

Total costs can now be compared, as follows:

	Traditional Approach		ABC Approach	
	Spanish Blend	French Roast	Spanish Blend	French Roast
Direct material	$3.00	$4.00	$3.00	$4.00
Direct labor	.50	.50	.50	.50
MOH	1.58	1.58	.7125	5.05
Total	$5.08	$6.08	$4.2125	$9.55

The explanation for the differences is that under the traditional approach, Spanish Blend was picking up a lot of the MOH that was more appropriately associated with French Roast. Under ABC, with more purchase orders and more batches, French Roast received more overhead. Also, even though it had fewer packaging hours, its hours per pound turned out to be higher, and that made the overhead cost per pound higher.

COST DRIVERS IN NONMANUFACTURING SETTINGS

A similar approach to distinguishing between cost measurement and cost management also can be used in nonmanufacturing settings. Although the cost drivers do not relate to *manufacturing* overhead per se, they frequently relate to an overhead activity that needs to be managed, a price setting function, or even a direct cost that could be managed more effectively when thought about as a cost driver. Let us look at each situation separately.

Overhead Activities in a Merchandising Organization

A company such as Amazon.com, although technically a merchandising organization, engages in many manufacturing-like activities: purchasing, material movements, batch assemblies, and quality control, for example. Although the costs of these activities are not absorbed into the "product" (an order shipped to a customer), they still must be managed, and the prices the company charges must reflect them. With its expansion into nonbook items such as electronics, Amazon.com has product diversity. It also has volume diversity (some customers order only one book, and others order many). Also, the relative costs for purchasing, material movements, and package assembly differ from one order to the next.

Is Amazon.com setting its prices at the right level when these various overhead costs are considered? Is it managing its overhead costs appropriately? An ABC system no doubt would help answer these questions, especially since industry standards for traditional bookstores no doubt would be quite inappropriate for a company with such a nontraditional business model.

Direct Costs in a Service Organization

In a hospital, the cost drivers are not nursing personnel, dietitians, housekeepers, or laboratory technicians but rather a set of six *activities:*[10]

- Type of case—a patient's diagnosis
- Volume—the number of patients of each case type

- Physician orders—the resources used to treat a patient of a particular case type (the number of days of hospital stay, the number of lab tests, etc.)

- Efficiency of resource delivery—the time needed to provide each resource (e.g., the number of technician minutes needed to complete a test in the laboratory)

- Factor prices—the cost per unit of each resource (e.g., nursing wage per minute)

- Programs—readiness to serve patients, including the hospital's administrative overhead

Many hospitals have shifted their thinking away from the traditional line items (such as nursing) and toward these types of cost drivers. In doing this, they effectively have moved toward an ABC-like system.[11]

 PROBLEM Try to construct a similar classification of the factors that influence costs in a university. Consider only the teaching activities of the university, not its research activities.

ANSWER There no doubt are several possible cost driver arrangements that one might construct. One possibility, similar to that for hospitals in the example given above, is the following:

- Type of student, for example, undergraduate versus graduate or international versus domestic

- Volume—the number of students of each type

- Curriculum requirements—the number and type of courses taken per student

- Efficiency of course delivery—the number of students per course

- Factor prices—the cost per unit of each resource (e.g., faculty salaries per course)

- Programs—readiness to serve students (a Ph.D. program, a Latin American studies program, etc.), including the university's administrative overhead

As in a manufacturing context, there is no "correct" classification scheme. The key idea behind classifying costs in this way is to shift from the traditional departmental structure of most organizations to a cost driver framework, that is, a listing and classification of the activities that cause the existence of costs. Some of these activities quite likely will transcend traditional departmental boundaries.

As the last few examples indicate, because organizations differ in their strategies and structures, they also differ in terms of the number and nature of their cost drivers. To a great extent, senior management's choice of a set of cost drivers depends on the organization's manufacturing or operating strategy and the way in which that strategy causes costs. Even here, however, there is considerable room for managerial judgment. Nevertheless, an ABC approach allows a company to shift its thinking from percentage increases in line items to an assessment of the kinds of activities that will be needed to support strategic objectives, the cost of each activity, and ultimately the organization's total costs.

Fireman's Fund illustrates how this process can work. Fireman's, which is among the top 20 U.S. property/casualty insurance companies, supplemented routine expense information from its regular accounting system by periodically sampling its costs for different products, activities, and tasks. Since most of the company's costs were staff-driven, it focused its sampling efforts not on the line item of "salaries" per se but on gaining a clear picture of how employees spent their time. This allowed the company to develop estimates of how much time was devoted to various products, activities, and tasks. Not only did this give Fireman's a more accurate picture of its internal costs so that managers could make more informed "make-versus-buy" decisions, but it helped the company adjust staffing needs for local offices on the basis of an office's particular mix of business.[12]

ABSORPTION COSTING VERSUS VARIABLE COSTING

Both GAAP and tax regulations require manufacturing companies to use an absorption costing system. Under this type of system, fixed MOH is treated as a product cost. That is, it is assigned (or attached) to products during the manufacturing process and *absorbed* into inventory. It remains attached to the products in the work in process inventory and subsequently in the finished goods inventory until the products are sold. At that time it is removed from finished goods inventory and placed on the income statement as part of the cost of goods sold.

A company that treated its fixed MOH as a period cost, that is, did not assign it to products but expensed it on the income statement in the period when it was incurred, would receive a qualified opinion on its audited financial statements. In effect, by not attaching fixed MOH to products but instead expensing it when the products were sold, it would violate GAAP's matching principle.

Absorption costing therefore must be used to compute cost of goods sold and value inventories for financial statements, and it must be used for tax purposes as well. This does not mean that it has to be used for managerial purposes, however. For internal reporting and control purposes, management can use any kind of information it wishes. There is only one criterion: The information must be useful. Because of the complexities associated with absorption costing, many companies have chosen to use a technique called *variable costing* for internal purposes. For some managers, variable costing is more intuitive than absorption costing and therefore is an approach that they find more managerially useful.

The difference between the two types of costing lies exclusively in the treatment of fixed manufacturing overhead. This is illustrated in Exhibit 5-1. As this exhibit indicates, absorption costing treats fixed manufacturing overhead as a *product* cost, whereas variable costing treats it as a *period* cost. Otherwise, there is no difference between absorption costing and variable costing.

The difference between these two forms of costing can have a significant impact on the financial statements. Consider two companies that are identical in every respect except one: Company A uses absorption costing, whereas Company V uses variable costing. In month 1, both companies produce and sell 1000 units of their products. In month 2, both produce 1500 units of their products but sell only 1000 units. In month 3, both pro-

EXHIBIT 5-1

Absorption Costing versus Variable Costing

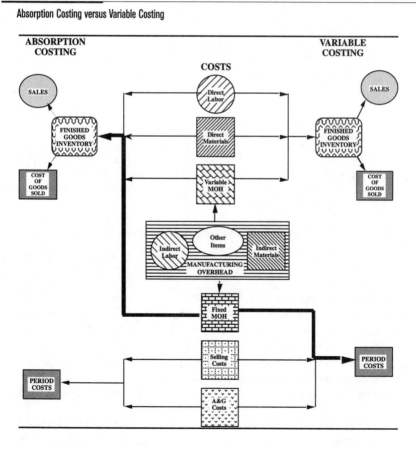

duce 500 units but sell 1000 units (obtaining the remaining 500 units from the finished goods inventory left over at the end of month 2).

To keep things simple, we will use only variable and fixed manufacturing overhead (i.e., no direct manufacturing cost), plus selling, general, and administrative costs. Assume the following:

	Company A	Company V
Selling price (per unit)	$220	$220
Variable manufacturing overhead (per unit of production)	$100	$100
Fixed manufacturing overhead	$60,000	$60,000
Selling, general, and administrative costs	$20,000	$20,000
Production, sales, and finished goods inventory during		
Month 1 Beginning balance	0	0
Production	1,000	1,000
Sales	1,000	1,000
Ending balance	0	0
Month 2 Beginning balance	0	0
Production	1,500	1,500
Sales	1,000	1,000
Ending balance	500	500
Month 3 Beginning balance	500	500
Production	500	500
Sales	1,000	1,000
Ending balance	0	0

Let us now prepare a statement of the cost of goods manufactured for each company for month 1. It will take a form slightly different from that in Chapter 4 because we have simplified the cost structure, using only variable and fixed MOH costs.

Cost of Goods Manufactured for Month 1

	Company A	Company V
Product costs		
Variable manufacturing overhead ($100 × 1,000)	$100,000	$100,000
Fixed manufacturing overhead	60,000	0
Total manufacturing costs this period	$160,000	$100,000
Plus: beginning balance of work in process inventory	0	0
Equals: total manufacturing costs this plus prior periods	$160,000	$100,000
Less: ending balance of work in process inventory	0	0
Cost of goods manufactured	$160,000	$100,000

We also can calculate a *product cost* per unit for each unit manufactured, as follows:

Total costs =	$160,000	$100,000
Total units manufactured =	1,000	1,000
Cost per unit =	$160.00	$100.00

We now can prepare an income statement:

Income Statement: Functional Classification for Month 1

	Company A	Company V
Sales revenue ($220 × 1,000 units)	$220,000	$220,000
Less: cost of goods sold		
Beginning balance of finished goods inventory	$0	$0
Plus: cost of goods manufactured	160,000	100,000
Equals: goods available for sale	$160,000	$100,000
Less: ending balance of finished goods inventory	0	0
Equals: cost of goods sold	160,000	100,000
Gross margin	$60,000	$120,000
Less: period costs		
Fixed manufacturing overhead	0	60,000
Selling, general, and administrative	20,000	20,000
Income before taxes	$40,000	$40,000

As one might expect, given identical sales and costs and no building of inventories, the two income statements show the same income before taxes. Now the plot thickens, however.

 PROBLEM Prepare a set of statements for month 2 comparable to the ones above.

ANSWER The two statements would look as follows:

Cost of Goods Manufactured for Month 2

	Company A	Company V
Product costs		
Variable manufacturing overhead ($100 × 1,500)	$150,000	$150,000
Fixed manufacturing overhead	60,000	0
Total manufacturing costs this period	$210,000	$150,000
Plus: beginning balance of work in process inventory	0	0
Equals: total manufacturing costs this plus prior periods	$210,000	$150,000
Less: ending balance of work in process inventory	0	0
Cost of goods manufactured	$210,000	$150,000

Product cost per unit for each unit manufactured is as follows:

Total costs =	$210,000	$150,000
Total units manufactured =	1,500	1,500
Cost per unit =	$140.00	$100.00

The income statement would look as follows:

Income Statement: Functional Classification for Month 2

	Company A	Company V
Sales revenue ($220 × 1,000 units)	$220,000	$220,000
Less: cost of goods sold		
Beginning balance of finished goods inventory	$0	$0
Plus: cost of goods manufactured	210,000	150,000
Equals: goods available for sale	$210,000	$150,000
Less: ending balance of finished goods inventory*	70,000	50,000
Equals: cost of goods sold	140,000	100,000
Gross margin	$80,000	$120,000
Less: period costs		
Fixed manufacturing overhead	0	60,000
Selling, general, and administrative	20,000	20,000
Income before taxes	$60,000	$40,000

*For Company A, this is 500 units × $140.00 per unit = $70,000.
For Company V, this is 500 units × $100.00 per unit = $50,000.

 PROBLEM Why is income before taxes higher for Company A? As part of your explanation, prepare calculations to reconcile the $20,000 difference ($60,000 – $40,000) between the two statements.

ANSWER The difference is in the fixed manufacturing overhead. With $60,000 of fixed overhead in Company A and 1500 units produced, each unit carries $40 of fixed overhead ($60,000 ÷ 1,500). Since 500 of those units are in inventory, there is $20,000 of fixed overhead (500 × $40) in inventory. By contrast, all $60,000 of fixed overhead has been expensed during the period (the month) in Company V.

 PROBLEM Now prepare a similar analysis for month 3, including an explanation for any difference between the two income-before-taxes figures.

ANSWER The cost of goods manufactured statement would look as follows:

Cost of Goods Manufactured for Month 3

	Company A	Company V
Product costs		
Variable manufacturing overhead ($100 × 500)	$50,000	$50,000
Fixed manufacturing overhead	60,000	0
Total manufacturing costs this period	$110,000	$50,000
Plus: beginning balance of work in process inventory	0	0
Equals: total manufacturing costs this plus prior periods	$110,000	$50,000
Less: ending balance of work in process inventory	0	0
Cost of goods manufactured	$110,000	$50,000

Product cost per unit for each unit manufactured is as follows:

	Company A	Company V
Total costs =	$110,000	$50,000
Total units manufactured =	500	500
Cost per unit =	$220.00	$100.00

The income statement would look as follows:

Income Statement: Functional Classification for Month 3

	Company A	Company V
Sales revenue ($220 × 1,000 units)	$220,000	$220,000
Less: cost of goods sold		
Beginning balance of finished goods inventory	$70,000	$50,000
Plus: cost of goods manufactured	110,000	50,000
Equals: goods available for sale	$180,000	$100,000
Less: ending balance of finished goods inventory	0	0
Equals: cost of goods sold	180,000	100,000
Gross margin	$40,000	$120,000
Less: period costs		
Fixed manufacturing overhead	0	60,000
Selling, general, and administrative	20,000	20,000
Income before taxes	$20,000	$40,000

The 500 units that Company A placed in inventory during month 2 came out this month and were sold. They carried $20,000 of fixed costs (500 × $40 per unit) with them. Those costs were added to the $60,000 in fixed costs that were included in the 500 units *manufactured and sold* this month, meaning that a total of $80,000 in fixed costs was included on Company A's income statement. This is in comparison to $60,000 of fixed costs on Company V's income statement and accounts for the $20,000 difference between the two income statements.

Reasons for Differences

As the examples above indicate, the reason for the differences between absorption costing and variable costing lies in the treatment of fixed manufacturing costs. The more general question, however, is why fixed costs behave in the way they do.

 PROBLEM   Review the above 3 months of data and try to extract a general principle that can be used to determine if income before taxes, other things equal, would be higher or lower under absorption costing than under variable costing.

ANSWER   The general principle is stated in Exhibit 5-2. As this exhibit indicates, when production exceeds sales, a company builds inventory. When a company builds inventory, as both companies did in month 2, some fixed costs will enter inventory under absorption costing and not go on the income statement that month. Other things being equal, this means that income under absorption costing will be higher than will income under variable costing.

Similarly, when sales exceed production, a company is reducing inventory. When this happens, fixed costs that had been placed in inventory come out and go on the income statement, and income under absorption costing will be lower than it is under variable costing.

EXHIBIT 5-2

Relationship among Production, Sales, and Income Absorption versus Variable Costing

IF PRODUCTION *EXCEEDS* SALES

then

INCOME *HIGHER* WITH ABSORPTION COSTING THAN WITH VARIABLE COSTING

•••

IF PRODUCTION *IS LESS THAN* SALES

then

INCOME *LOWER* WITH ABSORPTION COSTING THAN WITH VARIABLE COSTING

•••

IF PRODUCTION *IS THE SAME AS* SALES

then

INCOME IS *THE SAME* IN BOTH APPROACHES

As the problem above demonstrates, this relatively simple difference—the treatment of fixed manufacturing overhead—can have a profound effect on a company's income statements and balance sheets (via the inventory account). Thus, the decision to use variable costing instead of absorption costing is one that managers need to consider carefully. Managers who choose to use variable costing should recognize that the information they see for internal management purposes frequently will not correspond to the information that appears on financial statements prepared according to GAAP.

Product Costs versus Overhead
Volume Variances

In considering the use of variable costing, many managers confuse two issues:

1. The impact of having fixed costs treated as product costs under absorption costing and as period costs under variable costing

2. The impact of overhead volume variances when one is using an absorption system

In reality, these are two separate issues. Specifically:

■ There will be a difference between income under absorption costing and income under variable costing *when production is not the same as sales.* When this is the case, fixed manufacturing overhead will either enter or leave inventory under absorption costing.

- There can be an MOH volume variance *under absorption costing only*. This happens *when the actual volume of production differs from the expected volume*. Recall that an MOH *volume* variance is associated with the fixed MOH, which does not exist as a product cost in a variable costing system. (The MOH *budget* variance, if there is one, will be the same under either approach.)

Advantages of Variable Costing

Variable costing has three important advantages over absorption costing:

1. It is easier to understand. There is no need to absorb fixed MOH into products and therefore no confusion associated with the expansion or contraction of manufacturing inventories.

2. Sales and net income tend to move in the same direction. Note, for instance, that in the example above sales remained constant in all 3 months. Net income also remained constant under variable costing, but it fluctuated considerably under absorption costing, depending on whether production was greater or less than sales.

3. The separation of fixed costs and variable costs in the relatively clean way used in variable costing is intuitively more understandable to production managers and other middle managers. If those individuals are being asked to exert control over costs, it is helpful to have cost information that they can understand easily.

Implications for Just-in-Time Manufacturing Environments. Although the third reason is an important one for any company, the first two reasons are important only if a company expects to build or reduce inventory. Companies with just-in-time (JIT) manufacturing keep inventories close to zero, thus minimizing inventory carrying costs. Frequently, under a JIT system, raw materials are received the day before (or of) their use and finished goods are shipped immediately upon completion. Thus, the only inventory of any potential consequence is work in process.

The financial statements for companies that use JIT manufacturing will be approximately the same under either absorption costing or variable costing. The fact that fixed costs are held in a finished goods inventory until the product is sold is of little consequence to a company whose finished goods inventory is very small. Thus, whether fixed manufacturing overhead costs are treated as product costs or period costs has little significance for a company that uses JIT.

Disadvantages of Variable Costing

Variable costing has three disadvantages:

1. As was discussed above, for companies that do not have JIT manufacturing systems, variable costing results in internal financial statements that differ from those used for external reporting purposes. When the changes in inventory are slight from one period to the next and when expected and actual production levels are about the same, these differences are not great. Nevertheless, managers who decide to use variable costing need to be aware of these potential differences.

2. Since variable costing treats fixed manufacturing overhead as a period cost, it understates the full production cost. To the extent that full production cost is used as a basis for setting prices, as it is in many organizations, variable costing may lead managers to set prices that are unrealistically low. However, it should be kept in mind that even absorption costing excludes nonmanufacturing costs, and these costs also must be considered in setting prices.

3. Organizations that use variable costing still must use absorption costing for financial statements prepared according to GAAP and for tax reporting purposes. Therefore, when variable costing is used, an organization must maintain an accounting system that provides both sets of information. This type of system may be more costly to operate.

Overall, as with many management accounting decisions, there is no correct answer to the question of whether a company should supplement absorption costing with variable costing. The two most important questions for senior management to address are the following:

1. Will variable costing provide useful information for senior management decisions?

2. Will variable costing help line managers better understand and/or control costs?

If the answers to either of these questions is yes, the argument for developing a variable costing system is a strong one.

NOTES

1   For details, see Robin Cooper, "The Two-Stage Procedure in Cost Accounting: Part One," *Journal of Cost Management for the Manufacturing Industry,*

Summer 1987, pp. 43–51; Robin Cooper, "The Two-Stage Procedure in Cost Accounting: Part Two," *Journal of Cost Management for the Manufacturing Industry,* Fall 1987, pp. 39–45; and George J. Beaujon and Vinod R. Singhal, "Understanding the Activity Costs in an Activity-Based Cost System," *Journal of Cost Management,* Spring 1990, pp. 51–72.

2 For a discussion of the characteristics of a system in which a single rate is inappropriate, see Robin Cooper, "You Need a New Cost System When. . . . ," *Harvard Business Review,* January–February 1989, pp. 77–82.

3 For a detailed discussion of these factors, see Robin Cooper, "The Rise of Activity-Based Costing—Part Three: How Many Cost Drivers Do You Need, and How Do You Select Them?" *Journal of Cost Management,* Winter 1989, pp. 34–46.

4 See Robin Cooper and Robert S. Kaplan, "Profit Priorities from Activity-Based Costing," *Harvard Business Review,* May 1991.

5 A particularly good source for additional information is Robin Cooper and Robert S. Kaplan, *The Design of Cost Management Systems,* Englewood Cliffs, NJ: Prentice-Hall, 1991. Two readings in that book that apply directly to the topic of implementing ABC systems are Robin Cooper, "Implementing an Activity Based Cost System," *Journal of Cost Management,* Spring 1990, pp. 33–42, and Michael D. Shields and S. Mark Young, "A Behavioral Model for Implementing Cost Management Systems," *Journal of Cost Management,* Winter 1989, pp. 17–27.

6 For a full discussion, see Cooper and Kaplan, *The Design of Cost Management Systems,* pp. 269–272.

7 David A. Kunz, "3M Revisited: Evolving for the '90s," *Management Accounting,* October 1992.

8 Joseph A. Ness and Thomas G. Cucuzz, "Tapping the Full Potential of ABC," *Harvard Business Review,* July 1995.

9 One of the earliest articles to identify this idea—and an article that in a sense set the stage for much of the work on ABC—is Robert Kaplan, "Yesterday's Accounting Undermines Production," *Harvard Business Review,* July–August 1984. See also Robin Cooper, "Does Your Company Need a New Cost System?" *Journal of Cost Management,* Spring 1987, pp. 45–49.

10 These factors are explained in greater detail in David W. Young and Leslie Pearlman, "Managing the Stages of Hospital Cost Accounting," *Healthcare Financial Management,* April 1993.

11 For additional discussion, see Anthony and Young, *Management Control in Nonprofit Organizations,* Chapters 13 and 14. See also Young and Pearlman, "Managing the Stages of Hospital Cost Accounting."

12 Michael Crane and John Meyer, "Focusing on True Costs in a Service Organization," *Management Accounting,* February 1993.

CHAPTER 6

Responsibility Accounting: An Overview

$\mathbf{A}$s was discussed in previous chapters, an organization's accounting staff prepares financial statements for use by outsiders and cost analyses for use by line managers and senior management. The accounting staff also undertakes ad hoc analyses of cost and revenue data—usually of a differential nature—for internal use in making alternative choice decisions. These analyses frequently are done with guidance from senior management and line managers so that the analyses meet their needs.

Routine report preparation and ad hoc analyses are accounting activities that help managers in their day-to-day decision making. A third activity—*responsibility accounting*—goes beyond this type of decision making to assist in the ongoing management of the organization. Responsibility accounting focuses on the resources for which a manager has been given responsibility. As such, it distinguishes between revenues and costs that are controllable by a manager and those that are not. In its broadest sense, responsibility accounting is concerned with *planning and controlling* rather than *measuring* the resources used in an organization. Clearly, measurement is important in planning and control, and so the two cannot be separated completely. Nevertheless, the focus shifts in this chapter to the themes of planning and control.

Discussion of these topics, requires consideration of both the *structure* of an organization's responsibility accounting system and the *process* followed in its use. These terms will be defined and explained in this chapter.

The chapter begins with an analysis of the relationship between cost accounting and responsibility accounting. This allows us to explore the distinction between measurement and control. The chapter then looks at the various factors that must be considered in the design and use of a good responsibility accounting system.

Next we turn to the question of the responsibility accounting structure, which consists of the organization's *network* of responsibility centers. The chapter discusses the different types of responsibility centers and assesses the rationale for choosing one type in preference to another. The chapter then addresses the topic of the management control process, breaking it into four separate phases: programming, budgeting, measuring, and reporting. Each phase is discussed briefly in terms of its individual characteristics and its relationship to the other phases.

COST ACCOUNTING AND RESPONSIBILITY ACCOUNTING

The relationship between cost accounting and responsibility accounting rests in large part on the concept of resources. The discussion of cost accounting in Chapters 1, 4, and 5 focused on measuring the resources expended for a particular endeavor (called the cost object). Differential cost accounting, which was discussed in Chapters 2 and 3, also focused on measurement, but that discussion was expanded to include the question of how costs vary with changes in volume.

Responsibility accounting, by contrast, focuses on the managers who are responsible for controlling the use of an organization's resources. This concept of responsibility requires senior management to establish a network of *responsibility centers*. A responsibility center is an organizational unit headed by a manager who has been charged with achieving some agreed-upon results. The nature of those results is discussed later in the chapter.

It would be useful if the structure for accumulating full cost information were also the structure for accumulating responsibility center information. Unfortunately, this is rarely the case. Consider, for example, the cost of a day of inpatient care in a hospital. From a cost accounting perspective, we would add together the various resources that went into that day: room, board, nursing care, medications, and so on.

By contrast, from the perspective of responsibility accounting, we are concerned with the individuals who *control* those resources. For example, physicians have a major responsibility for the use of resources: They order medications, decide on the level of nursing care, order tests and procedures, and determine a discharge date. A nursing director or supervisor, who determines the efficiency and staffing patterns of nurses, has some additional responsibility. The director of housekeeping, who is responsible for the efficiency and quality of the cleaning effort, also bears some responsibility.[1]

Beginning in this chapter, we will focus on matters of control and will consider cost and revenue information in terms of how it can help the manager of a responsibility center exert control over the resources for which he or she is responsible.

RESPONSIBILITY ACCOUNTING SYSTEMS DEFINED

The goal of a responsibility accounting system is to help assure the effective and efficient use of an organization's resources. *Effectiveness* involves accomplishing what the organization wants to do. The more of an organization's objectives a responsibility center accomplishes, the greater its effectiveness is. *Efficiency* involves accomplishing an organization's objectives at a low cost and can be measured by a ratio of outputs to inputs, that is, the amount of output achieved per unit of input. Efficiency is measured without regard to whether the output supported the organization's objectives. Thus, an organization can be effective without being efficient, and vice versa. Outputs usually are measured in terms of revenue; inputs usually are measured in terms of expenses.

In practice, organizations display a wide variety of responsibility accounting systems. Sometimes those systems function well, and sometimes they do not. Sometimes the responsibility accounting system consists of highly formal procedures and regularly scheduled activities, and sometimes it is informal and sporadic. Sometimes the system involves a great deal of time on the part of senior management, and sometimes senior managers are only marginally involved. Sometimes a great deal of decision-making autonomy is delegated to divisional, departmental, or program managers, and sometimes these line managers have almost no authority or responsibility for decisions concerning the use of resources.

These differences arise because the characteristics of a responsibility accounting system are determined principally by the amount of autonomy and flexibility senior management wishes to give to line managers. In part these types of decisions relate to the amount of stability or turbulence that exists in an organization's environment or even within the organization's industry, and in part they relate to senior management's preferences and management style.

Because of these differences, there is no easy way to specify precisely the characteristics of an organization's responsibility accounting system. As is the case with many principles of management, responsibility accounting principles are incomplete and occasionally contradictory. Moreover, because they are concerned with the behavior of people, managerial motivation, and the role of information, they do not lend themselves easily to experiments or "proof."

Despite these limitations, responsibility accounting principles provide a way of thinking about an important set of management problems; consequently, it probably is better for managers to consider them than to ignore them. In general, managers have found responsibility accounting principles useful in designing systems that assist with resource planning and control.

As these comments suggest, although there are principles, there is no single correct way to design a responsibility accounting system. Many successful organizations operating in the same industry and competing for the business of the same customers have very different responsibility accounting systems. Some organizations, for example, use a very formal reporting process, providing managers at all levels with information pertaining to their activities, and expect close adherence to the financial objectives established in the equally formal budget formulation process. Other organizations use the budget as a rough guide and look only at a manager's performance at the end of the year to see whether it is satisfactory. There are many other variations.

The idea that there is no "right" responsibility accounting system came about both as a result of direct observation by management researchers of the activities of successful companies and as part of a new way of thinking about organizational design in general called contingency theory. Contingency theory holds that there is no right way to organize but rather that the most suitable organizational form is one that provides a "fit" with (1) the environment in which the organization operates, (2) the organization's general strategic thrust, and (3) the values and motivations of senior management. A similar fit must be attained for the organization's responsibility accounting system.

What, then, is a responsibility accounting system? Equally important, what can be said about it that will help managers of small and large organizations alike think about both its design and its fit with their strategies and organizational structures?

Answering these questions requires examining the structure and process of a responsibility accounting system. At the most fundamental level any system consists of a structure and a process. Structure is what the system is; process is what it does. The system of the human body, for example, comprises anatomy (its structure) and physiology (its process). Similarly, a responsibility accounting system can be thought of as having an anatomy and a physiology.

THE RESPONSIBILITY ACCOUNTING STRUCTURE

The structure of a responsibility accounting system can be assessed in terms of groups of individuals within an organization who work together to accomplish one or more of the organization's objectives. Each group, called a responsibility center, generally is led by a manager who has overall responsibility for its performance. Indeed, from the perspective of the structure of a responsibility accounting system, an organization can be thought of as a collection, or network, of responsibility centers. More specifically, since everyone in an organization is responsible for something and since most firms organize their employees into groups (divisions, departments, programs, etc.), each group can be thought of as a responsibility center. As a result, the key question in designing the structure of a responsibility accounting system is, "For what is the group responsible?" Senior management's objective is to design the organization's network of responsibility centers in such a way that individuals are responsible for the activities over which they exercise a reasonable amount of control. As we will see, this simple-sounding task is quite complex in practice.

Types of Responsibility Centers

One reason the design of responsibility centers is complex is that there are five types of responsibility centers—revenue centers, standard expense centers, discretionary expense centers, profit centers, and investment centers—and the selection of the most appropriate one for a particular organizational unit is by no means clear. The principal factor determining senior management's selection of one type instead of another is the kind of resources controlled by the responsibility center manager. Exhibit 6-1 lists the five possible types of responsibility centers and the financial objectives of each.

As Exhibit 6-1 indicates, if a manager has a great deal of control over revenue, as ordinarily is the case in a sales office, his or her department generally is considered to be a revenue center. This is the case even though the responsibility center incurs some expenses. That is, the manager's *performance* is evaluated in terms of the revenue generated by the department. On the other hand, if a manager has a great deal of control over his or her department's expenses but has no ability to generate revenue, the department ordinarily would be an expense center.

There are two types of expense centers: standard and discretionary. A standard expense center is appropriate when a manager can control the expense per unit of output but not the number of units of output. The laundry in a hotel, for example, might be a standard expense center. As such, the manager would be responsible for the expense per unit of activity, such as a pound of laundry, but not for the total expenses of the department. This is the case because total expenses depend on the number of units of activity ordered (pounds of laundry), which is not under the department's control.

A discretionary expense center, by contrast, is an organizational unit in which there is no easily measurable unit of activity, such as a personnel

EXHIBIT 6-1

Types of Responsibility Centers and Financial Objectives of Each

Type	Responsible for	Examples
Revenue center	Revenue earned by the center	A divisional sales office The development office in a university
Standard expense center	Expenses per unit of output, with a flexible budget used to compute total allowable expenses for each period	Many manufacturing plants The laundry in a hotel
Discretionary expense center	Total expenses incurred by the center regardless of the volume of output	An accounting department A corporate staff department
Profit center	Total revenues minus total expenses of the center	A product line in a large company A school or college in a large university
Investment center	Total revenues minus total expenses of the center, computed as a percentage of the assets used by the center, i.e. the center's return on assets (ROA)	A division in a multidivisional conglomerate

or accounting department. In these circumstances the department ordinarily receives a fixed budget that is negotiated with senior management but is not tied to any units of activity. The manager would be expected to adhere to this amount during the budgetary period (usually a year).

If the manager has control of both revenue and expenses, the center ordinarily would be a profit center. Many large and even some small organizations use profit centers as a way to give their managers incentives to both control expenses and attempt to generate additional revenues. Indeed, in many organizations profit centers have been extended to service departments, such as publications or computer support services that sell their services internally at transfer prices.

Even nonprofit organizations are finding that the creation of profit centers can have a dramatic impact on managerial behavior. For decades, Harvard University has designated its individual schools as profit centers, for example, as many hospitals do with their clinical departments, such as surgery and pediatrics. A particularly creative approach was taken by a manager in the repair garage of the New York City Sanitation Department, who was able to create a profit center mentality among the department's employees even though the department was a public sector agency with no earned revenue. To do this he used market prices in outside repair garages to create a pseudo revenue figure and then compared that amount to each operating unit's expenses. That arrangement led to a dramatic increase in the productivity of the affected units.[2]

Finally, a manager also may exert some control over the acquisition and management of certain assets, such as machines, other production equipment, accounts receivable, or inventory. If this is the case, the manager reasonably can be expected to have control over the productivity of those assets in addition to the center's revenue and expenses. This implies that the center should be an investment center. When this happens, the manager is responsible for the profit earned in his or her center in relation to the center's assets, sometimes computed in terms of the center's return on assets (ROA).

Role of Senior Management

Senior management weighs many factors in determining the best formal organizational structure, which is a prerequisite for designing the network of responsibility centers. Some of those considerations include the most appropriate division of tasks, the duties of specialized staff units, the activities that should be the responsibility of line managers, the decisions that should be made at or near the top of the organization, and the decisions that should be delegated to lower levels.

In some organizations senior management spends considerable time designing the formal organizational structure and then delegates to the accounting staff the job of determining the network of responsibility centers that overlays the structure. Or, worse, senior management fails to be explicit about the network of responsibility centers, leaving department heads and other managers to figure out the design for themselves on the basis of discussions in budget meetings or other similar activities. Both approaches can leave an organization without a network of responsibility centers that supports and reinforces senior management's strategy, structure, and desired culture.

It is important for senior management to spend time and energy defining the network of responsibility centers since by design or default all but very small organizations have not just a network but a *hierarchy* of responsibility centers. The hierarchy ranges from sections or other small units at the lowest level to departments and ultimately divisions. Indeed, since organizational units with some sort of responsibility exist in almost all organizations, the central question senior management must ask is not whether there *are* responsibility centers but whether their design facilitates the organization's ability to achieve its goals in an effective and efficient fashion.

The consequences of poor design of responsibility centers are visible in organizations where, for example, (1) some responsibility centers have overlapping goals and objectives that frequently are in conflict, (2) some of the organization's important goals and objectives have not been assigned to any responsibility center, (3) the transfer pricing and other policies for "buying and selling" relationships among responsibility centers have not been defined clearly, or (4) managers of particular responsibility centers are not given appropriate incentives to achieve their centers' objectives.

Clearly, the decision about the type of responsibility center that is appropriate for a particular organizational unit is extremely important, as is the design of a variety of other related features, including an appropriate incentive system to reward a manager and his or her subordinates for good performance. Thus, in conjunction with determining the desired formal organizational structure, senior management also must overlay it with a network of responsibility centers.

In addition, when an organization's strategy shifts, as occasionally is the case, senior management must *reconsider* its responsibility center design. In doing this, it must ask itself a key question: *Does the current responsibility center arrangement motivate managers to take actions that are in the best interest of both their individual responsibility centers and the organization as a whole?*

If the answer is yes, an appropriate responsibility center design most likely exists. If the answer is no, a redesign effort is called for.

The Decentralization Issue

Senior management's design of responsibility centers typically begins with the fundamental premise that the organization as a whole is an investment center. That is, an organization must obtain a sufficiently high ROA to (1) help finance asset acquisition and replacement, (2) provide the cash needed to support growth, (3) provide for unexpected contingencies ranging from an economic slowdown to a flood in the warehouse, and (4) satisfy investors. Even nonprofit organizations need an ROA to satisfy the first three of these requirements.[3]

The need for a satisfactory ROA means that the fundamental design question is how to decentralize investment responsibility among the various organizational units: divisions, departments, sales offices, manufacturing plants, and so forth. For example, many Fortune 100 companies have decentralized investment responsibility to their divisions. At General Motors, since the days of Alfred Sloan,[4] each division (e.g., the Chevrolet Division) has been an investment center. Other organizations decentralize

profit responsibility only; they hold their divisions accountable for budgeted profitability goals but not for ROA. In some organizations one or
more profit centers may be budgeted to incur a loss or only a small profit,
based on the idea that their products and services are needed to support
other organizational activities that earn substantial profits. Many cell
phone companies, for example, earn very little on the phones themselves
(sometimes giving them away) but make considerable profits on airtime
usage.

These sorts of decisions about responsibility centers cascade throughout the organization. For example, at the divisional level in General Motors
a similar set of responsibility design questions must be answered with
regard to marketing departments, sales offices, manufacturing plants, and
so forth.

To illustrate the tricky nature of process of responsibility center
design, consider the following problem.

 PROBLEM Energy International (a fictitious name) manufactures a wide variety
of energy-saving devices, which it sells nationally to distributors for final sale
through hardware and appliance stores. The company has two principal organizational units: sales and manufacturing. In its manufacturing plant the company
produces to order, and it attempts to maintain very small raw material and finished goods inventories. The lack of a finished goods inventory is further justified
financially by the extremely wide variety of devices the company manufactures
and the expense it would incur if it tried to maintain a finished goods inventory.

EI operates in an extremely competitive market in which its prices are very
close to its production costs. With little effort, its competitors can produce the
same kind and quality of devices as it can, such that any attempt to raise its prices
over the "market" price would result in a loss of business. Since EI must accept
the market price, the keys to its success are (1) keeping production costs low, (2)
minimizing the finished goods inventory, and (3) selling a large volume of
devices.

Distributors choose producers on the basis of price (no higher than the market), quality (which is relatively standard from one manufacturer to the next),
and service (delivery time). Since distributors do not want to store the devices in
inventory either, they order from the manufacturer that can deliver an order most
quickly. Energy International's sales force knows the distributors and their needs
and frequently asks the company's manufacturing manager to produce a relatively small order quickly to meet a distributor's urgent request. Because of high
setup requirements, small orders can be very costly to produce. However, failure
to fill a small order may mean the loss of larger orders from the distributor in the
future.

Who is responsible for revenue at EI? For costs? Who ultimately is responsible
for profits and for EI's return on assets? More specifically, what kind of responsibility center should a sales office be? A manufacturing plant?

You need not prepare answers to these questions yet, but please keep the questions in mind as you continue reading. We will return to this problem after some further discussion.

Designing Responsibility Centers

Questions such as those mentioned above for EI are also appropriate for many other companies that wish to determine an appropriate network of responsibility centers. In each instance, senior management must examine the basic elements of ROA and assess who controls each one. As we will see in the following discussion, although the methodology is pretty simple, the analytical effort needed to implement it is anything but simple.

Disaggregating ROA. To answer the question about how best to decentralize responsibility, we can turn to the basic elements of ROA and assess who controls each one. The answers will guide our responsibility center choices.

In any organization ROA is determined by a combination of five factors: (1) price, (2) volume (the number of units sold), (3) variable costs per unit (such as supplies and generally some labor costs), (4) fixed costs (such as managerial salaries, rent, and depreciation), and (5) asset levels. At the macro level, ROA can be calculated as follows:

$$ROA = profit \div assets$$

Determining the assets that are associated with a given responsibility center can be a bit tricky at times, since some assets frequently are shared among two or more responsibility centers. If the organization's cash is maintained centrally, for example, it is virtually impossible to determine how much of it should be attributed to a given responsibility center.

However, many assets can be associated directly with a particular responsibility center. The machines in a plant are clearly within the province of the plant, and, assuming the plant manufactures products for a single division, they also are the responsibility of that division. Accounts receivable probably can be linked to individual divisions, as can inventories and many other assets.

Once the assets associated with a responsibility center have been isolated, the next question concerns profit. Here the analysis becomes somewhat complicated. Let us begin with the basic equation for profit:

$$Profit = revenue - fixed\ costs - variable\ costs$$

Revenue is price multiplied by volume, variable costs are variable costs per unit multiplied by volume, and fixed costs do not depend on volume as long as they remain within the relevant range. These relationships allow us to unbundle the calculation:

Profit = (price × volume) − fixed costs − (variable costs per unit × volume)

This framework can be used to determine which elements of the profit formula a specific responsibility center manager can control or which elements senior management *wants* the manager to control. That determination in turn will help guide senior management's decision about what kind of responsibility center the unit should be. In some instances, the ability of the manager to control certain elements of the equation is quite clear. In others, however, there is considerable ambiguity. In still others, a choice must be made between two (or more) possible arrangements, either of which can be appropriate, depending on other design choices in the overall responsibility accounting system.

Ambiguity and choice arise because every organization is unique in terms of its strategy, its culture, its programs or product lines, and a wide variety of other characteristics. An important principle in designing responsibility centers is to align responsibility with control, but it sometimes is difficult to determine which elements of the ROA formula a given responsibility center manager can control or how best to give a manager control over the elements senior management wants him or her to control. As a result, senior management may spend considerable time debating the most appropriate responsibility center arrangement.

In addition, senior management must be careful to assure that the entire responsibility accounting system is designed in such a way that line managers have a level of control and decision-making authority that corresponds to their type of responsibility center. If this is not the case, these managers most likely will feel—quite correctly—that they are being held responsible for resources they cannot control. This can lead to considerable stress and frustration within the organization.

 PROBLEM   Newport Theater, a division of the drama center of Alston University, has been designated as a profit center. Its manager is responsible for devising a marketing strategy to bring in revenue and also is responsible for controlling the theater's expenses to make sure they do not exceed revenue. Each month approximately 20 percent of the administrative expenses of the drama center are allocated to Newport Theater. Those expenses are allocated by using bases of allocation that everyone at the university, including the manager of the theater, agrees are fair. Some use square footage, others use salary dollars, and others use work orders (for work by the buildings and grounds staff, for example). What problems do you think might arise with this arrangement?

ANSWER   Although the cost accounting system seems to be well designed, the responsibility accounting system is not. The distinction senior management must make here is between measurement and control. The cost accounting system appears to have done a good job of *measuring* the theater's "fair share" of the drama center's administrative expenses. However, since the manager of the theater cannot control the allocated portion of the drama center's expenses, the theater's ability to earn its budgeted profit has been impeded. That is, even though the allocation bases are considered by all to be fair, the full-cost accounting system is allocating some expenses to the theater that its manager cannot control.

In this regard, senior management must be certain to distinguish between the performance of an organizational unit, such as the theater, and the performance of its manager. The *theater's* financial performance can be assessed by combining its revenue with its full costs (from the full-cost accounting system). The *manager's* performance, in contrast, relates to the resources he or she can control. Techniques such as transfer prices and budgeted (rather than actual) cost allocations can be used to give the manager greater control. We will discuss some of these techniques later in the chapter. For the moment, however, it seems clear that considerable conflict will arise over who is responsible for controlling the theater's share of the administrative expenses of the drama center and that senior management may spend a considerable amount of time dealing with those conflicts.

A Working Example

Let us now look at some responsibility center decisions in the context of a hypothetical book publisher, Roper & Howe, Inc. (RHI). As Exhibit 6-2 shows, RHI is organized into four divisions. Each division is identical in structure to the Children's Book Division: It has some sales offices and

EXHIBIT 6-2

Organizational Structure of Roper & Howe, Inc.

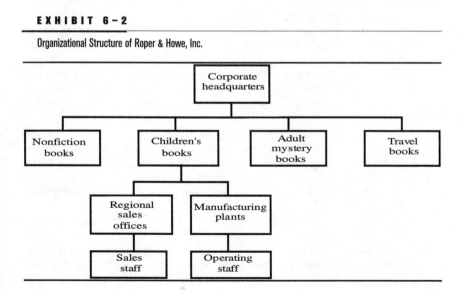

some manufacturing facilities. The problems below describe the kinds of issues senior management would face in designing a responsibility center structure for RHI.

 PROBLEM 1 The New York sales office of the Children's Book Division of RHI has a manager and a staff of six salespersons, all of whom are salaried. The office sells no books itself; instead, salespeople call on customers, promote the company's books, take orders from customers, and notify the division's manufacturing plant of the need to produce a certain number of books with a particular title. What kind of responsibility center should the office be?

ANSWER Although it is quite likely that the office manager's responsibilities include managing the expenses of the sales staff and the office, most of the expenses of Roper & Howe are in the writing, editing, and printing of the books. Thus, the office's responsibility extends principally to revenue, and the office most likely would be considered a revenue center: The office's performance would be measured according to the amount of revenue it generated from the sale of books. The manager might decide to make each salesperson in the office a separate revenue center, thus decentralizing responsibility within the office.

 PROBLEM 2 Books are printed and bound in the Newark, New Jersey, plant of the Children's Book Division. The plant manager receives requests from the salespeople in the division to produce a certain number of books with a particular title. The manager and the plant staff set up the printing presses, print the books, bind them, and store them in inventory before shipping them to distributors and bookstores throughout the country. What kind of a responsibility center should the plant be?

ANSWER It appears that the goal is for the plant to produce each order in accordance with some predetermined expense per book. If this is the case, the manager's responsibility is related only to expenses, not to revenue. Since the predetermined expense per book is based on a combination of factors (size, length, number of copies being printed), the plant most likely is expected to produce each order at or below the predetermined amount. Therefore, the plant quite likely is a standard expense center. The manager also might decentralize responsibility within the plant to natural groupings of activities, such as printing and binding.

As a standard expense center, the plant would not have a fixed budget. Instead, the controller's office of RHI would determine how many books the plant produced during a month. The controller then would multiply that figure by the predetermined expense per book to arrive at a performance budget. Therefore, the plant's budget would change each month in accordance with the number of books produced.

The process of preparing the performance budget each month could be made more sophisticated in two ways. First, a cost formula such as the total cost formula discussed in Chapter 2 might be used. If this happened, the budget would have both fixed and variable cost elements; this would be more realistic than having a single cost figure per book. Second, there might be different variable cost figures for different titles, reflecting the fact that large books tend to cost more to produce than do small ones, that hardbound books are more costly than paperbacks, and so forth. In all instances, however, the plant would remain a standard expense center; there simply would be greater sophistication in calculating the monthly performance budget.

 PROBLEM 3   The responsibility of the director of RHI's Children's Book Division is to manage both the sales offices located in various cities throughout the country and the production plant for the division. What kind of responsibility center should the division be?

ANSWER   Since the manager is responsible for both revenue (from the sales offices) and expenses (in the production plant), it appears that the division should be a profit center. This seems appropriate in that the manager has a reasonable amount of control over both revenues and expenses. Although responsibility has been decentralized to both the sales offices (which have been designated as revenue centers) and the plant (which is a standard expense center), the manager nevertheless has overall responsibility for the division's profits.

 PROBLEM 4   The division's director's responsibilities include a major role in decisions such as when to build a new plant, when to replace production equipment, what types of machines to purchase, how large an inventory to carry, when to extend credit to customers, and how large an accounts receivable balance to maintain. What kind of responsibility center should the division be?

ANSWER   Since the manager's responsibilities now extend to certain assets, he or she probably would be an investment center and would be responsible for earning a satisfactory percentage return on the assets under his or her control.

As these problems illustrate, large organizations frequently have a network or hierarchy of responsibility centers, including units, sections, departments, branches, and divisions. Except for activities at the lowest levels of the organization (book sales, maintenance of machines, and the like, in the problems above), each responsibility center consists of aggregations of smaller responsibility centers. A significant managerial activity for senior management in any organization, regardless of its size, is to design, coordinate, and control the work of all these responsibility centers.

ENERGY INTERNATIONAL

Let us now return to the situation faced by Energy International that was presented earlier in the chapter. Recall that one of the company's most significant ongoing operating decisions is whether to produce a small order for a distributor who, although new, might make much larger orders in the future. How can senior management design the company's responsibility centers so that the sales and manufacturing managers, acting in their own best interests, are simultaneously acting in the company's best interest with regard to this decision?

 PROBLEM Reread the Energy International example earlier in the chapter and answer the following questions. Be sure to focus on the economics of the industry and consider which organizational units in EI control which elements of the profit formula. Be sure to analyze question 3 (a key question for EI) in light of your responsibility center design decisions in questions 1 and 2

1. What kind of responsibility center should a sales office be?
2. What kind of responsibility center should a manufacturing plant be?
3. What kind of behavior on the part of a sales office manager and a plant manager would your responsibility design promote when there is a small order from an important, or potentially important, customer?

ANSWER In answering these questions, we can turn first to the basic elements of profit and look at who controls each one. That analysis might lead to the following conclusions:

- The sales force has very little, if any, control over price. It does not appear that a sales person can raise the price much above the market level if a distributor has a small order, since there is always the possibility that the distributor will turn to another supplier that will offer the market price. In almost all respects, then, prices are controlled by the market.

- The large number of different types of devices means that it would be extremely expensive to store them all in inventory. Thus, the company cannot achieve any economies of scale with regularly scheduled, long production runs. It will use long production runs when it can, or perhaps for a few high-volume items, but when there is a request for a small quantity of devices that it does not have in inventory, it either must turn the order down or sacrifice its economies of scale. However, if it turns down too many small orders, it may lose important customers (who would have placed large orders in the future) to its competitors.

Given these conclusions, should the sales offices of EI be revenue centers? Should the plant be a standard expense center? Should one or the other be a profit center, and if it becomes one, what should the other be?

The first step in the decision-making effort is to assess each of the elements of the profit formula from the perspective of EI and analyze who or what controls it.

- Price is controlled by the market.
- Unit variable costs and fixed costs are controlled by the manufacturing manager.
- Volume is the principal question.

If senior management decides that the sales force controls the volume of devices sold, it quite likely would set up its sales offices as revenue centers, since revenue will be determined almost entirely by the volume of sales. It then would establish its plants as standard expense centers, with standards determined in accordance with the type and number of devices ordered for each production run. The manufacturing manager's performance will be assessed in terms of a comparison between these standard expenses and the actual expenses of each production run. This is the traditional design that we saw with the book publisher Roper & Howe earlier in the chapter.

But what then? Would the manufacturing manager ever have an incentive to produce a small order? That is, would he or she ever be willing to sacrifice economies of scale and therefore exceed the standard expense for a given type of product in return for a potentially large downstream order? That is not likely. It is more likely that there would be ongoing conflict between sales and manufacturing over these small orders and that senior management would have to intervene regularly to resolve the differences. Moreover, when senior management sided with sales, it would need to adjust the standard expense for the small order or create a situation in which the manufacturing manager could not control a factor (unit variable cost) for which he or she was being held responsible.

However, senior management might decide that volume is related to service and quality and that service (which includes producing a small order on occasion) and quality govern sales. In these circumstances the manufacturing manager has a great deal of control over all relevant variables in the profit formula, and the plant therefore should be a profit center. If the manufacturing manager also controls some assets, the company might designate the plant as an investment center.

This is a very counterintuitive design that many senior managers no doubt would question. Indeed, at first blush it appears to fly in the face of all responsibility center design logic. To understand its counterintuitive logic, one must consider the behavior of the manufacturing manager when there is a small order. If the plant was a standard expense center, the manufacturing manager would have no incentive to accept a small order since the standards presumably would have been established with long production runs in mind. If the plant was a profit center, however, the manufacturing manager would have at least some motivation to look at the longer-run picture and analyze the relevant economics. That is, by turning down a small order, the manufacturing manager might lose a highly profitable order sometime in the not too distant future. As a profit center manager, he or she might decide to accept some small orders from potentially valuable customers. As a minimum, he or she would be motivated to assess the downstream consequences of the decision to accept or reject a small order.

Obviously, there is no right answer to this design question. In the case of EI, however, the shift from a standard expense center to a profit center arrangement for the plant led to exactly the kinds of behavioral changes discussed above. More generally, the example makes clear how important it is for senior management, rather than the accounting staff, to assess who controls the variables of the ROA formula and to consider how the responsibility center design decisions will motivate the affected managers.

The conclusion that can be drawn from this discussion both reinforces the contingency approach to the design of a responsibility accounting system and takes the contingency idea a step further. Not only will an organization's environment, strategy, and organizational design decisions influence the way it designs its responsibility accounting system, but even when these factors are incorporated into the analysis, many of the decisions will remain matters of judgment. They will depend (be contingent) on the way management views the relevant variables, its assessment of who controls those variables, and its view of how its design decisions will motivate the affected managers. In the end, responsibility accounting concepts can provide a framework for decision making, but senior management will always have to exercise its own judgment in determining the specific responsibility accounting structure.

THE RESPONSIBILITY ACCOUNTING FRAMEWORK

As several of these examples have suggested, much of what goes on in a responsibility accounting system must take place in the context of the organization's overall strategic direction. More specifically, according to Robert Anthony, an emeritus professor at Harvard Business School who is widely considered the conceptual father of responsibility accounting, managers engage in three different types of planning and control activities: (1) strategic planning, (2) task control, and (3) management control. Anthony identified and described these activities in *Planning and Control Systems: A Framework for Analysis*, a landmark book that both defined the field of responsibility accounting and gave it a clear direction.[5]

The Strategic Planning Process

During the strategic planning process, senior management determines the organization's goals and the general nature of the activities needed to achieve them, frequently undertaking a SWOT (organizational strengths and weaknesses in comparison to environmental opportunities and threats) analysis. Since environmental opportunities and threats do not arise in orderly, predictable ways, however, strategic planning decisions are not made according to a prescribed timetable. As a result, the strategic planning process is irregular and unsystematic.

The Task Control Process

At the other end of the spectrum from strategic planning is a set of activities used in carrying out the day-to-day operations of an organization, in particular the performance of specific tasks. Task control is the process of assuring that those operations are carried out effectively and efficiently. Although task control varies with the nature of an organization's operations, it generally involves activities such as maintaining adequate levels of inventory, sending out invoices in a timely way, collecting accounts receivable and depositing funds, and issuing paychecks on payday. Many task control activities do not involve managers. If they are automated, they do not even involve humans except to assure that the activity is functioning properly and to deal with matters not included in the automated process. For example, many organizations with sizable inventories, such as Wal-Mart, rely on a computer to place an order directly with the appropriate vendor whenever the quantity of an item in inventory decreases to a preset level.

The Management Control Process

The management control process sits between strategic planning and task control. It usually begins with the goals determined in the strategic planning process and focuses on how best to attain them. Thus, it addresses both the programs (or product lines) that can help move the organization toward its strategic goals and the budgets for those programs or product lines (as well as for other activities, such as computer support services). It also is concerned with the collection of data and the design and preparation of reports that present those data to line managers and others so that they can assess whether their responsibility centers are meeting budgeted projections. Increasingly, as will be discussed below, the process focuses on both financial and nonfinancial items that have to be measured and reported to line managers.

Unlike strategic planning, the management control process is regular and systematic, with steps repeated in a predictable way. Unlike task control, which may not involve humans directly, management control is fundamentally behavioral. In large measure it is a process in which line managers interact with a variety of people in the organization, particularly other managers. In many organizations line managers also interact with professionals such as engineers, scientists, computer programmers, and physicians.

This balance between the optimum allocation of resources and the behavior of managers, professionals, and others means that the management control process is governed partially by the principles of economics and partially by the principles of social psychology. Not only are the principles in these two disciplines quite different, their relative importance to the management control process varies greatly in different situations.[6]

Formal versus Informal Activities.   As with matters of structure, much of the management control process is informal. Meetings, ad hoc memoranda, and hallway and lunchtime conversations all can influence how managers make decisions about the use of resources. Nevertheless, in most organizations there also is a more formal process. This process usually consists of a set of regularly scheduled activities in which decisions are made about the kinds and quantities of products and services the organization expects to produce during an upcoming period of time and the resources needed to generate that output. During each fiscal year records usually are kept on actual results (revenues and expenses), and most organizations prepare regular reports on those results that senior and middle managers can use as a basis for determining whether corrective action of some sort is needed.

Formal Management Control Activities. In most organizations, these activities are considered part of the formal management control process. They can be classified into four separate phases:

1. Programming
2. Budget formulation
3. Operating and measurement
4. Reporting and evaluation

These phases recur in a regular cycle and build on each other, as is indicated in Exhibit 6-3. Thus, by describing each phase, we can gain an appreciation for the nature of the formal aspects of the management control process. The remainder of this chapter discusses the four phases briefly. They are discussed in greater detail in subsequent chapters.

Programming

In the programming phase of the cycle, decisions of a long-term nature are made that concern the kinds of product lines the company will produce, the kinds of programs it will engage in, and the amount of resources it will devote to each. In general, as Exhibit 6-3 indicates, these decisions are made within the context of the organization's overall strategy, coupled with whatever information is available concerning new opportunities, increased competition, new or pending legislation that might affect the organization's efforts, and a variety of similar considerations.

To understand the nature of the programming phase of the cycle, consider the case of Overdales, a hypothetical large department store chain in a large state, with stores in all major cities. Senior management is considering the addition of bakeries to each of its stores. The bakeries would offer fresh bread, pastries, pies, cakes, and a variety of other baked goods. Making this addition would require an investment of approxi-

EXHIBIT 6-3

Phases of the Management Control Process.

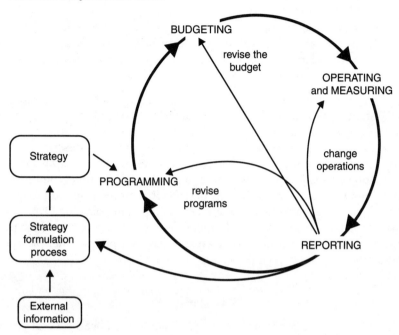

mately $500,000 per store to convert the space, purchase the necessary display counters, and buy the associated equipment.

This example illustrates several important aspects of programming:

- The decision is a programming one because it involves a new product line.

- A decision such as this is not easily reversible once it has been implemented; thus, it requires careful analysis.

- For two reasons, the decision has a clear strategic component. First, the store believes that it can compete with smaller neighborhood bakeries and can persuade shoppers who have come to purchase department store goods (clothing, bedding, appliances, etc.) to buy food as well. Second, the store also believes that it can develop the necessary new skills. That is, the food business involves management skills different from those necessary to run a department store—concern with freshness and taste, for example, in contrast to style and appearance.

- The decision will subject the store to a new form of regulation. Specifically, the bakery will have to meet the standards of the state's department of public health.

- The decision requires a capital investment and therefore requires, among other efforts, that an analysis be made of the return on the proposed investment (a technique for calculating this return is discussed in Chapter 8).

For these reasons, programming decisions ordinarily are considered "long-range" decisions, and the programming phase of the management control process frequently looks ahead by as much as 5 or 10 years. The program planning document generally is a lengthy one, describing each proposal in detail, estimating the resources necessary to accomplish it, and calculating its expected returns to the organization. In this type of "economic analysis" there may be many benefits that are very difficult to quantify, which complicates the decision. For example, in assessing Overdale's bakery product line, we must ask ourselves about the extent to which persons using the bakery will become aware of the company's other products and then purchase some of them.

Budgeting

In contrast to the programming phase, which looks ahead several years, the budgeting phase generally looks ahead only 1 year. It accepts product lines and programs as givens and attempts to determine the amount of revenues and expenses that will be associated with each. In many organizations, product lines and programs fall neatly into responsibility centers, and so each responsibility center manager can be charged with preparing a budget for each of his or her product lines or programs. Sometimes a program and a responsibility center are identical. For example, each of several departments in a bank might be designated as a responsibility center: current accounts, international banking, mortgages, and commercial loans. Each department also might have one or more programs. For example, the mortgage department might have one program for developers of apartment buildings, another for individual home owners, and a third for commercial properties. Current accounts might have one program for checking accounts and another for savings accounts.

In formulating the bank's budget, senior management might ask each program manager to develop a budget for his or her program. These budgets can be grouped into departmental budgets and finally into a master budget for the bank.

In this organization the fit among programs and responsibility centers would be fairly clean. In many organizations the fit among programs and responsibility centers is not nearly this neat, and a more complicated budgeting process is necessary. This frequently happens when programs cut across several responsibility centers. For example, many graduate schools of management run an MBA program, a doctoral program, a program for senior-level managers, a program for middle-level managers, and a research program. In many business schools the responsibility centers are not only programs but departments as well. There are departments of accounting, operations management, marketing, and organizational behavior, among several others.

Each program typically uses one or more faculty members from each of the departments, and faculty members in each department work in more than one program.

 PROBLEM How do you think programs and departments are incorporated into the budget formulation process in this kind of organization?

ANSWER Budget formulation here must involve a balance between the plans of program managers and those of departmental managers. Each program manager can specify how many faculty members are needed for his or her program, and each department manager can indicate how many faculty members he or she wants in the department, as well as their salaries. However, there must be a balance between the needs of the two. This type of matrix management will be discussed in greater detail in Chapter 7.

Characteristics of a Good Budget Formulation Process. Because of these differing kinds and levels of complexity, each organization must develop a budget formulation process that meets its specific needs. Regardless of its specific elements, however, a good budget formulation process generally has several key elements:

- A set of guidelines that are developed by senior management and communicated to line managers. This is the first step in the annual process. It usually is done in writing and sets forth a timetable for the rest of the process.

- A participatory element in which all middle managers have an opportunity to prepare budgets for their responsibility centers and discuss them with their superiors.

- A central staff (usually in the controller's office) responsible for coordinating the activities, carrying out many of the technical aspects of the process, and occasionally providing analyses that serve as "checks and balances" against projections by responsibility center managers.

- A hierarchy of information that begins with the smallest responsibility center and accumulates budget information by progressively larger responsibility centers, eliminating excessive detail at each step in the hierarchy.

- A negotiation phase in which, if necessary, each responsibility center manager has an opportunity to defend his or her budget against anticipated reductions.

- A final approval and sign-off by senior management authorizing responsibility center managers at each level to carry out the budget as agreed on in the preparation and negotiation phases.

In general this final approval constitutes a commitment between each responsibility center manager and his or her superior that the budget will be adhered to unless there are "compelling reasons" to change it. Compelling reasons include large and unanticipated changes in volume, a lengthy strike, fuel shortages and resulting large price increases, a fire in the main building, and any number of similarly significant or catastrophic events.

As anyone who has participated in a budget preparation effort knows, the process frequently has a certain gamelike quality to it. This in part is the reason senior management uses staff analyses in addition to the information submitted by responsibility center managers. The intent is to eliminate any "slack" in the budget so that the final budget amounts are as realistic as possible. Overall, the budget for each responsibility center should be relatively difficult to attain but attainable nevertheless.

Operating and Measurement

Once programs have been established and a budget has been agreed on, the organization commences operating during the budget year. This is, of course, an oversimplification, since all organizations except newly established ones operate continuously. However, if some new programs have been approved or if new funds have been made available for existing programs, it is likely that a variety of new or different operations also will commence at the beginning of a new budget year.

From a responsibility accounting perspective, new or different types of operations have important implications. Specifically, if the budget is to be adhered to, managers must receive information concerning their responsibility centers' performance compared to budgeted objectives. Consequently, both the new activities and the ongoing ones must be measured. More specifically, data must be collected about both financial and nonfinancial activities, and this information must be incorporated into the responsibility accounting system. The operating and measurement phase of the process, then, involves putting plans into effect and measuring the relevant inputs and outputs.

Role of the Accounting System. If the measurement aspect is to be effective, the organization must have a well-developed accounting system. Not only must the accounting system keep records of revenues and expenses, but those records must be modified each year to include new programs or product lines. Moreover, the system must be designed so that the information can be used for several purposes:

1. To prepare financial statements. Here certain rules are imposed on the organization by outside agencies (e.g., the Financial Accounting Standards Board or the Securities and Exchange Commission) that govern how the information is to be presented.
2. To prepare cost analyses that allocate overhead to products and services for purposes of computing full costs.
3. To classify revenues and expenses by programs and responsibility centers. Information on programs is used for evaluating the programs and for future programming decisions. Information classified by responsibility centers is used to measure the performance of the managers of these centers, that is, for comparing actual performance to budgeted performance.

Although the information has multiple uses, it must be integrated. That is, although data collected for one purpose may differ from those collected for another or certain data elements sometimes will be reported in a detailed fashion and sometimes in summaries, in all instances the data must be reconcilable from one report to another. This requires careful and thoughtful design of the information coding structure at the outset and a cautious, systematic process for including new data elements when the system must be modified. This means that in designing and modifying the accounting system, the organization's accounting staff (which usually designs such systems) must be managed carefully to ensure that it is aware of the multiple uses of the information.

In general, the system is built on a financial base; that is, amounts are stated in monetary units, since these units are generally the easiest to collect, maintain, and integrate with each other. Nevertheless, managers also may wish to see a variety of nonmonetary measures, such as minutes, percentages, number of clients, spoilage rates, and sales returns. These nonmonetary items make the measurement system somewhat broader than the accounting system.

Finally, it must be remembered that information itself is a resource. As with all resources, it has both a cost and a use to which it can be put. Senior management must assure itself constantly that the information's value exceeds its cost.

From a responsibility accounting perspective, senior management is concerned with the information that flows to responsibility centers and program managers and its role in facilitating their decision making. Thus, the goal of the measurement phase of the responsibility accounting system is to determine the appropriate information to gather to meet the needs of those managers. This goal is complicated by two factors: (1) Different managers in an organization make different kinds of decisions, and (2) any individual manager will make a variety of decisions depending on the particular circumstances he or she faces at various times in the operating year. These factors mean that the measurement phase of the management control process must be flexible and dynamic: In any growing or evolving organization, the information needed by senior and middle managers not only will differ from one responsibility center or program to the next but will be changing constantly.

Reporting and Evaluation

The final phase of the management control process is the presentation of information to program and responsibility center managers. The information collected in the measurement phase of the cycle thus is classified, analyzed, sorted, merged, totaled, and finally reported to operating managers. The resulting reports generally compare planned outputs and inputs with actual ones and thus allow both responsibility center managers and their superiors to evaluate performance during the operating period. This information, along with a variety of other information (from conversations, informal sources, industry analyses, etc.), generally leads to one of three possible courses of behavior, as indicated in Exhibit 6-3.

Change Operations. If the operating manager or his or her supervisor is not satisfied with the results shown on the reports, corrective action of some sort may be needed. This can include activities such as examining sources of supply to attempt to obtain lower prices, asking supervisors about the use of overtime, and speaking with salespersons about customer satisfaction or dissatisfaction with the product. Action also can include praise for a job well done, constructive criticism, reassignment, or, in extreme cases, termination.

Revise the Budget. In some instances certain key aspects of the activities in a responsibility center are not under the control of the manager of the center. For example, if the volume of production in a factory is determined exclusively by the sales force and the orders that salespeople submit, the factory manager has little ability to control that volume. If supply prices are the responsibility of the purchasing department or if wage rates are determined by senior management in its negotiations with unions, the managers of the affected responsibility centers generally will have little control over variations from the budget. Moreover, the effect of a strike or a natural disaster may mean that it is all but impossible for a responsibility center manager to meet the budget. In these instances some organizations will revise the budget.

Revise Programs. The reports also can be used as a basis for program evaluation and revision. For any of a number of reasons, the programming decisions made by the organization may not be optimal. The anticipated demand for the product or service may not exist, competition may be stronger than the organization thought it would be, technological improvements may have made the product or service obsolete, or the organization may not be able to develop the skills necessary to revitalize the program. In extreme situations the reports may indicate not only a need to revise or discontinue one or more of the organization's programs but a need to change the organization's overall strategy as well.

Because the reporting and evaluation phase has this feedback characteristic, the loop shown in Exhibit 6-3 is a closed one. As a consequence, the process tends to be rhythmic: It follows a pattern which, although variations may exist, is about the same every year. Managers learn this pattern and adjust their activities to it.

NOTES

1 The health-care application of some of the management control principles and concepts discussed in this chapter and Chapter 7 are available on an interactive CD-ROM. See David W. Young, *Financial Control Systems in Health Care*, CD-ROM. Cambridge, MA: Crimson Press Curriculum Center, 1997. For a more general nonprofit application, see Robert N. Anthony and David W. Young, *Management Control in Nonprofit Organizations*, 7th ed. Burr Ridge, IL: Irwin/McGraw-Hill, 2003.

2 For details, see the "New York City Sanitation Department" case in Anthony and Young, *Management Control in Nonprofit Organizations*.

3 This idea is discussed in David W. Young, "Nonprofits Need Surplus Too," *Harvard Business Review*, January–February 1982. See also Mary T. Ziebell and Don T. DeCoster, *Management Control Systems in Nonprofit Organizations*. San Diego: Harcourt Brace Jovanovich, 1991, and Regina E. Herzlinger and Denise Nitterhouse, *Financial Accounting and Managerial Control for Nonprofit Organizations*. Cincinnati: South-Western Publishing, 1994, p. 152.

4 Alfred E. Sloan, *My Years with General Motors*. New York: Macfadden, 1965.

5 Robert N. Anthony, *Planning and Control Systems: A Framework for Analysis*. Boston: Division of Research, Graduate School of Business Administration,

Harvard University, 1965. For a more recent description of these activities, see Robert N. Anthony, *The Management Control Function*. Boston: Harvard Business School Press, 1988.

6 For a more detailed discussion of the management control process, see Robert N. Anthony and V. J. Govindarajan, *Management Control Systems*, 10th ed. Burr Ridge, IL: Irwin/McGraw-Hill, 1999.

CHAPTER 7

Key Issues in Designing the Responsibility Accounting Structure

Chapter 6 discussed some of the basic design considerations in developing or reconfiguring a responsibility accounting structure. It raised but did not discuss in depth several complex matters. Among those issues are the link between the responsibility center structure and the organization's motivation system, the development of appropriate transfer prices, the problem with using return on assets (ROA) as a basis for measuring the performance of the managers of investment centers, and some of the informal matters that arise in the context of decentralizing responsibility in large and/or complex organizations. This chapter addresses those considerations.

The chapter begins with the issues senior managers must consider if they are to make profit centers or investment centers work to the overall benefit of the organization, including some tricky design matters in matrixlike organizations. Next, the chapter takes up the general topic of motivation and discusses some recent thinking on various ways to reward managers and others for good performance. The argument is made that one of the principal objectives in designing a responsibility accounting system is to attain congruence between the organization's overall goals and the personal goals of operating managers. A number of matters must be considered to attain this "goal congruence," one of which is the design of a motivation system.

The chapter then addresses some specific situations to illustrate the difficulty of designing appropriate transfer prices. It also uses an example to illustrate how *residual income* can substitute for ROA in measuring the performance of investment center managers. Inadequate attention on the part of senior management to these two topics in particular—either individually or in combination—explains why many responsibility accounting systems fail to achieve the goal of encouraging managers to do what is in the organization's best interest.

The chapter concludes with a brief discussion of some of the informal aspects that can influence the success of a responsibility center design. In particular, it looks at ways in which individuals in organizations gain power and influence outside the formal responsibility center network.

MAKING PROFIT AND INVESTMENT CENTERS WORK

If senior management designates an organizational unit as an investment or profit center, it must pay careful attention to five design issues that affect that unit's ability to succeed.

Issue 1: The Fairness Criterion

A profit center's manager must be able to exert *reasonable* influence over the revenues and expenses of his or her center. If the center is designated as an investment center, he or she also needs to have reasonable control over the assets included in measuring the center's performance. This does not imply that the manager must have *complete* control over those items, since few, if any, responsibility center managers have that kind of control. However, a profit or investment center manager should be able to exercise a "reasonable" degree of control over the center's volume of activity, work quality, variable costs, and direct fixed costs as well as (depending on market conditions) the prices charged. In a *Harvard Business Review* article that some consider a classic, Richard Vancil called this the "fairness criterion."[1]

The Newport Theater problem in Chapter 6 illustrated a fairly typical violation of the fairness criterion. Recall that senior management allowed the accounting staff to allocate a portion of actual corporate overhead costs to the theater. In doing that, it effectively had asked the theater's manager to be responsible for some costs that he or she could not control. This problem could have been solved by using transfer prices for those overhead services for which a unit of activity could be "purchased" (e.g., legal) and allocating a portion of corporate overhead agreed to in the budgeting phase of the management control process for those services for which transfer prices were inappropriate (e.g., administration and general). These types of changes would have satisfied the fairness criterion.

Issue 2: The Goal Congruence Criterion

The term *goal congruence*, which is borrowed from social psychology, describes the idea of aligning the goals of managers of individual responsibility centers with the goals of the organization as a whole. Other terms, such as *aligning incentives*, often are used to describe the same idea. A lack of goal congruence is present when a responsibility center manager takes actions that serve his or her own center's interests but are not in the best interests of the organization overall. This usually means that some changes are needed in the responsibility accounting system, although not necessarily in the design of the responsibility centers.

When senior management sees the need for cooperative actions among profit center managers, it can promote them by designing the motivation process so that they have a positive impact on the profit center's reported performance or at least do not affect it adversely. For instance, some organizations have promoted cooperation with a policy that no profit center manager will receive a bonus unless *all* profit centers meet or exceed their budgeted profitability targets. In other organizations, profit performance is one of several items considered in the motivation process and a manager's bonus depends on adequate performance along all dimensions. In all instances the design leads to enhanced goal congruence. We will return to this issue later in the book.

Issue 3: An Absence of Dysfunctional Incentives

Related to matters of fairness and goal congruence are a variety of considerations that must be managed carefully if an organization is to avoid dysfunctional behavior by profit or investment center managers. For example, some managers may pay too much attention to the revenue side of the equation or cut expenses without concern for the longer-term consequences of those cuts. A classic example is a profit center manager who suspends machine maintenance, reasoning that doing that will increase the center's profits and that he or she will be promoted to another division before the machines begin to break down.

In addition, the competitive spirit the profit center concept fosters may have dysfunctional consequences for the organization. For instance, a profit center manager may be unwilling to cooperate with other responsibility centers in the way senior management wants and may make decisions that add to the profit of his or her own unit while causing profit reductions in other units. The manager may be reluctant to incur overtime costs, for example, even though the output of his or her center may be badly needed by other responsibility centers.

Issue 4: A Well-Designed Set of Transfer Prices

Intraorganizational transactions can exist between two profit centers in a relatively small organization or between two divisions in a large multidivisional corporation. A transfer price is appropriate in a hospital when, say, the department of pediatrics orders a test from the laboratory. In a corporation such as General Motors it is used when, say, the Chevrolet Division "purchases" batteries produced by the Delco Division.

Transfer prices constitute a monetary way of measuring the amount of a responsibility center's internally furnished services. Indeed, if there are internal transactions and no transfer prices, it is not appropriate to designate the unit that is providing the service as a profit center, since it does not have the ability to generate revenue. An internal audit organization, for example, usually provides services without charge and therefore is not a profit center. Similarly, if senior management requires or strongly encourages operating units to use the services of certain staff units, such as the information services department, those staff units probably should not be profit centers, at least not until operating units accept the value of the services and are willing to pay for them.[2]

Arriving at satisfactory transfer prices is one of the most complicated aspects of designing a responsibility accounting structure. The basic problem with setting a transfer price, the potential for conflict that transfer prices create, and some issues for senior management to consider in developing an effective transfer pricing system are discussed later in this chapter. Different organizations use different approaches to address these issues, depending on a variety of circumstances, such as the availability of market price information and the effect of the choice on each manager's motivation.

Issue 5: A Clear Cross-Subsidization Policy

When an organization has investment or profit centers, senior management must decide whether there will be cross subsidization among them. Investment or profit centers that are independent, that is, do not cross-subsidize each other, and have managerial rewards linked to bottom line performance constitute a powerful motivating device in an organization. In effect, they create a series of small business units sometimes referred to as "every tub on its own bottom" or ETOB.

Unfortunately, an ETOB structure occasionally can create a fortress-like mentality among the affected responsibility center managers, leading to a culture quite different from the one that would exist in an organization with cross subsidization among its responsibility centers. The ETOB approach might be appropriate in a conglomerate with relatively unrelated business units, such as General Electric, but likely would be inappropriate for a strategy that entailed cross subsidization among divisions, as in corporations that have adopted the Boston Consulting Group model of stars, dogs, cash cows, and question marks. In short, senior management must be certain that its cross-subsidization policy is in line with the organization's strategy.

DESIGN COMPLICATIONS

Determining the appropriate responsibility centers for a company's product lines would be relatively easy if each product line (1) sold its services to the outside, (2) was staffed by personnel who worked for no other product line, and (3) was the responsibility of a manager who had reasonable control over hiring and other personnel decisions as well as over decisions on supply and material purchases. In these circumstances each product line most likely would be designated as an investment or profit center.

Most organizations are not set up in a way that permits such a tidy and well-defined formal structure. Many companies operate over large geographic areas and must consider that fact in designing their structures. For example, does a multidivisional corporation have one manager of its home appliance division with broad geographic responsibilities or several area managers, each with responsibility for all the products in his or her area, including home appliances?

In general, a separate formal structure is needed when the responsibility for a product line's success involves more than one supporting functional unit. For example, the director of a master's degree program in a large university draws on faculty members from several different departments (e.g., accounting, marketing, organizational behavior) who work in the program. Moreover, although faculty members may teach in a particular program, their reporting relationships within the organization generally are not to the director of one program only. Similar blurring of product and functional lines takes place in companies such as Boeing Aircraft and McKinsey Consulting, where project managers may need personnel from several functional units to carry out their projects successfully.

Matrix Organizations

Although the product line structure need not match the organizational structure, there typically is a manager who has identifiable responsibility for each program, project, or product line. This need for a fit between the organizational structure and the "product line" structure often results in a matrix organization. The matrix consists of product lines along one dimension and functional units along the other. It is illustrated in Exhibit 7-1.

In this sort of arrangement each product line manager is accountable for his or her line's profitability. Functional unit managers, by contrast, are held accountable for the skill mix in their units. In this example, most employees would have a home base in a functional unit, but they also would be "purchased" at a transfer price by one or more product lines. Since product line managers call on functional units for work to be done on their products, responsibility is divided between the functional units

EXHIBIT 7-1

A Typical Matrix Structure

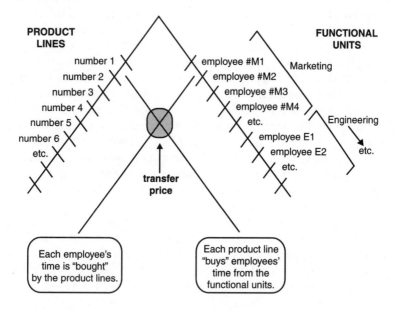

PRODUCT
LINES

number 1
number 2
number 3
number 4
number 5
number 6
etc.

transfer
price

employee #M1   Marketing
employee #M2
employee #M3
employee #M4
etc.   Engineering
employee E1
employee E2   etc.
etc.

FUNCTIONAL
UNITS

Each employee's
time is "bought"
by the product lines.

Each product line
"buys" employees'
time from the
functional units.

and the product lines. The product line managers, whose units probably are designated as profit centers, would be responsible for the profitability of their lines. The functional unit managers might be either standard expense centers or profit centers with a goal of zero profitability. In both instances they would be responsible for recruiting the needed skill mix and undertaking the requisite training to meet the needs of the product lines. In some instances the need for a functional unit specialist might be for a relatively short period, such as on a consulting project. In others, such as the construction of an aircraft, the functional specialist might spend a year or more working for a particular product line.

One of the most interesting juxtapositions of product lines and functional units occurred in the U.S. Department of Defense (DOD) in the 1960s, where functional responsibility lay with the secretary of the army, the secretary of the navy, and the secretary of the air force, but with defense programs cutting across functional lines. For example, the DOD had a strategic mission that was related to a possible nuclear exchange with the Soviets. Different parts of that program were the responsibility of the Army (antiballistic missiles), the Navy (Polaris submarines), and the Air Force (strategic missiles and bombers). The DOD needed a mechanism that facilitated decision making for the program as a whole.[3] The result was a matrix structure.

The Contingency View

As this discussion suggests, there is no single "right" answer to the problem of responsibility center design. Each organization is unique in terms of its strategy, management philosophy, culture, programs and/or product lines, and a wide variety of other characteristics. The guiding principle is that of aligning responsibility and control, but no clear-cut prescriptions can be given. As a result, senior management in many organizations spends a considerable amount of time debating the most appropriate responsibility center structure for a given strategy and organizational structure. Moreover, when either the strategy or the organizational structure shifts, as it frequently does, senior management must reconsider the responsibility center structure. In doing this, it must ask itself a very fundamental question: *Does the responsibility center structure motivate managers to take actions that are in the best interest of both their individual responsibility centers and the organization as a whole?*

If the answer is yes, an appropriate responsibility center structure most likely exists. If the answer is no, senior management must engage in a redesign effort.

RESPONSIBILITY CENTERS AND MOTIVATION

As the above discussion suggests, a responsibility accounting structure can provide a powerful motivating force for middle- and lower-level managers in an organization. It therefore is extremely important that senior management consider the incentives that underlie the structure. Indeed, unless there is a motivation system in place that rewards managers for good performance and either does not reward, or penalizes, them for poor performance, the type of responsibility center chosen is immaterial.

There is considerable disagreement about how to design a good motivation system. What motivates people to perform well in organizations, how senior management designs appropriate *motivation* (as distinct from *compensation*) packages, and what role monetary compensation plays in this effort are all controversial. Despite the disagreements, one fact stands out from all the rest: Financial compensation is not everything. Indeed, Stanford's Jeffrey Pfeffer, who has studied the impact of compensation on performance, concludes in *The Human Equation* that a firm's compensation system is a *relatively unimportant* factor. He cites employee surveys showing that a pleasant, challenging, and empowering workplace often has a greater impact on employee behavior than do monetary incentives.[4]

Harvard's Dorothy Leonard and Tufts's Walter Swap make a parallel argument in their book *When Sparks Fly*. They emphasize the importance of employees' passion for work that leads them to lose the distinction between work and play. They give the examples of 3M, where research and development (R&D) employees are allowed to use 15 percent of their time to pursue any individual project they want, and Hewlett-Packard (H-P), where R&D employees may set aside 10 percent of their time to work on individual projects. As a result, they argue, both 3M and H-P are among the most innovative companies in the world.[5]

The Role of Contingent Compensation

Although these authors and others consider financial rewards to be of secondary importance, most observers tend to agree that when they are present, financial rewards work best when they take the form of incentive—or contingent—compensation. The potential incentives can range from piece rates to stock options. Even Jeffrey Pfeffer, who espouses the importance of a pleasant workplace as a motivational force, agrees that contingent compensation is a powerful motivator, referring to the positive experiences of companies such as Home Depot and Southwest Airlines. In Pfeffer's view, when employees receive a share of the profits (whether with bonuses, stock options, or some other means), they work to keep costs low and seek ways to increase revenues.[6]

Judith Bardwick, a clinical professor of psychiatry at the University of California at San Diego, takes the idea of contingent compensation a step further, suggesting that job *insecurity* can be a powerful motivating force. In her view, senior management needs to find a balance between security and anxiety if it is to get high performance from employees.[7] She cites the example of Intel, whose commitment to its employees includes a willingness to assist them in "making intelligent career choices," which includes not providing a guarantee of continued employment. Intel employees are expected to review the company's quarterly business updates to determine where the company is growing and shrinking and to use that knowledge to focus their career decisions and training activities.

General Electric (GE) and Microsoft have variations on this "job continuation" incentive program. At GE, anyone who cannot operate as a team player; is not prepared to work up, down, and across the organization; and is unwilling to work with both customers and suppliers should plan to seek a job elsewhere.[8] Microsoft's employees are rewarded solely on the basis of performance. Management understands that people spend 50 percent of their time doing something that is destined to fail, and as a result, Microsoft expects failures from everybody. At the same time, nobody can rest on his or her past successes; people are rewarded only for their most recent performance. Because of the rapid growth of the company, there are always opportunities for promotion. The open positions are not filled by the people with the most seniority, however, but by the best people available. One result is that managers always have a powerful incentive to do a good job. Moreover, as they move up the hierarchy, the competition increases dramatically. Only the best survive.[9]

These examples can be combined with some well-established conceptual principles related to motivation. For example, Abraham Maslow's "hierarchy of needs" begins with most basic physical needs (food, clothing, etc.) at the bottom and rises to "self-actualization" at the top.[10] It is clear, though, that not all of a firm's employees will see their jobs as being related to the same level in Maslow's hierarchy. Indeed, not all employees will be self-actualized no matter what kind of motivation process senior management designs.

Maslow's concept of a hierarchy of needs is supported by Douglas McGregor's notion of Theory X and Theory Y, two contrasting assumptions about what motivates employees' behavior.[11] Managers who believe in Theory X think employees are motivated only by their basic needs, not by a desire to contribute to the organization's success. By contrast, managers who believe in Theory Y see employees as motivated by "higher-order growth needs." In fact, looking at McGregor's dichotomy in conjunction with Maslow's hierarchy suggests at least the possibility that some employees *are* motivated by basic needs, whereas others—those who have moved up Maslow's hierarchy, perhaps because they have reached positions of greater responsibility in the organization—have more lofty aspirations.

Clearly, people are far more complex than some of these bifurcated theories would suggest. For example, as David McClelland has argued, most employees (indeed, most people) have some combination of three motives: achievement (the need to seek tasks that will provide a sense of accomplishment), power (the need to be in charge of and influence others), and affiliation (the need to have social and interpersonal relationships).[12] An ideal motivation process would target each employee's mix of these three motives and align itself with them. A challenging task, indeed.

Overarching Themes

In light of these different theories, it is not surprising that so much has been written about the topic of motivation. However, most managers would agree that no theory or combination of theories can be used to eliminate the difficult (perhaps impossible) task of designing an appropriate motivation process for each employee in an organization. There are, however, three basic themes that can be of use to senior managers who are designing (or redesigning) an organization's motivation system.

Theme 1: There Are Two Basic Sources of Rewards: Extrinsic and Intrinsic. Other than financial rewards, extrinsic rewards can include praise, recognition, a gold watch, and a variety of other nonfinancial items. Intrinsic rewards, by contrast, come from within the employee himself or herself and relate to how well he or she believes a task was performed. A good motivation system will incorporate both sources. Certainly, for example, 3M and H-P employees receive an intrinsic (as well as an extrinsic) reward if they find that their investment of time in a budding idea has resulted in a new and popular product. Similarly, a promotion at Microsoft, though extrinsic, no doubt also is a clear indication that a task has been performed well.

Theme 2: Employees Need Feedback. Regardless of the set of rewards and recognition activities senior management uses, it needs to find ways to provide employees with feedback on their performance. Feedback allows employees to satisfy several needs, such as relating rewards to the effort they have expended or comparing rewards to an external standard of some sort.

Theme 3: Procedural Justice Is Important. Employees need to believe that a fair process was used to determine the distribution of rewards among them. The complexity of this issue is illustrated dramatically by the example of a small but rapidly growing start-up company called Cambridge Technology Partners (CTP).[13] At CTP the sales personnel were receiving large commissions in return for bringing business to the firm. At the same time the technical and operations people were being asked to work night and day to meet the demands of the growing business while receiving no supplemental compensation other than stock options in a nonpublic company. As a result, the technical people complained about a lack of distributive justice until the firm went public and they all had a sizable share of its equity. At that point the salespeople (who had no equity) complained about a lack of distributive justice. Clearly, where one stands on this issue depends on where one sits!

Link to the Responsibility Accounting System

In addition to the three themes discussed above, a fourth appears to be important, although it rarely is discussed in the business literature, and then only in a tangential way: *The motivation system must fit with a firm's responsibility accounting system.* Without this sort of fit it is likely that senior management will be sending mixed messages to employees or that a lack of goal congruence will arise.

In short, senior management has to recognize that the design of the motivation system depends to a great extent on the organization's strategy and the nature of its responsibility centers. Entrepreneurial behavior by profit center managers will be difficult to achieve, for instance, unless the motivation process provides appropriate rewards for the kinds of risks being taken and the measurement phase of the management control process assigns costs to profit centers in a way that managers perceive as fair.

Finally, as will be seen in subsequent chapters, to the extent that employee attitudes, customer satisfaction, and operational performance are important to a company and are a basis for rewarding employees, the management control process has to support the motivation system. This support can come through the budgeting effort, in which senior management can build incentive compensation into each responsibility center's budget. Support also can come by way of the measurement and reporting phases of the process. For example, besides paying its sales staff on commission, the retailer Nordstrom prints that number on each employee's check stub and ranks each sales clerk's performance on the employee bulletin board in terms of revenue per sales clerk (rather than per square foot, which is the more common industry measure). One result is that the turnover of productive clerks tends to be low, whereas that of unproductive clerks is high.[14]

Similarly, citing the example of Pioneer Petroleum, Robert Kaplan and David Norton argue that the "Balanced Scorecard," which is discussed more fully in Chapter 11, is most useful when it is linked to a reward system. Pioneer tied 60 percent of its executives' bonuses to financial performance (which consisted of a weighted average of five components: operating margins, return on capital, cost reduction versus plan, growth in existing markets, and growth in new markets). The remaining 40 percent was based on the scorecard's indicators concerning customer satisfaction, internal process improvements, and employee learning and growth.

FAIRNESS AND GOAL CONGRUENCE PROBLEMS

In these situations and others, one of the primary driving forces is the desire to achieve fairness and goal congruence. Indeed, a *lack* of one or the other frequently plagues an organization's responsibility accounting system. Violations of these criteria appear in a variety of situations; two of the most common involve transfer prices and capital investment decisions. Let us look at each one separately.

Transfer Prices

The responsibility accounting structure frequently contains several responsibility centers that engage in "buying and selling" transactions among themselves. As a result, the prices at which those transactions take place—

the transfer prices—become important elements of the responsibility accounting structure.

Fairness Problems. To illustrate how transfer prices can affect fairness in a responsibility accounting system, let us begin with a relative simple but very common situation.

 PROBLEM The department chairs in a school of management were being encouraged to have their faculty members use the school's copy center for the reproduction of research papers and for other copying needs. At a meeting of the department chairs one chair reported that the cost of making 100 copies of a research paper was $20 more using the school's copy center than it would have been if the work had been done at a private copy center about one block from the department's offices.

This kind of situation happened several times a week in each department, adding up to many thousands of dollars a year. The school's copy center had prepared a detailed breakdown of its costs for photocopying the research paper:

Direct materials		$90
Direct labor		25
Variable overhead	2	
Fixed overhead	17	19
Total costs		$134
Markup		13
Price		$147

The private copy center did work that was equal in quality and speed to that of the school's copy center. Its manager had informed the chair that it would have charged $127 for the job described above. The chairs knew that the school's copy center had the capacity to produce about 300,000 copies a week but was operating at a level of only about 250,000 a week.

What is the lowest price the school's copy center should charge for this job? What is the highest price the department should pay? What should be done about the school's transfer pricing policy for its copy center?

ANSWER This is a relatively straightforward transfer pricing problem. The market price is known and is higher than the variable costs of the in-house entity (the school's copy center). Quality appears to be similar between the two options, the fixed overhead costs of the in-house entity have been identified clearly, and the in-house entity has excess capacity. In practice, it is much more difficult to identify fixed overhead, capacity is a bit more elusive, and comparability of quality is rarely this clear. Moreover, market price at times is below the in-house entity's variable costs.

In the school's set of circumstances it is possible to establish a transfer price that would promote fairness, that is, would give department chairs greater control over the costs for which they are being held responsible. To do this, the lowest price a department should pay would be the copy center's variable costs, as follows:

Direct materials	$90
Direct labor	25
Variable overhead	2
Total variable costs	$117

There frequently is some debate about the *highest* price that should be paid. The normal argument is that it should be the market price: $127 in this situation. If the transfer price were set at the market price, the copy center would cover its variable costs and some, but not all, of its fixed overhead. However, the department would be better off since it would not be paying a price above market and hence would perceive the transfer price as "fair." The school would be financially better off since no resources would flow to the private copy center.

In this situation it was possible to determine the market price and ascertain that all other factors (quality, turnaround time, etc.) were comparable. This is not always the case. If a market price is unavailable or if there are differences in some of these other factors, the transfer pricing decision becomes more complicated.

Sometimes there are goal congruence problems. If for some reason the private copy center's price were *below* the school copy center's variable costs, an argument could be made that the lowest price the departments should pay would still be the market price. In these circumstances, however, there is a clear signal to the school that its copy center is being run inefficiently or that the cost computations are erroneous. However, if the cost figures are accurate, the school will be better off having the work done by the private copy center, since it will not incur any of the variable costs (which exceed the market price) and possibly could eliminate some or all of the fixed overhead.

As the following problem demonstrates, transfer pricing can create some fairly serious goal congruence problems.

 PROBLEM   The Automated Component Division (ACD) and the Laboratory Testing Division (LTD) are two divisions within a larger company; both have been designated as profit centers. The ACD charges outside customers $11 for a component that is used in manufacturing a camera. The full cost of the component includes all direct materials and labor (both of which are minimal), purchased services, and a fair share of overhead. The ACD adds a small profit margin to this full cost amount to arrive at the $11 price.

A sophisticated test is needed to analyze the component and assure that it meets tolerances before it is shipped. This test currently is "purchased" by the ACD from the LTD. The LTD charges all the company's divisions $6 for this test or ones like it. The price is based on variable costs of $2 per test (mainly supplies and labor), plus $3 of fixed costs and $1 of profit.

The ACD's manager has discovered that tests of comparable quality and with equivalent turnaround time can be obtained for $4.50 from a laboratory nearby that is not part of the company. The following table shows each profit center's financial performance under the two options as well as the company's overall financial performance under the two options.

	Automated Components Division	Laboratory Testing Division	Company Overall
Option 1: Buy from the Laboratory Testing Division			
Revenue	$11.00	$6.00	$11.00
Variable cost	6.00	2.00	2.00
Contribution	$5.00	$4.00	$9.00
Option 2: Buy from the Independent Laboratory			
Revenue	$11.00	$0.00	$11.00
Variable cost	4.50	0.00	4.50
Contribution	$6.50	$0.00	$6.50

What is the problem depicted in the figures in this table? Specifically, where is there an absence of goal congruence?

ANSWER   The problem is that if the ACD improves its financial performance by having the tests done by the independent laboratory, the company's overall profits decline. The company pays $2.00 "out of pocket" for every test that is done for the ACD by the LTD. All other costs are fixed. Therefore, each test done by the LTD reduces the company's profits by $2.00.

If the ACD buys tests from the independent laboratory, the company incurs an out-of-pocket cost of $4.50 instead of $2.00, and its profit therefore is reduced by $4.50. This is the case because when the tests are purchased from the independent laboratory, the price includes not just variable costs but a portion of the fixed costs of the independent laboratory, plus a profit margin. Clearly, the company would prefer to have the ACD purchase tests from the LTD rather than from the independent laboratory.

Remember, however, that when the ACD purchases tests from the LTD, it is charged $6.00, not $2.00. As a result, for each test the ACD purchases from the LTD, the ACD's profits fall by $6.00, compared with only $4.50 if it purchased the tests from the independent laboratory.

In summary, if the ACD purchases from outside the company, that division's profit increases, but the company's overall profits fall. Forcing the ACD to buy from the LTD maximizes the company's overall profits but reduces the profits of the ACD. If the ACD's manager is paid a bonus that is based on profits, the bonus is reduced. Clearly, the ACD manager's goals are not congruent with those of the company as a whole.

Issues to Consider in Setting Transfer Prices

The resolution of transfer pricing problems such as these is one of the most complicated aspects in designing a responsibility accounting structure. In arriving at a transfer price, senior management typically chooses among three options: (1) market price, (2) full cost, and (3) marginal cost.[15] Different organizations use different options, depending on factors such as the availability of information concerning market price and the effect of the choice on managers' motivation. Therefore, there is no option that can be called the "right" option.

Although there is no right option, there are five basic issues that senior management must consider in making a transfer pricing decision.

- *Issue 1: Strategic importance:* Decisions about transfer pricing frequently are affected by an organization's strategy. For example, assume that the company in the last problem had decided that for strategic reasons it needed to have an in-house laboratory testing division. If it were to allow the ACD and other divisions to purchase tests at outside laboratories and if all the divisions did that, there would be no activities taking place in the LTD. Or suppose that having the tests in question done at an outside laboratory would reveal a trade secret. In either of these circumstances senior management probably would require the ACD and other similar divisions to use the in-house laboratory. However, it still might be possible to require the LTD to set its price at "market." In these circumstances management might ask the LTD only to break even each year rather than attempt to earn a profit and to use a measure other than profit as a basis for determining the LTD manager's annual bonus.

- *Issue 2: Autonomy versus central control* Assuming an in-house laboratory is not required for strategic reasons, senior management must decide how much autonomy it wishes to give to its individual divisions. Will it allow them to set their own prices without intervention, or will it intervene to set prices? Will it allow purchasing divisions to go outside if they can get a better arrangement (price, quality, service, etc.) than internal selling divisions offer them?

  If senior management gives its selling divisions the autonomy to set prices at the level they choose and gives purchasing divisions the autonomy to buy from the outside, it must be prepared to lose some intraorganizational transactions. As in the example above, the loss of those transactions may cause corporate profits to fall in the short run. Senior management therefore must believe that the increased autonomy will give individual division managers the motivation to increase their profits and that the resulting increases will more than offset the short-run declines in the company's overall profits caused by the use of outside purchases.

If, in contrast, senior management intervenes in the price setting and outside purchase decisions of its divisions, it must be
prepared to engage in many of those interventions. It thus must
have a process to address the conflicts that will arise between and
among divisional managers.

- *Issue 3: Rules of the game:* The "rules of the game" must be clear.
  Managers must know their options at the beginning of the budget year. If they must buy from inside the organization, this
  needs to be well understood and agreed to. As was discussed
  previously, many organizations have a rule that the transfer price
  must be at the market price. However, this approach is not
  always possible because of the unavailability of market price
  information for some internally provided goods and services. In
  these circumstances, some other price or a transfer pricing formula must be determined and incorporated into the budgeting
  phase of the management control process.

- *Issue 4: Incentives:* When the price (or pricing formula) is established during the budgeting phase of the management control
  process and is held constant throughout the budget year, a manager who is purchasing internally does not pay for inefficiencies
  in a selling unit that cause its actual costs to exceed its budgeted
  costs. Allowing selling units to pass along their inefficiencies to
  buying units would remove any incentive for selling units to control their costs.

- *Issue 5: Standby capacity:* Transfer prices frequently are affected by
  the need for standby capacity. In the problem above, for example,
  the in-house laboratory incurs some fixed costs simply by being
  "ready to serve" the other divisions. These costs can include both
  depreciation on the laboratory equipment and the costs of some
  technicians and other staff that must be present, perhaps on a 24-
  hour-a-day basis and on weekends.

   To deal with this kind of situation some organizations establish a two-part transfer price. At the time budgets are prepared
each division that expects to use the in-house entity's services
projects how much of those services it plans to use. The selling
division's fixed costs are determined, and each buying division
agrees to pay its "fair share" of those costs each month regardless
of its use of the selling division. That is, those divisions agree to
pay the selling division for being available to them when they
need it. Then, when they use the selling division's services, they
pay only the variable costs associated with the services used.
Thus, one part of the transfer price is fixed each month and the

other part is variable, based on actual use of the selling division's services.

Clearly, there can be many complications in adopting a two-part transfer price. Separating fixed costs and variable costs can be tricky. Determining a buying entity's fair share also can be complicated; some divisions may require 24/7 availability, for example, whereas others may not. There also can be game playing in which some buying entities deliberately underestimate their needs in order to pay a lower share of the fixed costs. In general, all these problems are resolvable if senior management believes that the two-part approach will promote greater fairness in the system, enhance goal congruence, or both.[16]

Overall, the key question is whether an organization's transfer pricing policies motivate managers to take actions that are in the best interests of *both* their individual responsibility centers *and* the organization as a whole. If this is the case, the policies would seem to be appropriate. If it is not, senior management quite likely needs to consider modifications to enhance fairness, goal congruence, or both.

Capital Investment Decisions

Many of the issues associated with capital investment decision making are discussed in introductory finance textbooks. They also will be covered briefly in Chapter 8. There is one issue, however, that relates directly to the responsibility center decision and its impact on goal congruence. This issue surfaces in the case of investment centers when the performance of an investment center manager is measured in terms of ROA. Consider the following situation.

 PROBLEM Atrium, Inc., is a multidivisional corporation. The Sporting Goods Division (SGD) manufactures a variety of sports equipment that it sells to retail stores throughout the United States and abroad. It has been designated as an investment center. All of Atrium's investment center managers are paid bonuses that are based on ROA percentages. Specifically, for each 1 percent increase in actual ROA over budgeted ROA, a manager is paid $20,000 of bonus dollars.

Since some divisions have greater profitability potential than others, each has a different budgeted ROA target. The SGD's target is 22 percent. Overall, Atrium, Inc. has an ROA of 15 percent.

Although it uses investment centers, Atrium, Inc., also requires central office approval for any capital investment over $200,000. As in many multidivisional companies, senior management uses this approval process to exercise control over major asset acquisitions to be certain that they are in line with corporate strategic objectives.

As the SGD entered its third quarter of operations, its actual ROA was 25 percent. The division general manager (DGM) expected to be able to maintain that figure throughout the remainder of the fiscal year. Midway through the third quarter the manager of SGD's home recreation unit presented the DGM with an investment opportunity. By spending $500,000 for some specialized equipment and inventory, the unit could produce a new line of products oriented toward the teenage market. The equipment could be in place by the end of the third quarter so that the division could earn a full quarter's worth of profits, which the unit manager estimated would be $28,750. The division's market research staff agreed with the unit manager and also told the DGM that the $28,750 could be sustained in future quarters so that the annual profit potential from the investment was about $115,000. At present, the assets in the SGD totaled approximately $10,000,000.

The DGM knew that if the division moved ahead with this venture, Atrium's accounting staff would make the appropriate adjustments in ROA calculations so that he would not be penalized for a midyear investment, that is, for the fact that he would earn profits on the investment for less than a full year. The accounting staff usually did this by multiplying the profits for any given time period by an appropriate factor in order to annualize them.

Assuming the unit manager's estimates are correct, will the DGM submit this proposal to the central office for approval? Why or why not? If so, do you think it will be approved? If not, why not?

ANSWER   The DGM's annual bonus with and without the investment is as follows:

	Without Investment	With Investment
Division profit	$2,500,000	$2,615,000
Division assets	$10,000,000	$10,500,000
Division ROA	25.0%	24.9%
Less: budgeted ROA	22.0%	22.0%
Difference	3.0%	2.9%
Bonus @ $20,000 per percentage point	$60,000	$58,000

The profit without the investment is computed by multiplying assets (given at $10,000,000) by 25 percent (the given ROA). Profit with the $500,000 investment is $115,000 more (on annualized basis), thus lowering the division's ROA to 24.9 percent. Thus, the investment will cost the DGM $2000 in bonus dollars, making it unlikely that he or she will submit this proposal to the central office.

At the same time, the project has an ROA of 23 percent ($115,000 ÷ $500,000), which is 8 percent above the company's overall ROA of 15 percent. It therefore is likely that the central office would approve this project since it seems consistent with the organization's strategy and would improve the company's overall ROA.

This example illustrates one of the primary problems associated with the use of ROA for measuring the performance of investment center managers. Any time a proposed project is below a center's existing ROA, it is unlikely that the division manager will submit the proposal to senior management even if the investment would improve the company's overall ROA. Once again, there is a lack of goal congruence.

Residual Income.   In an effort to avoid this lack of goal congruence, some companies have employed the technique of residual income (RI). With the RI approach, an investment center is assessed a fee for the assets it uses. The investment center's *net* profit—or residual income—then is computed by deducting that fee from its *gross* profit.

 PROBLEM   Assume that the Sporting Goods Division is charged a fee of 22 percent (the budgeted ROA) for the assets it uses. Compute the division's residual income.

ANSWER   When this approach is used, the division's RI is as follows:

	Without Investment	With Investment
Division profit before fee	$2,500,000	$2,615,000
Less: fee (22% of assets)	2,200,000	2,310,000
Residual income	$300,000	$305,000

If we assume that the DGM's bonus is based on the division's RI, he or she now will have an incentive to undertake the investment, and most likely will propose it to the central office. Thus, the RI approach makes the DGM's goals congruent with those of the organization overall while retaining the investment center idea.

RELATING THE RESPONSIBILITY ACCOUNTING STRUCTURE TO INFORMAL AUTHORITY AND INFLUENCE

Responsibility centers can be very powerful forces in helping an organization achieve its strategy. No matter how carefully responsibility centers are designed, however, informal matters will always be present. These matters include unwritten rules concerning, for example, the decisions that are appropriately made by a profit center manager, those that require approval from a higher level, and those that require consultation with (but not necessarily the approval of) staff offices or higher-level managers. In general, senior managers tend to give more autonomy to subordinates whom they know well and whose judgment they trust. As a result, despite the presence of a variety of formal devices in an organization, some profit center managers may have considerably more autonomy and/or influence than others do.

In addition, as was discussed earlier, the responsibility center network is linked with the organization's culture and conflict management processes. Rapid cultural change can result from shifting the organization's responsibility center structure from, say, independent (ETOB) profit centers to an elaborate cross-divisional subsidization scheme or vice versa. Dramatic cultural change also can result from centralizing revenue and establishing a series of expense centers. Moreover, investment or profit center arrangements with cross subsidization almost certainly will produce conflict about the appropriate size of the subsidies. This conflict will have to be managed, as will conflicts concerning transfer prices.

Managing culture and conflict requires addressing this more informal side of the organization and thinking about how it relates to the formal responsibility accounting structure. Indeed, attention to these informal relationships can be extremely helpful in improving the functioning of the responsibility accounting system overall.

Most often, informal relationships are described in terms of power and influence, which people in organizations may gain for reasons other than their formal positions in the hierarchy or the nature of their responsibility centers. As John Kotter, one of the leading authorities on power and influence, has observed, "a manager can be dependent in varying degrees on superiors, subordinates, peers in other parts of the organization, the subordinates of peers, outside suppliers, customers, competitors, unions, regulating agencies, and many others."[17] Clearly, the lines on the organizational chart fall far short of depicting all these relationships. Indeed, as Kotter goes on to observe, even the lines are not always reliable "because virtually no one in modern organizations will passively accept and completely obey a constant stream of orders from someone just because he or she is the 'boss.' " As Herbert Simon observed over 50 years ago in the book that contributed to his receipt of the Nobel Prize in Economics, "authority is only one of a number of forms of influence. Its distinguishing characteristic is that it does not seek to convince the subordinate, but only to obtain his acquiescence. In actual exercise, of course, authority is usually liberally admixed with suggestion and persuasion."[18]

Kotter describes four ways in which managers and others gain power in organizations and thus make their influence felt outside the formal lines of authority.

1. Through a sense of *obligation*. In effect, people build up and use "chits" all the time in organizations.

2. Through *expertise*. A manager with in-depth knowledge in a functional area such as production, marketing, or finance has power based on that knowledge. Similar power might accrue to someone who has knowledge about a particular product, a set of customer concerns, or a competitor's strengths and weaknesses.

3. Through *identification with their ideas*. Some managers are more charismatic than others, and people will follow their lead even though they may not completely accept the particular direction in which the manager is going. Managers who use this technique frequently will be more visible in the organization

through means such as their attire, their body language, the speeches they give, and the meetings they chair.

4. Through *perceived dependence*. Some managers will create the perception that they are able to acquire resources and make them available, *if they choose*, to help another person be successful. People in the organization who need those resources tend to accord power to those managers.

In short, although an organization chart may identify the formal authority arrangements and although a clear network of responsibility centers may exist, both can and frequently do exclude many key decision makers, especially in team- and knowledge-based organizations, where authority is much more informal. For example, in some hospitals (which are basically knowledge organizations) physicians who admit a large number of patients have a great deal of influence in organizational decision making even though they may be independent practitioners and not even appear on the organization chart. Their influence comes in large measure from their ability to admit their patients to another hospital and thus to cause a significant shift in the revenue streams of both hospitals.[19]

Similarly, in some consumer product organizations the R&D department has considerably more power than the organization chart might indicate, since much of the organization's future is dependent on its successful endeavors. More generally, the idea that power lies in areas of uncertainty perhaps was best illustrated by Michel Crozier in his classic study of organizational power and influence. Crozier identified low-level maintenance workers in a manufacturing plant as having a great deal of power because of their ability to control machine downtime, a critical success factor for the organization.[20]

As these comments suggest, informal decision-making processes generally are unwritten and frequently are somewhat mysterious. They encompass a network of interpersonal relationships that has important implications for management. Because they are unwritten, however, the informal processes generally are difficult to identify and certainly are hard to manage.

NOTES

1 See Richard F. Vancil, "What Kind of Management Control Do you Need?" *Harvard Business Review*, March–April 1973.

2 This issue is especially important with the information services department, which research has shown moves through various stages on its way to acceptance by operating units. See Cyrus F. Gibson and Richard L. Nolan, "Managing the Four Stages of EDP Growth," *Harvard Business Review*,

January–February 1974, and Richard L. Nolan, "Managing the Crises in Data Processing," *Harvard Business Review,* March–April 1979. For a more recent perspective, see Richard L. Nolan, "Connectivity and Control in the Year 2000 and Beyond," *Harvard Business Review,* July–August 1998.

3 Robert N. Anthony and David W. Young, *Management Control in Nonprofit Organizations,* 7th ed. Burr Ridge, IL: Irwin/McGraw-Hill, 2003.

4 Jeffrey Pfeffer, *The Human Equation: Building Profits by Putting People First.* Boston: Harvard Business School Press, 1998.

5 Dorothy Leonard and Walter Swap, *When Sparks Fly: Igniting Creativity in Groups.* Boston: Harvard Business School Press, 1999.

6 Pfeffer, op. cit.

7 Judith M. Bardwick, *In Praise of Good Business.* New York: Wiley, 1998.

8 Robert Slater, *Jack Welch and the GE Way.* New York: McGraw-Hill, 1999.

9 David Thielen, *The 12 Simple Secrets of Microsoft Management: How to Think and Act Like a Microsoft Manager and Take Your Company to the Top.* New York: McGraw-Hill, 1999.

10 Abraham H. Maslow, *Motivation and Personality.* New York: Harper & Row, 1954.

11 Douglas McGregor, *The Human Side of Enterprise.* New York: McGraw-Hill, 1960.

12 David C. McClelland, "Business Drives and National Achievement," *Harvard Business Review,* July–August 1962.

13 Teresa Amabile, George Baker, and Michael Beer, *Cambridge Technology Partners (A) and (B).* Boston: Harvard Business School Publishing, 1995.

14 Frederick F. Reicheld, *The Loyalty Effect: The Hidden Force Behind Growth, Profits, and Lasting Value.* Boston: Harvard Business School Press, 1996.

15 Transfer pricing has been the subject of many articles and treatises in the accounting literature. One of the best management-oriented descriptions can be found in David Solomons, *Divisional Performance: Measurement and Control.* Homewood, IL: Richard D. Irwin, 1965. This book is considered a classic in the responsibility accounting literature.

16 The book by Solomons mentioned in the previous note contains a section on two-part transfer pricing. For an application of this idea to integrated delivery systems in health care, see David W. Young, "Two-Part Transfer Pricing Improves IDS Financial Control," *Healthcare Financial Management,* 51, no. 8, August 1998.

17 John P. Kotter, "Power, Dependence, and Effective Management," *Harvard Business Review,* July–August 1977.

18 Herbert A. Simon, *Administrative Behavior.* New York: Free Press, 1945.

19 For a discussion of power and influence in hospitals, see David W. Young and Richard B. Saltman, *The Hospital Power Equilibrium.* Baltimore: Johns Hopkins Press, 1985.

20 Michel Crozier, *The Bureaucratic Phenomenon.* Chicago: University of Chicago Press, 1964.

CHAPTER 8

Programming

$\mathbf{C}$hapter 6 briefly described two phases of planning in the management control process: programming and budgeting. Those phases represent long-range and short-range planning activities, respectively. In the programming phase of the cycle, an organization's long-range decisions frequently involve investments in fixed assets that senior management expects will be used over a future period (usually several years) and will result in a "payback" of some sort to the organization. The end result of the programming phase ordinarily is a *capital* budget and frequently a commitment to initiate new programmatic endeavors, such as a new product line or a new service-related program.

By contrast, the budgeting phase of the process typically has a 1-year focus and is concerned only with operating activities. It usually results in an *operating budget* and a *cash budget*. This chapter will look in some depth at programming; operational budgeting is reserved for Chapter 9. Cash budgeting issues typically are discussed in financial accounting and finance textbooks.

The chapter begins with an overview of the programming phase of the management control process, positioning it as a key activity in implementing an organization's strategy. Programming decisions that call for the purchase of new capital (such as a new plant or new equipment) usually rely in part on one or more analytical techniques that incorporate the relatively long period over which the new or replacement assets will be used. We look at some of these techniques, including the payback period, net present value, and the internal rate of return. Although there are some instances in which an organization may decide to make a capital investment without giving much formal consideration to the analysis, the use of one of these analytical techniques is an important aspect of most programming decisions.

Next, we examine two issues that are very important in capital investment decision making: the impact of accelerated depreciation and the choice of a discount rate. This leads into the issue of risk and the way companies deal with risk in assessing a capital investment proposal.

The chapter concludes with a discussion of the political, behavioral, and other considerations that can influence senior management's choice of a proposal, including ways in which programming links to both an organization's culture and its conflict management processes. Appendix B discusses the concept of net present value.

PROGRAMMING: AN OVERVIEW

In the programming phase of the management control process, senior management makes a variety of decisions of a long-term nature concerning the product lines the company will manufacture, the programs it will undertake, and the approximate amount of resources it will devote to each one. As was discussed in Chapter 6, these decisions are made within the context of the organization's overall strategy, coupled with whatever information is available concerning new opportunities, increased competition, new or pending legislation that might affect the organization's efforts, and similar considerations.

Frequently, each division in an organization prepares its own strategic plan in which it defines its business elements, competitors, and competitive advantages and disadvantages. This plan establishes a framework for the organization's programming activities.[1]

Because programming decisions generally are long range in nature, the programming phase of the management control process frequently looks ahead by as much as 5 or 10 years. In some large organizations there is a lengthy program planning document that describes each program proposal in detail, estimates the resources needed to accomplish it, and calculates the expected returns.

Programming also can be an inherently creative activity, bordering on strategic change. Gary Hamel, a leading strategic thinker, demonstrates this when he contrasts programming at Nabisco (stuffing "twice as much white gunk between two chocolate cookies as you used to" to get Double Stuf Oreos) with programming at The Gap (which "went from selling Levi jeans and a motley assortment of teen clothing in an undistinguished mall format to owning a portfolio of couldn't-be-cooler brands sold in some of the freshest retail digs around").[2]

CAPITAL BUDGETING TECHNIQUES

The programming phase must focus on the long term, since decisions about fixed assets almost always involve multiyear commitments. A new piece of equipment, for example, usually will last for 3 to 5 years, sometimes longer. A new or renovated facility may last 10 to 20 years.

In making decisions with multiple-year commitments, it is important to recognize that although an investment in, say, a new piece of equipment will have benefits that extend over several years, a financial benefit received at some point in the future is not worth as much as the same amount received today. This section discusses why that is the case, introducing the concept of *present value*, a technique that frequently is used to deal with the problem of looking at future financial benefits in today's terms.

Capital Investment Decision Making

A decision to purchase a fixed asset can have a major impact on an organization's financial statements in both the short run and the long run. In the short run it may affect cash management through a reduction in the cash account to purchase the fixed asset or in terms of an increase in debt to finance the asset's acquisition. If debt is used, assuming it is of a long-term nature, the short-term impact on cash is mitigated somewhat, resulting only in annual debt service outlays (principal and interest payments) rather than the large outlay of cash that otherwise would be necessary.

The longer-run effect comes about as a result of the impact of the new fixed asset on annual cash flows. That is, the acquisition of a fixed asset—generally a piece of equipment or machinery but occasionally a new or renovated facility of some sort—almost always will result in some positive effects on cash flow. These effects can result from decreased operating expenses or increased revenues that exceed the associated increase in expenses. In most instances the effects will be felt for several years—over what is called the *economic life* of the new asset.

The decision to purchase a new fixed asset entails a variety of considerations that are difficult to quantify. In many organizations, for example, strategic and competitive concerns, regulatory mandates, employee morale, union grievances, and the like, play a major role in such decisions. In some companies, each division prepares a strategic plan early in the fiscal year. Then, later in the year, the firm develops an overarching plan that looks ahead into the next calendar year and establishes the framework for its capital budgeting activities. In these organizations, as in many others, the programming phase tends to span several months.

In addition to strategic considerations, an important aspect of almost all capital investment decisions is financial feasibility: comparing the cash inflows from the investment with the purchase price of the asset. The three most common techniques used to do this are payback period, net present value, and internal rate of return. Some organizations use all three techniques.

Payback Period. The payback period is the easiest technique. It entails simply dividing the net investment amount by the estimated annual cash inflows attributable to the investment. The quotient is the number of years of cash inflows necessary to recover the net investment.

The net investment amount generally is defined as the cost of the new asset, plus the installation costs, plus the disposal costs of the asset being replaced, minus any revenue received for the asset being replaced. Annual cash flows are the reduced expenses or increased contribution attributable to the new asset.

 PROBLEM Nido Escondido Bank is considering the purchase of a $100,000 piece of equipment for its check processing activities. The new equipment will replace an existing piece of equipment that the vendor has offered to repurchase for $20,000. It also will result in labor savings of approximately $40,000 a year. How long will it take the bank to "pay back" the investment?

ANSWER The net investment amount is $80,000 ($100,000 − $20,000 for the old equipment). The labor savings of $40,000 a year constitutes the cash inflows attributable to the investment. The resulting payback period is 2 years ($80,000 ÷ $40,000).

The principal advantage of the payback period approach is its simplicity, and it frequently is used to get a rough estimate of the feasibility of a particular investment opportunity. Its main disadvantages are (1) its failure to recognize profitability, (2) the difficulty it presents for making an assessment of the financial feasibility of different capital investment projects, particularly for comparing the return from alternative projects, and (3) its exclusion of the time value of money.

These disadvantages are related; they rest on the notion that a dollar saved 1 year from today is not as valuable as a dollar saved today, a dollar received 2 years from today is worth even less, and so on. If the payback period is relatively short, as it was in the example above, this is not a particularly serious limitation, but with longer payback periods the technique's utility is quite limited.

Net Present Value. The net present value technique avoids these limitations by incorporating the time value of money into the analysis. It does this, as its name implies, by calculating the present value (i.e., the value in today's terms) of future cash inflows. In effect, it recognizes that cash flows received in the future do not have as much value as do those received today. (If you do not understand the concept of present value, read through Appendix B before going any further.)

A capital investment analysis using the technique of net present value involves five steps:

1. Determine the estimated annual cash inflows from the investment. Those inflows may be either increased contribution (increased revenues less the associated increase in expenses) or decreased costs to the organization, but they must result *exclusively* from the investment itself, not from any activities that would have taken place without the investment.

2. Determine the estimated economic life of the investment. This is not the *physical* life of the new asset but rather the period over which it will generate the cash flows. This has become an important consideration in purchasing personal computers, which tend to have a long physical life but a very short (2 to 3 years) economic life.

3. Determine the *net* amount of the investment. This is its purchase price, plus installation costs, plus disposal costs for the old asset, less any cash received from the sale of the old asset.

4. Determine the required rate of return. As a general rule, this is at least the organization's weighted cost of capital (discussed later in the chapter) and generally will be increased to reflect whatever level of risk is associated with the investment. That is, the riskier the investment, the higher rate of return needed to justify it.

5. Compute the net present value according to the following formula:

Net present value = present value of cash inflows
– net investment amount

A variety of hand-held calculators have present value functions that can be used to make these computations. Most spreadsheet software packages also include present value functions. For our purposes here we will use present value factors, which are given in Tables A and B in Appendix B. In those tables the formula is slightly different from the one given above:

Net present value = (cash inflows × present value factor) – net
investment amount

or

$$NPV = (CF \times pvf) - I$$

Present value factors for *one-time* cash flows are given in Table A, and present value factors for *even annual* cash flows are shown in Table B. The present value factor lies at the intersection of the year row and the percent column selected in steps 2 and 4 above.

 PROBLEM   Nido Escondido Bank has an opportunity to purchase some equipment that will result in labor savings of approximately $33,000 a year. The equipment has a purchase price of $120,000 (net) and is expected to produce the labor savings for approximately 5 years. The bank's board has decided that an acceptable project must produce a rate of return of at least 8 percent a year. Is the proposed investment financially feasible?

ANSWER   The computations are as follows:

1. Annual cash flows = $33,000
2. Economic life = 5 years
3. Net investment amount = $120,000
4. Rate of return = 8 percent
5. $NPV = (CF \times pvf) - I$
   = $33,000 \times 3.993) - \$120,000$
   = $131,769 - \$120,000$
   = $11,769$

The investment therefore is financially feasible; that is, the present value of the annual cash flows is greater than the amount of the investment.

Several important points should be made about a net present value analysis such as this one. First, once we have determined the desired rate of return, a project that yields a net present value of zero or greater should be acceptable to us. That is, it is not important for the project to produce a present value greater than zero since if this were the case, the implication would be that we should raise the desired rate of return.

Second, although an analysis of this kind appears to be quite precise, we should recognize that its significant elements are estimates or guesses and may be quite imprecise. Specifically, cash flow projections beyond a period of 2 to 3 years ordinarily are not very precise, and the same is true of estimates of the economic life of most investments. Thus, we should be careful about attributing too much credibility to the precision that the formula seems to have. Because of this, even though an NPV of zero should be acceptable, many managers look for the NPV to be a *comfortable margin* above zero to compensate for these uncertainties. Of course, what is comfortable for one manager may not be comfortable for another.

Third, inflation is a factor. Because of potential increases in wage rates, it is likely that the labor savings from an investment will be greater 5 years from now than they are today. If we are to adjust the cash flow factor for the effects of inflation, however, we also need to adjust the required rate of return to reflect the need for a return somewhat greater than the rate of inflation. By excluding inflation from both the cash flow calculations and the required rate of return, we neutralize its effects and thus do not have to undertake the somewhat complex calculations that otherwise might be necessary.

Fourth, the financial analysis is only one aspect of the decision-making process. Clearly, there are many more considerations, including political and strategic analyses. Managers must be careful not to let the financial analysis dominate a decision that has strategic consequences that cannot be quantified or at least cannot be quantified easily. In these instances a manager's judgment and "feel" for the situation may be as important as the quantitative factors. Moreover, if a project is *required* for nonquantitative reasons (e.g., to meet required health and safety standards), its net present value is all but irrelevant. In short, almost all capital budgeting proposals involve a wide variety of nonquantitative considerations that influence the final decision. The use of present value or any related techniques serves mainly to formalize the quantitative part of the analysis.

Internal Rate of Return. The internal rate of return (IRR) method is similar to the net present value method, however, instead of determining a required rate of interest for making the calculations, we set net present value equal to zero and calculate the *effective* rate of return for the investment. Although this method is slightly more complicated than the net present value approach, it has the advantage of providing an exact rate of return rather than simply concluding that a proposed project meets or fails to meet an organization's stipulated rate of return. This makes it easier to rank proposed projects in terms of their financial benefits. Since an organization may not have sufficient capital investment funds to undertake all desirable projects, the IRR approach can help it determine its financial priorities more easily.

The IRR approach begins with the net present value (NPV) formula:

$$NPV = (CF \times pvf) - I$$

but sets NPV equal to zero so that

$$CF \times pvf = I$$

or

$$pvf = I \div CF$$

Once the present value factor has been determined, it can be located in Appendix B, Table B, in the row corresponding to the number of years of economic life of the project. The resulting interest rate, or rate of return, can be determined from the column in which pvf is found. Some calculators and spreadsheet programs have functions that can compute IRR quite easily, and so the approach here is more cumbersome than need be the case in practice.

 PROBLEM   Nido Escondido Bank wishes to determine the rate of return for the project described in the last problem. Do the calculations.

ANSWER   The computations are as follows:

$$pvf = I \div CF$$
$$pvf = \$120,000 \div 33,000$$
$$pvf = 3.636$$

Looking at Table B in Appendix B, in the row for 5 years (the economic life of the investment), we find the present value factor of 3.791 in the column for an interest rate of 10 percent and a present value factor of 3.605 in the column for an interest rate of 12 percent. Thus, the project's IRR is about 11 percent.

Effect of Taxes

The tax effects of the project are an important consideration. That is, any time an organization is able to realize some cost savings, the resulting increase in income will be taxed. As a result, the organization does not receive the full effect of the cost savings. Similarly, depreciation serves as a "tax shield," reducing the amount of taxes that otherwise would be paid. It does this by increasing the organization's expenses; which, other things being equal, reduces income before taxes.

 PROBLEM   Nido Escondido is in a 37 percent tax bracket. How does this change the cash flow described in the previous example? Be sure to include both the *increased* income before taxes arising from the cash flows and the *reduced* income before taxes arising from depreciation.

ANSWER   Of the $33,000 in anticipated cost savings (which will become taxable income), $12,210 ($33,000 × 0.37) will be taxed. Additionally, however, with annual depreciation of $24,000 (120,000 ÷ 5), $8,880 ($24,000 × 0.37) of tax savings will be realized. The net effect of the analysis is as follows:

1. Annual cash flow   = $33,000
   Less: taxes: (0.37 × $33,000)   =   (12,210)
   Plus tax savings ($24,000 × 0.37)   =   8,880
                                               $29,670

Alternatively, the computations can be done as follows, which is perhaps somewhat more intuitive:

	Income Statement	Cash Flow
Annual increase in income from cost savings	$33,000	
Annual cash flows from cost savings (assuming all are in cash)		$33,000
Less: depreciation	24,000	
Taxable income	$9,000	
Less: income tax (at 37%)	3,330	3,330
After tax income	$5,670	
After tax cash flow		$29,670

2. Economic life = 5 years
3. Net investment amount = $120,000
4. Rate of return = 8 percent
5. NPV = (CF × pvf) – I
   = ($29,670 × 3.993) – $120,000
   = $118,472 – $120,000
   = ($1,528)

The investment is no longer financially feasible.

Impact of Accelerated Depreciation

Accelerated depreciation often is advocated by economists as a public policy measure to stimulate investment. Let us look at how accelerated depreciation would affect this decision.

 PROBLEM   Nido Escondido Bank uses the sum-of-years-digits method to calculate its depreciation for tax purposes. The result is the following annual depreciation expense figures:

Year	Rate	Beginning Book Value	Depreciation Expense	Ending Book Value
1	5/15 = .333	$120,000	$39,960	$80,040
2	4/15 = .267	80,040	32,040	48,000
3	3/15 = .200	48,000	24,000	24,000
4	2/15 = .133	24,000	15,960	8,040
5	1/15 = .067	8,040	8,040	0

How will this change the analysis of the proposed investment? To work out the solution, it is necessary to make separate present value computations for each of the 5 years.

ANSWER Because the depreciation expense is different each year, we need to compute the present value on an annual basis, using Table A in Appendix B. The computations are as follows:

Year	Cash Flow	Depreciation Expense	Taxable Income	Income Tax Expense	Net Cash Flow	pvf	Discounted Cash Flow
1	$33,000	39,960	$(6,960)	$(2,575)	$35,575	.926	$32,943
2	33,000	32,040	960	355	32,645	.857	27,977
3	33,000	24,000	9,000	3,330	29,670	.794	23,558
4	33,000	15,960	17,040	6,305	26,695	.735	19,621
5	33,000	8,040	24,960	9,235	23,765	.681	16,184
Totals	$165,000	$120,000	$45,000	$16,650	$148,350		$120,282
Less amount of investment							120,000
Net present value							$282

The investment now is financially feasible.

There are several points worth noting about this example:

- The totals are the same whether we use straight line or accelerated depreciation. Under accelerated depreciation, the depreciation expense totals $120,000; taxable income is gross cash flows minus the depreciation expense, or $45,000; income tax expense is $16,650; and net cash flow is $148,350. Under straight line depreciation, the totals are the annual amounts time five. Thus, for example, taxable income is $9,000 × 5 = $45,000 and net cash flow is $29,670 × 5 = $148,350.

- Over a 5-year period the only differences between the two approaches are the gross and net present values. The gross present value is higher under accelerated depreciation because of the earlier cash flows ($32,943 in year 1 for accelerated depreciation, for example, compared with $29,670 under straight line depreciation).

- Because of the earlier cash flows, the total gross present value is $120,280 under accelerated depreciation, compared with $118,472 under straight line depreciation. The difference of $1808 is enough to make the project acceptable with accelerated depreciation and unacceptable with straight line depreciation.

This minor difference explains why economists advocate accelerated depreciation as an incentive to spur investment. Other things being equal, the use of accelerated depreciation will make some otherwise marginal projects feasible. This is the case not because the totals change, however, but because the cash flows come earlier in a project's life.

CHOOSING THE DISCOUNT RATE

In the examples and problems discussed so far we have been using a discount rate of 8 percent. A question that arises in this context is "How does management determine this number?" Clearly, the discount rate can have a significant impact on a project's financial feasibility. Thus, the way it is determined is of considerable importance in the decision-making effort.

Weighted Cost of Capital

As a first step in choosing a discount rate, many companies calculate the weighted cost of capital (WCC). This approach is based on the fact that an organization's assets are financed by a combination of liabilities and equity. Some liabilities, such as accounts payable, are usually interest-free, but short-term debt and long-term debt carry an interest rate that the organization must pay. Equity generally comes in two forms—contributed capital and retained earnings—and there can be considerable debate about the proper interest rate to use for it.

Conceptually, the interest rate attributed to equity should be the amount that shareholders of the company's stock expect to earn on their investment. Thus, it would be higher in a company in a high-risk business than in a company in a low-risk business. However, these rates are not easy to determine, and so choosing the appropriate rate for equity is a matter of judgment. Many companies use an opportunity cost approach, looking, for example, at what their investments have earned historically and using that rate as the interest rate for equity. Others take a somewhat more arbitrary approach, although always, one would hope, with the interests of the shareholders in mind. In addition, as will be discussed in greater detail below, sometimes the equity interest rate is adjusted for upcoming plans to issue more equity, or perhaps the organization's environment has become more risky than it was in prior years.

In all instances, however, the analytical approach to computing the weighted costs of capital is the same. We begin with the cost of each of source of capital and weight it by its relative amount. For example, assume that the right side of an organization's balance sheet appears as shown below with the interest rates as shown there (this is an organization that has attributed a rate of 12 percent to its equity):

Item	Amount	Interest Rate
Accounts payable	$3,000	0.0%
Accrued salaries	2,000	0.0
Short-term note payable	10,000	12.0
Total current liabilities	15,000	
Long-term note payable	75,000	10.0
Mortgage payable	150,000	8.0
Total liabilities	240,000	
Contributed capital	150,000	12.0
Retained earnings	50,000	12.0
Total liabilities and equity	$440,000	

In calculating a weighted cost of capital, we (1) determine the percentage of the total liabilities and equity that each source represents, (2) multiply that number by the appropriate interest rate, and (3) add the resulting totals together. The calculations for the situation shown above would look as follows:

Item	Amount	Percent of Total	Interest Rate	Weighted Rate
Accounts payable	$3,000	0.6	0.0%	0.00%
Accrued salaries	2,000	0.5	0.0	0.00
Short-term note payable	10,000	2.3	12.0	0.28
Total current liabilities	15,000			
Long-term note payable	75,000	17.0	10.0	1.70
Mortgage payable	150,000	34.1	8.0	2.73
Total liabilities	240,000			
Contributed capital	150,000	34.1	12.0	4.09
Retained earnings	50,000	11.4	12.0	1.37
Total liabilities and equity	$440,000	100.0		10.17

The current weighted cost of capital is just over 10 percent.

Current versus Projected Weighted Cost of Capital

If the capital investment decision-making effort were carried out by using an organization's current cost of capital, it would fail to incorporate the cost of borrowing or additional equity offerings that the firm planned to undertake to finance the new projects. For this reason, many organizations use a *projected* weighted cost of capital. That is, senior management determines the magnitude of additional debt that the organization will incur and also determines whether it will issue additional stock. It uses the interest it will pay on the additional debt and applies the interest rate it has chosen for its equity as part of the calculation of a *projected* weighted cost of capital. This becomes the weighted cost of capital it uses for the upcoming capital investment decisions, which are the ones that will result in new assets going into place in the next year.

Once these financing decisions have been made, the company can choose its capital investments in light of the available funds. Present value and IRR techniques are useful in making these determinations, but they do not assist the organization in determining how much additional debt it can carry on its balance sheet or whether additional equity offerings should be made.

Incorporating Risk

Some proposed projects are riskier than others. Companies deal with this problem in one of several ways:

- Senior management increases the WCC by a few or many percentage points that reflect its sense of a project's riskiness. It may do this by classifying projects into risk categories (high, medium, and low) and assigning different discount rates to each category.

- Senior management heavily discounts the cash flows beyond the first few years. The reasoning here is that in dynamic environments or industries in which competition is increasing, any cash flow projections after a few years out are highly speculative. This approach biases the decision-making process against any project that has long-run benefits, however.

- Senior management uses a higher discount rate for projects that base their cash flow estimates on additional revenues and expenses, in contrast to those that base their cash flow estimates on cost savings. The reasoning here is that cost savings can be verified more easily. For example, management can verify a claim that a new piece of equipment will save labor costs, but it has a very difficult time verifying a claim that a new product line will sell as well as its advocates believe it will.

POLITICAL AND BEHAVIORAL CONSIDERATIONS

In most organizations, present value or IRR computations are only one aspect of the programming phase. As was mentioned earlier, most organizations include a variety of nonquantitative considerations in the decision-making process. These considerations can include (1) quality improvements; (2) the need for a full range of services, and (3) current or changing requirements by regulatory organizations such as the Occupational Health and Safety Administration and the Environmental Protection Agency.

Sometimes regulatory changes can work (or can appear to work) in the organization's favor. Certainly this was the impression in the airline industry and California's electrical utility industry, for example, when they were deregulated. The impact of deregulation on programming decisions can be significant. For instance, in 1980, when the Staggers Act partially deregulated the railroad industry, Burlington Northern Railroad changed the nature of its programming process. It introduced many new variables, such as long-term contracts, creative financing arrangements, partnerships in research and development, and the development of new types of equipment.[3]

Of course, organizations must be careful not to be seduced by deregulation. For example, in the case of Burlington Northern, some investments in railroad equipment were needed, primarily for safety reasons, regardless of their return on investment (ROI). Also, one might argue, some safety problems in the airline industry and blackout problems in California might have been averted through a focus broader than just ROI.

Beyond considerations such as these, there is an internal political dimension to capital budgeting that is not always well understood. For example, some managers may have the "ear" of senior management, run divisions that are seen as key to the company's future, or simply be more articulate or forceful than some of their colleagues. As a result, they may receive a favorable decision on a proposed project that has a much lower net present value or IRR compared with a project in another division with a manager who, for one reason or another, is not seen in such a favorable light. In short, it would be a naïve to assume that the types of financial analyses described above are totally deterministic. However, in most organizations they are important ingredients in the decision-making process, and in some they are given considerable weight.[4]

OTHER CONSIDERATIONS

Programs are one of the most readily observable aspects of an organization's strategy. Thus, if new programs and large capital expenditures are to remain consistent with strategy, line managers must understand the linkages between their activities and the organization's overall strategic directions. Indeed, if an organization's strategy is to evolve over time because of shifting environmental opportunities and threats and changing organizational strengths and weaknesses, senior management must find ways to monitor and manage the organization's programs so that they remain consistent with and supportive of the evolving strategy. Thus, although many large companies have decentralized a considerable amount of decision-making authority to their divisions, most of them require corporate approval for investments that exceed some threshold amount. Their reasoning is that these investments, if not considered carefully, may lead the firm in strategic directions that senior management does not want to take.[5]

The balance between centralization and decentralization in programmatic decision making in a large multidivisional corporation was addressed quite articulately by Alfred Sloan in his memoirs, *My Years with General Motors*.[6] Sloan recounted almost painfully the continual struggles he went through in trying to decide how much authority to give his division general managers. Some 40 years later Harvard's Joseph Bower found that the senior management of a large multidivisional firm was struggling with the same issue.[7] Bower went on to say, however, that decentralization could work if a "context" were created in which the "right" (i.e., beneficial to the corporation overall) decisions by division general managers were rewarded appropriately.

Link to Culture

More broadly, programming can be an especially important tool for managing an organization's culture in that senior management can use it to influence that culture quickly and significantly. Specifically, the constraints senior management establishes on programming and the way it makes use of the "programming purse" can have a profound impact on line managers' understanding of what is acceptable and what is unacceptable in the organization. This can help maintain or change the organization's culture.[8]

Link to Conflict Management

Because many of the benefits of new program proposals are difficult to quantify and because line managers (especially profit and investment center managers) tend to be quite optimistic about their program proposals, a bias toward new programs tends to characterize the programming phase of the management control process. In particular, many proposals tend to overestimate sales volume and prices. Some may tend to underestimate costs.

Senior management can counteract this bias by using its own staff to analyze the proposals. When this happens, there can be considerable friction between the planning staff and the line managers. Designing a conflict management process to deal with this friction and the political content so that the final result is a tough but realistic analysis may be one of the most challenging tasks senior management faces in programmatic decision making.

NOTES

1 Samuel C. Weaver, "Capital Budgeting," *Financial Management*, Vol. 18, Issue 1, Spring 1989.

2 "Feature: A Conversation with Gary Hamel (author of *Leading the Revolution*, Harvard Business School Press, 2000). Innovation Alert from Harvard Business School Publishing, July 11, 2000.

3 Gus Welty, "When Is It Time to Buy?" *Railway Age*, Vol. 192, Issue 10, October 1991.   ＊

4 For an excellent description of political and behavioral matters as well as a description of how senior management can *manage* them, see Joseph L. Bower, *Managing the Resource Allocation Process: A Study of Corporate Planning and Investment*. Boston: Division of Research, Graduate School of Business Administration, Harvard University, 1970.

5 For additional discussion of this issue, see David Solomons, *Divisional Performance: Measurement and Control*. Homewood, IL: Dow Jones-Irwin, 1965.

6 Sloan, Alfred E., *My Years with General Motors*. New York: Macfadden Books, 1965.

7 Bower, op. cit.

8 For additional discussion on this point, see David W. Young, "Managing Organizational Culture," *Business Horizons*, September–October 2000.

CHAPTER 9

Operational Budgeting

$\mathbf{A}$s long as there are scarce resources and alternative uses, organizations will face financial constraints. Most organizations deal with this issue by means of the annual budgeting activity. In contrast to programming, which looks ahead several years, budgeting generally is done for a single year. Ordinarily, it uses the new programs that emerged from the programming phase, along with existing programs, and attempts to determine the revenues, expenses, and nonfinancial outcomes that will be associated with each one.

In some organizations, programs fall neatly into responsibility centers so that each responsibility center manager prepares a budget for each of his or her programs. Alternatively, each program may be a separate responsibility center, most likely a profit center or investment center. When neither of these arrangements is possible, a more complex, matrix-like structure may be needed, such as the one discussed in Chapter 7.

Regardless of the specifics, it is important for the budgeting phase to fit with both the organization's strategy and the programming phase of its management control process. Additionally, by having line managers budget for nonfinancial as well as financial goals and objectives, senior management can relate each program to the organization's overall strategic direction. This is not a new idea. Ford Motor Company included nonfinancial items in its budgets some 35 years ago, and the approach was refined about 25 years ago by Texas Instruments. Today it is used in many companies in many different forms.

Despite these changes and the importance of budgeting to an organization's success, the budgeting phase of the management control process remains anathema to many senior managers. They see it as causing a loss of valuable time and as something to be finessed rather than taken seriously. As a consequence, many line managers devote considerable energy to game playing in the budgetary process rather than using the budget as a tool to help them improve their performance. When this happens, budgeting plays a far less valuable role than it could.

When separated from programming, budgeting typically is concerned only with operating activities, which are assessed in two ways: (1) The *operating budget,* which focuses on revenues and expenses on an accrual basis; this budget is used as a basis for measuring the financial performance of operating managers. (2) The *cash budget,* which analyzes cash inflows and outflows associated with ongoing operations; this budget is used by the controller's office as a way to forecast the organization's cash needs so that it can arrange for whatever financing is needed.

Understanding operating budgets requires knowledge of both the technical aspects of preparing a budget and the fit of the budgetary process with a variety of other aspects of the organization. Understanding the cash budget requires knowledge of the difference between accrual accounting and cash flows. This chapter addresses only the operating budget. Cash budgeting is discussed in most financial accounting and finance textbooks.

The chapter looks at operational budgeting through several lenses. The discussion begins with the broad context in which budgeting takes place and distinguishes between the mechanical and behavioral aspects of budgeting. We then look more closely at the mechanical aspects of building a budget; this is followed by a discussion of some of the behavioral issues, especially *budgeting linkages*—areas where the budgetary process must be linked to other organizational systems or processes.

THE CONTEXT FOR OPERATIONAL BUDGETING

During the operational budgeting phase of the management control process, line managers set out their plans for the upcoming year. In many organizations these plans—once they have been translated into a budget—become a central aspect of measuring managerial performance.

One of the most fundamental problems in budgeting is that the budget usually assesses only short-term, usually annual, financial performance. However, senior management also is concerned with the achievement of longer-run strategic and programmatic objectives, which are not measured by the budget in many organizations. As a result, these organizations treat budgeting mechanically, not allowing it to play the more powerful role that it could if organizational, strategic, and behavioral matters were incorporated into it.

Clearly, budgeting has "mechanical" aspects. Revenue forecasts must be made, the associated expenses must be estimated, and an overall profit or loss figure must be calculated. For organizations to use the budget as a managerial tool, however, senior management must view it from a more global perspective. We first look at this perspective and then use the resulting framework as a basis for discussing the mechanical aspects of budgeting.

The global perspective begins with the broad organizational context, within which there is a "budgeting context." A successful budgetary process flows from and reinforces these two contexts. This idea, which is shown schematically in Exhibit 9-1, explains why different organizations may take very different approaches to budgeting. To understand this exhibit, let us look at its key elements, beginning with the organizational context, moving to the budgeting context, and concluding with the more specific budget formulation and monitoring activities.

EXHIBIT 9-1

The Organizational Context for Budgeting

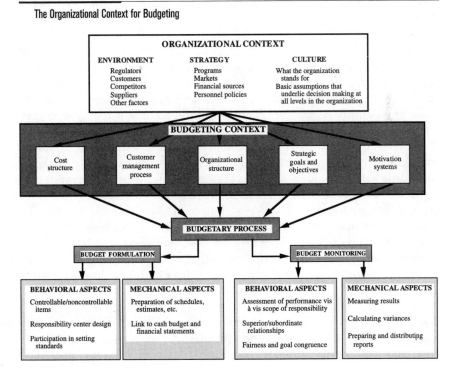

Organizational Context

One way of thinking about the context for a budget is in terms of the organization's environment, strategy, and culture.

Environment.   In many respects an organization's environment governs much of what happens in its budgeting process. An organization that operates in a highly regulated environment, such as a public utility, must gear its budget process in part to the needs of the regulatory agencies and the constraints they place on its activities. In contrast, an organization that operates in a highly competitive environment, such as an airline, quite likely needs a budgetary process that eliminates as much "slack" in its cost structure as possible. An organization that is the sole provider of a particular service in an environment that protects it in some way, such as a water authority, may not have to pay as much attention to its costs.

Strategy.   An organization's strategy also has a great deal to do with its budgetary process. A textile manufacturer operating in a rural area, being in close proximity to suppliers, selling to a regional market, and using many unskilled workers quite likely will have a different budgetary process than will a textile manufacturer operating in an urban area, being some distance from its suppliers, selling to a national market, and using a highly skilled work force.

Similarly, organizations that provide differentiated products may be less concerned with low costs and more concerned with the various features their products need if they are to remain differentiated from competitors' products. A company such as Intel, for example, will put most of its emphasis on the research and development required to stay far enough ahead of its competitors through product differentiation that it can charge a premium price. Similarly, Airborne Express, a company that differentiates itself by serving mainly large urban areas, promising second-day delivery for most of its customers, and providing warehouse space for some other customers at its wholly owned airport, will have a quite different budgeting process than will, say, Federal Express or United Parcel Service. A company such as Southwest Airlines, which differentiates itself on the basis of *very low* cost, will need to make sure that its budget addresses the various factors that allow it to maintain its competitive position, such as the activities needed to achieve short gate turnaround times.

Culture.   Some organizations have strong and well-understood cultures. They have a set of ideas and attitudes that embodies the notions of good and bad and identifies what is desirable or undesirable.[1] Indeed, if employees understand and believe in the organization's culture, they will tend to make decisions that are consistent with it. In these circumstances senior management needs to intervene less in line managers' decision making than is the case when line managers do not understand or believe in the culture.

In a 1945 book, Herbert Simon observed that most organizations engage in four activities to maintain their cultures: hiring, training, severance, and internal communication.[2] Organizations use those activities to influence the way in which middle managers, professionals, and others go about making decisions, including budget-related decisions. For example, Microsoft's policy is to hire only very smart, highly analytical people regardless of their computer expertise, reasoning that it can train them to do the job. To do this it uses a rigorous series of job interviews—mainly with the team with which a candidate will work if hired—to assure that there is a fit with the company's intense, market-driven high-technology culture.

Disney Company supplements its hiring activity with an intense training effort. Indeed, one of that company's core principles is to "train employees extensively and constantly reinforce the company's culture."[3] Moreover, at Disney training goes beyond formal classroom experience and extends into an employee's day-to-day activities. Each Disney employee receives constant on-the-job reinforcement by his or her "coach," who praises success and gradually instills Disney's basic cultural assumptions into the employee's behavior.[4] As is discussed below, these cultural factors not only have resource implications for an organization's budget, but they also influence the organization's budgeting process. Moreover, when combined with environmental and strategic factors, they create an organizational context that is unique for any individual organization.

Budgeting Context

The budgeting context arises out of the organizational context and consists of five features of the organization that both influence and constrain the way the budget is prepared.

Cost Structure. An organization's context influences its cost structure. For example, as was indicated above, Airborne Express, with its own airports but with limited pickup and delivery services, has a different cost structure from that of Federal Express. Similarly, if it is to continue to maintain its culture, Disney Company must build the cost of training into its budgeting effort. By contrast, a company, such as Crown Cork and Seal, that operates in an intensely competitive environment must have a budget process that squeezes as much slack as possible out of its expenses; an intimate knowledge of its cost structure and the ability to identify areas where there are leverage points for expense reductions thus are essential aspects of its budgetary process.

This does not diminish the importance of revenue forecasts. For example, at Lowe's Companies the sales budget is the key to the entire budgeting process. Since an accurate sales budget requires an accurate sales forecast, senior management considers a wide variety of sales-related factors: historical sales data and trends, market research studies, industry competition, general economic conditions, and movements of economic indicators. In addition, several groups prepare information for the creation of the sales budget: Merchandising estimates it at the product level, stores estimate sales volume at the store level, and the finance department uses regression analysis to create statistical forecasts of customer groups and total company sales. Once the sales budget is established, a first cut at profitability is taken. If this is insufficient, expenses must be reduced; it is not acceptable to assume that there will be additional revenue from increased volume, a higher-margin mix, or higher prices.[5] There are many companies like Lowe's that do not change their revenue predictions to achieve a bottom line target in the budget. Instead, the focus must be on expense reduction, and this again means having an in-depth understanding of the cost structure.

Customer Management Process.   Most organizations have a process that identifies customers and attempts to meet their needs at a price they perceive as fair. This process includes activities designed to attract customers to the organization as well as ones that take place within the organization to serve them. These activities combine both marketing and operations management and include product conception, design and manufacture, service scheduling and provision, price setting, facility siting, and after-sale service provision.[6] The way in which organizations interact with their customers both before and after the initial sale is coming under intense scrutiny in many quarters. In particular, recent advances in information technology and the presence of the Internet have affected not only what a company knows about its customers (and what they know about the company) but how a company defines both the goods it sells and the services it provides. At the same time, many companies are experiencing an upheaval in their production efforts. Reengineering, total quality management, continuous quality improvement, and the like, have affected the cost, quality, and delivery cycles of many companies' goods and services. Clearly, all these changes affect the budgetary process in significant ways, sometimes constraining it and sometimes opening up new possibilities for both revenue generation and expense reduction.

One of the acknowledged leaders in the effort to link marketing and production is Toyota, with its Toyota Production System (TPS). Toyota defines the ideal plant as one "where a Toyota customer could drive up to a shipping dock, ask for a customized product or service, and get it immediately at the lowest possible price and with no defects." If a plant does not achieve this ideal, the shortcoming "is a source of creative tension for further improvement efforts."

In the TPS environment anyone can challenge the established production process. A worker who encounters a problem is expected to ask for assistance at once. The problem is a signal that some sort of learning is needed either by the person on the assembly line or by his or her superiors in terms of a process improvement. If two or more line workers are involved in the problem, they are expected to collaborate in seeking a solution, using a superior as a coach if need be.[7]

From a budgeting perspective, the TPS implies that time will be spent on process improvements, conflict management, and data collection as well as on actual production activities. Moreover, since new measures are developed constantly to address the experiments taking place, the reports prepared for line managers and senior management are always in flux. This also will have budgetary implications.

In some companies the budget monitoring phase includes a focus on a customer's total contribution to the company's profits and identifies the reasons why some customers are not making the expected contributions. This raises the more strategic question of whether a particular customer is worth retaining. Some companies are finding that when the appropriate costs and revenues are considered, some customer relationships may contribute very little to the bottom line. The issue then is whether prices can be raised for certain aspects of the relationship or whether, counterintuitively, the company should be dissuading certain kinds of customers from purchasing its products.[8] At an extreme that many managers would consider excessive, Lan and Spar, a small Danish bank that adopted a strategy focused on white-collar workers, sent letters to its corporate customers asking them to move their accounts to another bank. Lan and Spar is now the most profitable bank in Denmark.[9]

Organizational Structure. The way an organization is structured also influences the way it goes about formulating and monitoring its budget. Some companies are organized into departments, whereas others have structures that are more product line or program based. Some organizations are highly authoritarian, whereas others are more collegial. All these factors influence how the budget is structured, who plays a role in its formulation and monitoring, and how much consideration is given to contrasting views during the budget formulation process.

In addition, if senior management has established investment or profit centers and expects line managers to take the budgeting process seriously, it must address several important issues in formulating the annual budget: (1) setting the profitability goal for each profit center, (2) deciding whether there will be cross subsidization among the profit centers, and

(3) if there is cross subsidization, determining the subsidy amounts. Reaching acceptable answers to these questions usually is quite difficult.

Similarly, as was discussed in Chapter 7, decisions about transfer prices can affect budgeting. For example, a "hands-off" approach to transfer pricing—allowing managers to purchase from outside the organization if they wish—will influence the budgeting activity differently from a "buy inside only" approach, as will the establishment of two-part transfer prices.

Strategic Goals and Objectives. Some organizations specify their strategic goals and objectives clearly, but others do not. When these goals and objectives are specified, the managers who are responsible for attaining them soon begin to develop relationships between their attainment and the costs associated with that attainment. When this happens, an organization has the opportunity to budget for both strategic goals and objectives as well as revenues and expenses and can begin to make trade-offs among them.

In particular, the types of nonfinancial information that senior management decides to measure and report can have an important impact on the organization's budgeting process. For example, if a company has chosen a "customer intimacy" strategy, it no doubt will want to collect and report regularly on matters involving customer satisfaction. It can use the budget to develop certain threshold scores and then hold line managers responsible for achieving them. Indeed, it has been argued that a Balanced Scorecard approach to budgeting, measuring, and reporting contributed to the turnaround at Sears a few years ago.[10] Similarly, as discussed in Chapter 7, Pioneer Petroleum based 40 percent of its managers' compensation on achieving BSC results. Clearly, the budget will need to contain these target figures.

Motivation Systems. Some organizations have reward systems that pay bonuses or provide stock options to key operating managers. Others encourage managers to behave in an entrepreneurial way and provide extra budgetary resources to those who are successful. There is a link between these kinds of motivation systems and the way budgets are formulated and monitored. For example, at 3M Company, where continual innovation is considered a key to success, research and development (R&D) employees who have an especially good idea can obtain an internal grant for as much as $50,000 to support their experimental efforts. Under these circumstances, the budget has to be formulated with recognition that several or many internal grants may be awarded.

In many organizations the budget is used along with actual results as a major tool for performance evaluation. When this is the case, managers' annual bonuses, stock options, salary increases, and promotions may be linked closely to how well they performed against their budgets. In particular, managers of investment and profit centers with contingent compensation need to consider the full range of factors that influence a unit's return on investment or profit. If the motivation process is well designed, these managers will think in the long term as well as the short term. In general, however, managers of revenue and expense centers with contingent compensation tend to think in the short-term only, and senior management leadership is needed to design a budgeting process that emphasizes long-term thinking as well.

Beyond this, if a portion of incentive compensation is based on performance against the budget, the organization must have reliable and detailed financial information. This information allows senior management and line managers to align the motivation system with the cost (and revenue) drivers under a line manager's control and to reward behavior that is in the best interest of the organization overall, thus enhancing goal congruence. Therefore, the budgeting effort is linked to both the motivation system and the measurement phase of the management control process.

To reinforce this linkage, some organizations identify their cost drivers (discussed in Chapter 5), link the budget to them, measure and report variances by cost driver in each responsibility center, and reward responsibility center managers on the basis of their performance with respect to the cost drivers under their control. Other organizations do not have this sort of rigor in the management control process. Instead, they formulate budgets more generally, perhaps using line items and trend analysis; measure and report financial and nonfinancial information in an equally general way; and reward responsibility center managers on the basis of something other than performance against the budget. Clearly, the motivation system will differ considerably between these two types of organizations.

Finally, if strategic goals are to be taken seriously, it is not sufficient simply to develop a Balanced Scorecard or engage in another means of programmatic measurement and reporting. Senior management also must link programmatic measurement and reporting with the motivation process. When this happens, managers are rewarded for more than financial performance. This link among the motivation process, the financial measurement and reporting activity, and the nonfinancial measurement and reporting activity thus becomes a key ingredient in an organization's budgetary process.

Budget Formulation

Budget formulation has both mechanical and behavioral aspects. We will discuss the mechanical aspect in greater detail later in this chapter. For the moment it is important to see it in its broader context.

Mechanical Aspects. All budgets have a mechanical aspect. Schedules and estimates of sales, hours, unit costs, and the like, all must be made. In recent years the use of spreadsheet technology has greatly facilitated the mechanical side of budget formulation. Managers can incorporate key budget drivers into a spreadsheet program in such a way that "what if?" scenarios can be tested for their budgetary implications. Moreover, when spreadsheets are used, decisions made in budget meetings about reductions or increases can be incorporated into individual managers' budgets quickly and accurately.

Behavioral Aspects. If a budget is to be useful as a management tool, its formulation must be more than a purely mechanical exercise, with arbitrary reductions across line items when the first pass leads to unacceptable results. Indeed, if the budgetary process is to be useful for managers at all levels in the organization, it must assist them in making a commitment to achieving a set of agreed-upon results. Because the "bottom line" does not measure performance fully, these results need to be of a strategic as well as a financial nature. In most instances, if managers are to commit themselves to achieving the strategic and financial aspects of the budget, they must have some degree of participation in setting the budget targets or standards.

The budget also can help different departments and divisions communicate their plans and needs to one another, and it can help managers at all levels anticipate potential problems. This *communication* aspect of the budgeting process is perhaps one of its most important benefits. When it is combined with the activities needed to assure managerial commitment, it gives the budget formulation process a significant behavioral aspect.

Budget Monitoring

The mechanical side of budget monitoring consists of measuring the same elements that were used to formulate the budget and structuring that information in a way that is useful for program and department managers. In many instances the most useful way to structure information is in terms of variances. In addition, this information must be distributed to the appropriate managers and used by them for decision-making purposes.

If senior managers want to use the information from the budget monitoring phase to manage the activities of their units, they must give careful consideration to some important behavioral aspects of the process. Subordinates' performance must be assessed in terms of the scope of their responsibilities, and individuals must be held accountable only for the variances they can control. In carrying out this process, managers need to be sensitive to the various superior-subordinate relationships that exist in the organization. In particular, both senior and middle managers must view the organization as holistically as they can and be careful not to place too much emphasis on the elimination of negative variances to the exclusion of the organization's more strategic objectives. For example, in a hospital, if too much emphasis is placed on reducing the negative variances in technician time per procedure in the radiology department, the technicians may respond by attempting to work faster and in so doing lower the quality of their work. As a result, many procedures may have to be redone, and this both costs the hospital more and lowers the overall quality of patient care.

Recent research on responsibility accounting systems has placed particular emphasis on this aspect of the budget monitoring effort. In many organizations, the management of quality has become as important as the management of costs and managers cannot focus exclusively on one to the exclusion of the other. We will discuss budget monitoring in greater detail in Chapter 10.

BUILDING A BUDGET: THE MECHANICAL SIDE

The mechanical side of preparing a budget is done in the organizational and budgeting contexts that were described above, combined with the decisions senior management has made about the organization's responsibility centers. For example, profit center managers will build their budgets differently than standard expense center managers, whose budgets will differ from those of managers who run discretionary expense centers or revenue centers.

In most organizations there is a budgeting timetable that typically includes the following seven steps or some variation on them:

- *Step 1: Dissemination of guidelines.* The corporate office distributes guidelines for managers to follow in preparing their budgets. Those guidelines include dates when various documents are due. Sometimes divisions are asked to submit partial budgets (such as revenue budgets) to corporate headquarters before preparing the remainder of their budgets. Sometimes divisions are asked to submit only complete budgets.

- *Step 2: Preparing the revenue budget.* Each division's first step usually is to prepare a revenue budget. Doing this provides the organization with reasonable assurance that anticipated revenue is based on realistic market expectations. If expenses were estimated first, there could be a tendency to assume that revenue would be high enough to cover them, which might be unrealistic.

In preparing the revenue budget, senior management in each division usually asks the revenue centers to estimate sales for the year. Sometimes these figures are reviewed and evaluated by the divisional staff to assure that they are realistic in light of economic conditions, competitive forces, production capabilities, and so forth. Sometimes, if there is the possibility that different divisions will assume sales to the same customers, the corporate staff will review the revenue forecasts made by all divisions. In many organizations, revenue budgets contain considerable detail about exactly which sorts of products will be sold and where.

- *Step 3: Preparing the production budget.* Once sales forecasts have been agreed to by the division's senior management, the manufacturing managers prepare production budgets. Manufacturing managers use the detailed sales budgets to forecast their need for raw materials and direct labor. They also estimate how much overhead they will need to operate the plants.

  In many organizations the production budget is a variable (or flexible) budget; that is, it is broken into fixed and variable costs. Frequently a product mix factor also is included in the variable budget so that its form is roughly like the one shown in Exhibit 9-2.

  As Exhibit 9-2 indicates, each plant budgets for its fixed costs in relation to a certain overall volume of anticipated production and also budgets for a certain amount of variable costs per unit of production for each product line.

- *Step 4: Preparing the discretionary expense center budgets.* The corporate staff prepares a budget for its activities. Since those activities are not related to production volume or mix, the budget is a fixed amount, based on assumptions about the kinds and amounts of

EXHIBIT 9-2

Variable Budget by Product Line

Plant	Direct Fixed Costs	Indirect Fixed Costs	Product Line	Variable Cost per Unit		
				Direct	Indirect	Total
A	$900,000	$200,000	1	$35	$10	$45
			2	20	5	25
			3	5	2	7
B	$300,000	$150,000	22	$11	6	17
			35	3	1	4

activities the staff will have to engage in during the year. For example, if there is litigation pending, the budget for legal services may be higher this year than it was last year. Or if there are plans to undertake a major revision of the management information system, the budget may be higher. Similarly, if activities that took place last year will not take place this year, the budget will have to be reduced.

- *Step 5: Preparing the divisional budget.* The division's budget is a summary of all the pieces described above. It is based on the sales forecasts of a certain volume and mix of products, which are used to both forecast revenue and predict the production budgets by using the fixed/variable breakdowns. The budgets of the discretionary expense centers are subtracted from the total to give the overall divisional profit that is expected for the year. An example of how this budget might look is shown in Exhibit 9-3.

- *Step 6: Preparing the master (or corporate) budget.* The various divisional budgets are assembled at the corporate level to determine the profit forecast for the year. Income taxes are estimated, and a return on assets (or equity) is computed. This budget usually is taken to the board of directors for approval.

- *Step 7: Revision and final approval.* If the master budget is not approved (usually because the return on assets or return on equity is not sufficiently high but sometimes because some flaws in forecasts have been identified), it may be returned to one or more divisions for reworking. When this happens, the divisions usually are not permitted to adjust their revenue forecasts. This is the case because it would be too easy—and usually unrealistic— simply to assume that sales will be higher than originally forecast and to use the higher sales forecast as a means to achieve a higher profit. Instead, divisions usually are required to reduce their expenses either in the plants or in the discretionary expense centers. Reduced expenses in the plants can result from lowering fixed costs or variable costs per unit but ordinarily not from assuming a different volume or mix of sales.

Important Features

The process described above is only a rough guide to what actually happens in most organizations, and there are many variations on the general theme. Despite the specific approach a company takes, however, several features of the mechanical side of budgeting can be found in most well-managed organizations:

EXHIBIT 9-3

Master Division Budget

		Product Lines								
Formula	Sales Office/Plant	1	2	3	...	22	35	...	Total	Profit
	Sales Office									
	New York									
1	Volume (000)	10	15	100		30	150			
2	Price	$70.00	$40.00	$10.00		$25.00	$8.00			
3 = 1 × 2	Revenue ($000)	$700	$600	$1,000		$750	$1,200		$4,250	
	Washington									
4	Volume (000)	5	10	50		15	80			
5	Price	$70.00	$40.00	$10.00		$25.00	$8.00			
6 = 4 × 5	Revenue ($000)	$350	$400	$500		$375	$640		$2,265	
	Boston									
7	Volume (000)	12	5	45		5	120			
8	Price	$70.00	$40.00	$10.00		$25.00	$8.00			
9 = 7 × 8	Revenue ($000)	$840	$200	$450		$125	$960		$2,575	
	Total Revenue									
10 = 1 + 4 + 7	Volume (000)	27	30	195		50	350			
11 = 2	Price	$70.00	$40.00	$10.00		$25.00	$8.00			
12 = 10 × 11	Revenue ($000)	$1,890	$1,200	$1,950		$1,250	$2,800		$9,090	
	Manufacturing Plant									
	Hartford									
13	Variable cost/unit	$45.00	$25.00	$7.00						
14 = 10	Expected volume (000)	27	30	195						
15 = 13 × 14	Total variable cost ($000)	$1,215	$750	$1,365						
16 = 12 – 15	Contribution to fixed costs	$675	$450	$585					$1,710	
17	Fixed costs ($000)								_1,100_	
18 = 16 – 17	Contribution to division profit									$610
	Atlanta									
19	Variable cost/unit					$17.00	$4.00			
20 = 10	Expected volume (000)					50	350			
21 = 19 × 20	Total variable cost ($000)					$850	$1,400			
22 = 12 – 21	Contribution to fixed costs					$400	$1,400		$1,800	
23	Fixed costs ($000)								_450_	
24 = 22 – 23	Contribution to division profit									_1,350_
25 = 18 + 24	Total contribution to division profit									$1,960
26	Division administrative costs									_950_
27 = 25 – 26	**Total Division Profit**									$1,010

- *The budget is taken seriously by senior management.* Senior management is involved in budget meetings with division heads and in setting the tone for the process. It does not turn the budget process over to the controller but instead relies on the controller to assemble the information and do any needed analyses.

- *The timetable remains roughly the same each year.* It is adhered to closely so that division managers and others who are involved know what to expect and when.

- *Staff analyses are used as a check.* These analyses verify or contradict forecasts by division mangers and their staffs. When staff analyses contradict the division's forecasts, neither is allowed to dominate the decision making. Instead, areas of disagreement are identified, discussed, and resolved. When corporate staff and division managers cannot resolve the differences between themselves, senior management makes the final decisions.

- *There is a negotiation phase.* Division managers have ample opportunity to present their case to senior management and defend their forecasts.

- *The final budget represents a serious commitment.* Division managers make a commitment to achieving the budgeted level of profit, usually with the stipulation that highly unusual circumstances, but nothing else, can result in a budget revision. Highly unusual circumstances can include acts of nature (such as floods) and events such as fires, prolonged strikes, and major economic events.

- *Within divisions, budgets also represent serious commitments.* Sometimes these commitments are different from the division's commitment to senior management. For example, if manufacturing plants are standard expense centers, plant managers are expected to adhere to budgeted levels of unit variable costs and total fixed costs but not to total costs, since those costs are affected by the volume and mix of orders. Sales office managers, by contrast, may be expected to adhere to budgeted revenue forecasts. They may be allowed to change the volume and mix of sales as long as total revenue forecasts are met.

- *The budget is monitored closely, and variances are identified.* Division senior management and corporate senior management take negative variances seriously and work to eliminate them.

 PROBLEM   Job Enrichment Division (JED) was a division of a company in southwest Texas that produced a wide variety of consumer products using electronic components. JED had been formed when the company realized that it needed a constant supply of low-wage labor. Most of its labor force consisted of immigrants, some of whom were illiterate and almost none of whom spoke English. Since manufacturing operations required employees who had a basic level of literacy in the English language, the company realized that it made economic sense to train recently arrived immigrants in both fundamental reading skills and English.

As a result of those needs, JED was required to conduct two different types of training programs: basic literacy and English as a second language. The division ran its programs for 40 weeks of the year, closing during the remaining weeks for breaks and vacations. Each program was managed by a separate program manager who also was a faculty member of that program. The remaining faculty members were hired on a per-session basis, based on the actual number of trainees in the session and the budgeted trainee:faculty ratio.

Budgeted data on the two programs for the upcoming fiscal year are shown below.

	Basic Literacy	English as a Second Language
No. of training sessions	4	2
Length of each training session (in weeks)	10	20
Average no. of trainees per session	100	30
No. of trainee-weeks	4,000	1,200
No. of trainees	400	60
Trainee:faculty ratio	20:1	10:1
No. of faculty needed	5	3
Average faculty salary	$20,000	$25,000
Workbooks per trainee	5	2
Average price per workbook	$15	$20

Administrative and general costs were projected to total $78,200 for the year.

QUESTIONS

1. Prepare a budget for the upcoming fiscal year. Try to set it up on a spreadsheet and to make it as formula-driven as possible, using what you consider to be the key cost drivers.

2. What kind of responsibility center should a training program be? Why? What kind of a responsibility center should JED be? Why?

ANSWERS

QUESTION 1

The budget should look something like the following:

	Basic Literacy	English as a Second Language	Total
Faculty			
5 @ $20,000; 3 @ $25,000	$100,000	$75,000	
Workbooks			
5 × 400 × $15; 2 × 60 × $20	30,000	2,400	
Program-related expenses	$130,000	$77,400	$207,400
Administration and general (A&G)			78,200
Total expenses			$285,600

The following issues were important in calculating the budget:

- Distinguishing between programs. Each program should be budgeted for separately.
- Distinguishing between program-related and A&G expenses.
- Presenting the budget in good form. The numbers should be relatively easy to follow and understand.

QUESTION 2

JED and its programs probably should be standard expense centers. There is no evidence to suggest that any revenue is associated with the programs. There is an easily measurable unit that drives program costs, however, and program managers can exert reasonable control over the use of faculty and books per trainee in their programs. Therefore, a standard expense center structure seems appropriate.

BUDGETING LINKAGES

Viewed in this context, the budgetary process is not only an integral part of an organization but an essential ingredient in the organization's success. Moreover, the role of budgeting depends to a large extent on its fit, or linkage, with a variety of other organizational elements. Seven linkages stand out as particularly important.

Linkage 1: Between the Cost Structure and the Budget Formulation Phase

In the formulation phase, a budget must be built around the cost structure faced by the organization. In addition, it must distinguish between costs that managers can control and those they cannot. For example, although some fixed costs are controllable in a typical budget period, many others are not. They exist because the organization has committed itself to be "ready to serve" and will continue to exist even if no units of service are provided. Classic examples of this situation include fire departments, hospital emergency rooms, fast food chains, and many retailers.

By contrast, most variable costs and some step-function costs *are* controllable, but only on a *per-unit* basis. As a result, it may be appropriate to ask a manager to control variable cost *per unit* but not *total* variable costs, since total variable costs are affected by volume, which frequently is outside a department manager's control.

Linkage 2: Between the Cost Structure and the Budget Monitoring Phase

In the budget monitoring phase the measurement and reporting system must specify the reasons that underlie a variance between budgeted figures and actual figures. Otherwise, a manager may find it difficult to determine the reasons underlying a deviation between budgeted performance and actual performance. A technique for making these computations, called variance analysis, will be discussed in Chapter 10.

Linkage 3: Between the Customer Management Process and the Budgetary Process

Most organizations are able to identify one or two factors that are crucial to or indicative of their ongoing success in managing customers. In an airline, it is occupancy (or "load factor"); in a health maintenance organization (HMO), it is hospital days used per thousand enrollees; for a fire department, it is response time; for a magazine publisher, it is renewal rate; for a restaurant, it is number of "covers" (paying patrons). And so on.

It is important to incorporate these critical success factors into the budgetary process. An airline that does not build load factors into its budget formulation and monitoring phases almost certainly will face serious difficulties. A fire department must include projected estimates of response time in its budgeting effort; otherwise, it may have difficulty making trade-offs between operating costs and its overall performance measures, such as loss of lives and property. Similarly, many HMOs have encountered serious financial problems when their hospitalization rates per 1000 enrollees exceeded the budgeted levels. A restaurant must build number of covers into its budget, since revenue can fluctuate greatly with only a small change in the average number of daily covers.

 PROBLEM Peppercorns, a family restaurant, is open 6 days a week, 50 weeks a year. Its revenue averages $30 per cover, and it has a staff of 50 waiters. Each waiter works one shift a day and serves an average of 40 covers per shift. How much will revenue be affected by a change to 41 covers per waiter over the course of a year?

ANSWER   Revenue changes by $450,000. The calculations are as follows:

Change in average number of covers/waiter (41 − 40) = 1
Number of workdays in a year = 300
Number of waiters = 50
Revenue per cover = $30
Change in revenue (1 × 300 × 50 × $30) = $450,000

Southwest Airlines has taken this way of thinking to a much more sophisticated level. At Southwest, gate turnaround time is a key element in the customer management process, and the company has developed a number of policies to reduce turnaround time to well below the industry average. When this lower turnaround time is multiplied by the number of flights Southwest has during a budget year, the result is a need for several fewer aircraft than would be the case if its gate turnaround time equaled the industry average. This reduction in needed assets (aircraft) helps Southwest earn a return on assets that is the envy of the industry.

Linkage 4: Between the Organizational Structure and the Budgetary Process

Many organizations have a product line structure that is overlaid on a functional structure. For these organizations the budgetary process must be designed to fit this structure. If it is not, managers who make decisions that can affect the budget may not have appropriate budgetary responsibility. For example, when the costs of a "mission" department (e.g., product line A) are affected by the costs in several service departments (e.g., maintenance and janitorial) but service department costs are allocated to product lines rather than being purchased by transfer prices, service department managers tend to take little responsibility for their departments' costs.

The budgetary process also must be designed to capture the intricacies of the organizational structure. This can be tricky when budgetary units either overlap or fall between organizational units, when the budget for a department has been disaggregated according to some sections within the department but not others, or when budgetary categories are established that do not correspond to organizational units.

 PROBLEM The Department of Medicine at Arlmont Hospital includes several sections: internal medicine, geriatrics, gastroenterology, and cardiology. Each section is managed by a chief of the specialty, and the department itself is under the direction of the chief of medicine. The budget report, which contains both budget and actual cost data, is prepared monthly and contains direct cost information classified into salaries, supplies, and depreciation. The information is broken down by ward, including two general medicine wards and a geriatrics ward. Each specialty chief is asked to prepare a budget and assist the hospital in its cost-containment efforts. What problems, if any, are there with this arrangement?

ANSWER Until the cost data are classified by specialty rather than by ward, only the chief of geriatrics will have the requisite information to prepare and monitor a budget. Additionally, to facilitate greater control, the budget categories may have to be disaggregated further to distinguish among types of personnel and supplies.

Linkage 5: Between Strategic Goals and Objectives and the Budgetary Process

Organizations that incorporate nonfinancial measures of performance into their budgetary processes have the opportunity to make explicit trade-offs between strategic objectives and financial constraints. Alternatively, these trade-offs may be resolved by default, as happens when budget cuts are necessary but managers do not have sufficient information to determine which products or product lines are most successful in meeting the organization's overall goals.

An explicit linkage can be established by designing the budgetary process to include a component in which department managers are asked to specify strategic objectives and commit themselves to their attainment in the same way they committed themselves to the financial objectives of the budget. Otherwise, managers may see the budget as a financial constraint rather than a pool of resources designed to assist them in the attainment of some strategic ends. Of course, to attain this linkage, an organization's senior management must make its strategic objectives explicit.

In some instances the creation of a "game-playing" culture can help provide the linkage. In the New York City Sanitation Department, for example, an especially creative manager developed pseudo profit centers by using outside garage prices as "revenue." This manager also faced a variety of union-related constraints on productivity, but by creating teams of mechanics, using the outside prices to compare each team's productivity with the cost of similar repair jobs in private garages, and making it a "game" to beat the private garages, the manager was able to achieve a dramatic increase in the department's productivity.[11] Similarly, in a large oil company, employees were asked to define their own performance objectives and the steps needed to achieve them. A portion of their compensation was based on their progress toward achieving those objectives.[12]

Linkage 6: Between the Motivation System and the Budgetary Process

The two examples discussed above move us into the territory of motivation systems. Although managers appear to derive at least some of their motivation from nonfinancial sources, the budget can play a role in providing them with incentives to work toward the organization's strategic goals and objectives. However, to the extent that managers are committed to strategic objectives that are not financially feasible or are encouraged to develop new product ideas that then are thwarted by the budgetary process, the linkage between the organization's motivation system and the budgetary process is weakened. When that happens, the budget may be seen as a hurdle to overcome rather than an integral part of the planning process.

Many organizations, especially those in the nonprofit sector, have difficulty finding a link between organizational strategy and rewards.[13] Some nonprofits seek that link by encouraging entrepreneurial behavior and providing supplemental resources to successful managers. Others, including some for-profit professional service firms, provide nonfinancial bonuses such as sabbatical leaves. The city of Phoenix, Arizona, uses a "gain sharing" approach. It has a suggestion program that encourages employees to submit ideas that promote cost savings or measurable improvements in productivity, product quality, employee morale, or safety and pays cash awards up to $2500. The Phoenix system has received several national awards.[14] These kinds of approaches also can work in the for-profit sector. At Pioneer Petroleum, as discussed previously, 40 percent of executive compensation is related to Balanced Scorecard indicators on customer satisfaction, internal process improvements, and employees' learning and growth.[15]

In some manufacturing plants, by contrast, the entire budgetary process in some departments is one of generating statistics in an attempt to convince the controller's office that the department will provide at least as much output as it did during the prior year. In many other organizations the budget is used as a way to obtain funds from corporate headquarters. In these instances the budget is not looked upon as a useful management tool by managers. Indeed, in circumstances such as these the budgetary process is at best divorced from other motivation systems in the organization; at worst, it is inconsistent or incompatible with them.

Although there is no simple way to attain a good fit between motivation systems and the budgetary process, organizations can attempt to interest their managers in budgeting through an attractive structuring of financial incentives. As was discussed in Chapter 7, a contingent compensation system seems to be a powerful mechanism. There undoubtedly are a variety of other mechanisms that could be used to improve the fit between the motivation system and the budgetary process. At Starbucks, for example, employees receive health benefits and stock options after only a few months on the job. One result, Starbucks claims, is that the organization has an employee turnover rate that is about half the industry average.[16]

A fascinating point that emerges from the example of Starbucks and organizations like it is the importance of incorporating line workers into the organization's budgetary system. If, for example, a senior manager can develop a budgetary system that includes line workers and enhances their motivation, he or she will have taken a major step toward bridging the gap between the organization's budgeting requirements and its line workers' need for greater involvement in the operations of the company.[17]

Linkage 7: Between the Budget Formulation and Budget Monitoring Phases

In addition to the linkages discussed above, which are between the budgeting context and the budgetary process, there is an important linkage *within* the budgetary process, especially between the formulation and monitoring phases. In particular, when managers have made strategic and financial commitments and are prepared to take them seriously, the budget monitoring phase must provide information that is complete (i.e., allows managers to assess the extent to which they are meeting their commitments), accurate, and timely. Unfortunately, the reporting process in many organizations operates with such long time lags that the information is of little managerial use when it arrives, and, as was mentioned above, even systems that are timely frequently do not provide sufficient detail on the reasons that underlie a budget variance. Managers in these organizations find it very difficult to assess the action that should be taken to correct a problem situation.

TOWARD MORE EFFECTIVE BUDGETING

Looked at in a broad context, if costs and revenues are to be planned and controlled effectively, an organization will need a sophisticated responsibility accounting system. At a minimum, this responsibility accounting system must address four factors:

- A budget *formulation* process that fits the organizational and budgeting contexts and, in particular, is built around the organization's cost drivers. This can be accomplished by incorporating product and/or service mix estimates into the planning process so that the volume of each type or category becomes the driving force in formulating the budget. These estimates can be converted through the application of standard resource inputs and standard efficiency factors to estimates of total resource requirements and ultimately into dollar amounts.

- A budget *monitoring* process that reports on the variances between budgeted and actual expenditures in each area so that reporting can be tied to performance. By comparing actual results to budgeted ones and doing this by area of control, the budget monitoring process can complement the budget formulation process. Senior management then can relate performance to responsibility and can hold managers responsible only for the cost (and revenue) drivers over which they exercise a reasonable amount of control.

- The inclusion of a variety of nonfinancial measures in the budgeting and reporting processes that are linked to the organization's strategic objectives.

- Budgeting and reporting processes that incorporate line managers and other employees into the decision-making process and reward them for good performance both of their departments and of the organization overall.

NOTES

1. For a definition and discussion of organizational culture, see Edgar H. Schein, *Organizational Culture and Leadership*, 2d ed. San Francisco: Jossey-Bass, 1992. See also David W. Young, "Managing Organizational Culture," *Business Horizons*, September–October 2000.

2. Herbert A. Simon, *Administrative Behavior*. New York: Free Press, 1945.

3. Bill Capodagli and Lynn Jackson, *The Disney Way*. Chicago: McGraw-Hill, 1999.

4. See James S. Doyle, *The Business Coach: A Game Plan for the New Work Environment*. New York: Wiley, 1999.

5. Keith A. Howell, "Lowe's Companies' Statistical Approach to Sales Forecasting," *Corporate Controller*, Vol. 3, Issue 5, May–June 1991.

6. These activities and the link between marketing and production have been discussed at length in the literature. In addition to any good textbook on marketing or operations management, see Theodore Levitt, "A Production Line Approach to Service," *Harvard Business Review*, July–August 1972; W. Edwards Deming, *Out of Crisis*. Cambridge, MA: MIT Press, 1986; K. Ishikawa, ed., *Guide to Quality Control*. White Plains, NY: Kraus International Publications, 1986; J. M. Juran, *Juran on Planning for Quality*. New York: Free Press, 1989; and Michael Hammer and James Champy, *Reengineering the Corporation*. New York: Harper Collins, 1993.

7. For a detailed discussion of the TPS, see Steven Spear and H. Kent Bowen, "Decoding the DNA of the Toyota Production System," *Harvard Business Review*, September–October 1999.

8. See Robert E. Wayland and Paul M. Cole, *Customer Connections: New Strategies for Growth*. Boston: Harvard Business School Press, 1997. See also Don Peppers and Martha Rogers, *Enterprise One to One: Tools for Competing in the Interactive Age*. Currency/Doubleday, 1997.

9. Reported in Constantinos C. Markides, *All the Right Moves*. Boston: Harvard Business School Press, 2000.

10. *The Balanced Scorecard at Sears: A Compelling Place for Feedback and Learning.* Harvard Business School case study, reported in Balanced Scorecard On-Line Report Summary, Harvard Business School, July–August 2000.

11. For details, see the case "New York City Sanitation Department" in Robert N. Anthony and David W. Young, *Management Control in Nonprofit Organizations*, 7th ed., Burr Ridge, Il: McGraw-Hill/Irwin, 2003.

12. Robert S. Kaplan and David P. Norton, *The Balanced Scorecard*. Boston: Harvard Business School Press, 1996.

13. Philip H. Mirvis and Edward J. Hackett, "Work and Work Force Characteristics in the Nonprofit Sector," *Monthly Labor Review*, April 1983.

14. Bob Nelson, *1001 Ways to Energize Employees*. Workman Publishing, 1997.

15. Robert S. Kaplan and David P. Norton, *The Balanced Scorecard.* Boston: Harvard Business School Press, 1996.

16. Howard Schultz and Dori Jones Yang, *Pour Your Heart Into It: How Starbucks Built a Company One Cup at a Time.* New York: Hyperion, 1997.

17. For additional discussion of this idea, see Jack Stack, *The Great Game of Business,* ed. Bo Burlingham. New York: Currency Books, 1992.

CHAPTER 10

Measuring and Reporting

As Chapter 6 indicated, responsibility accounting systems include both structure and process. Of particular importance in the area of process is the rhythmic flow of activities consisting of four separate but closely related phases: programming, budgeting, measuring, and reporting. Chapters 8 and 9 discussed programming and budgeting. This chapter builds on the concepts discussed in those chapters, concentrating on the *measuring* and *reporting* phases of the management control process.

The chapter begins with an overview of the measurement phase of the management control process, discussing the importance of aligning responsibility with control. It then discusses some measuring and reporting techniques, particularly flexible budgeting and variance analysis.

After the discussion of variance analysis, the chapter describes the criteria for a good reporting process. It then turns to the topic of measuring and reporting *nonfinancial performance*, an issue that is taking on increasing importance in many organizations.

THE MEASUREMENT PHASE

Among other things, managers are paid to make decisions. Ordinarily, an informed decision is better than an uninformed one. The difference between the two, of course, is information. For this reason, the measurement phase of the management control process is especially important. In many respects it is in this phase that managers' needs and accountants' skills merge. In particular, managers must be able to communicate their information needs to the accounting staff; otherwise, the accounting staff will not be able to design a measurement system that captures the appropriate information.

At the same time, both managers and accountants must recognize that different costs (and revenues) are used for different purposes. This means, for example, that it ordinarily is inappropriate to use full cost information for either alternative choice decisions or responsibility accounting purposes. Responsibility accounting focuses on the distinction between controllable and noncontrollable items, including both revenues and expenses.

Aligning Responsibility with Control

The controllable/noncontrollable distinction is important. Most costs in an organization are controllable by someone. As a consequence, the responsibility accounting system must be designed so that different managers are held responsible for controlling different costs. Ideally, the system is designed so that each manager is held responsible only for the costs over which he or she exercises a reasonable degree of control.

In part, this alignment between responsibility and control is attained through the choice of responsibility centers: as Chapters 6 and 7 indicated, this is by no means an easy task. In addition, however, the responsibility accounting system must attempt to assign only controllable costs to each responsibility center (along with revenues in the case of profit and investment centers). This also can be quite difficult, frequently requiring the accounting staff to measure the organization's costs in ways that differ from those used for full cost calculations.

Finally, if managers are to be asked to control costs, they must receive information pertaining to their responsibility centers in reports that are both useful and timely. This may mean augmenting the cost-collection process, or it may simply mean that data already being collected for full cost or other purposes are restructured for responsibility accounting purposes. In all cases, the way information is presented in the reports sent to a responsibility center manager is an important aspect of the responsibility accounting system.

MEASURING AND REPORTING TECHNIQUES

In the context of measuring controllable costs, two techniques stand out as particularly relevant and important: flexible budgeting and variance analysis. When used judiciously, both techniques can be helpful to managers at all decision-making levels.

Flexible Budgeting

The concept of flexible budgeting is derived from the distinction between controllable costs and noncontrollable costs. In standard expense centers individual department managers are expected to control both the department's fixed costs and the variable costs *per unit* of activity but are unable to control the *total units* of activity. As a result, they exercise little control over *total* variable costs. A common solution to this problem is the preparation of a budget that is adjusted for volume changes before measuring a manager's performance. This adjusted budget is known as a *flexible budget.*

A flexible budget contrasts with a *fixed budget,* which is a budget with no variable expense component; it typically is used in a discretionary expense center. In a discretionary expense center, the manager is held responsible for spending no more than the amount budgeted for each month or other reporting period and there are no volume factors per se that could cause actual expenses to exceed budgeted expenses. Of course, even in a discretionary expense center there can be compelling reasons to change the budget, such as a labor strike, a fire in one of the company's buildings, or another similarly catastrophic event.

A flexible budget is developed by classifying a responsibility center's expenses into their fixed and variable components. Rather than being a fixed amount, the flexible budget is expressed as a cost formula that uses agreed-upon fixed expenses and agreed-upon variable expenses per unit. An expected level of volume is specified to make sure the fixed expenses are within the relevant range. This gives rise to the original budget. The original budget then is "flexed" each month or other reporting period by applying the actual volume of activity to the cost formula. The result is a budget that can be used to measure the responsibility center manager's performance. Because of this it sometimes is called a *performance budget.*

 PROBLEM   The manager of Tanglewood Dentistry, Inc., a large dental group practice, estimated that 2000 patients would need examinations and cleanings each month and that each examination and cleaning would take approximately a half hour of a dental hygienist's time at an hourly rate of $20. Other costs associated with an examination and cleaning were supplies, electricity, and water, which totaled about $5 per cleaning. The monthly fixed costs associated with the examination and cleaning activity were $8000. The result was the following budget:

Estimated number of procedures	2,000
Hygienist cost (½ hour at $20/hour)	$10
Other variable costs	5
Total variable costs per procedure	$15
Variable cost budget	$30,000
Fixed costs	8,000
Total budget	$38,000

During the reporting period, a total of 2500 patients had an examination and cleaning and the department incurred total costs of $50,000. Prepare the flexible budget cost formula for Tanglewood and analyze the department's performance.

ANSWER   A flexible budget cost formula for the department would be TC = $8,000 + ($15 × number of procedures)

The "flexed" budget would look as follows:

TC = $8,000 + ($15 × 2,500) =	$45,500
Less actual expenditures	50,000
Spending variance	$ (4,500)

Note that although it appears initially that there was a budget overrun of $12,000 ($38,000 − $50,000), in fact only $4500 was a "spending" overrun. The remaining $7500 can be attributed to the volume change, which the manager could not control.

Factors Other Than Volume.   Although the flexible budget is a partial answer to the problem of aligning responsibility with control, it does not answer all the important questions. Returning to the example above, we still would have some questions about the negative $4500 spending variance. Among the possible explanations are (1) a higher hygienist wage rate, (2) higher per-unit supply costs, (3) more hygienist time per procedure, (4) more supply usage per procedure, (5) usage of different kinds of supplies, and (6) higher fixed costs.

Since the answer most likely is contained in one or more of these factors, we then could explore the issue further. If, for example, more hygienist time than budgeted had been used, we would want to know why. Were there new hygienists on the job who required training and thus were slower than anticipated in doing examinations and cleanings? Or were there some patients for whom examinations and cleanings were more complex than they were for others, resulting in more time needed to complete the procedures? Or perhaps patients arrived late, and scheduling was disrupted, slowing the hygienists down. Although accounting techniques cannot answer all these questions, the technique of variance analysis permits us to look into some of the possibilities.

Variance Analysis

Variance analysis is an accounting technique that permits a close examination of the difference between budgeted information and actual information. The technique allows us to break down the difference into categories that are potentially meaningful for managerial action. In this chapter we are concerned primarily with variances in *direct costs.* Variances in overhead costs were discussed in Chapter 4.

In most organizations the difference, or *variance,* between budgeted performance and actual performance can be explained by one or more of six factors:

1. Volume (number of units of output of goods or services)
2. Mix of units of output
3. Revenue per unit of output (selling price)
4. Rates paid for inputs (e.g., labor wages and cost per unit of raw materials)
5. Efficiency of inputs (usage of raw materials and productivity of labor)
6. Mix of inputs (e.g., different skills levels of labor or different kinds of raw materials)

Variance analysis can be used to determine the amount of the total change between budget and actual that is associated with each of these factors.

Ordinarily, the variance for each factor is considered separately. There are three reasons for the separation: (1) Each variance typically has a different cause, (2) different variances usually involve different responsibility center managers, and (3) different variances require different types of corrective action. Thus, if the responsibility for different factors has been assigned to different responsibility center managers, variance analysis helps senior management work with each of those managers to determine the reasons for the variance and the kinds of corrective action that might be taken.

Basic techniques for calculating these variances are shown below; more complex techniques are described in cost accounting textbooks. In many situations, computer programs are available or can be developed easily on a spreadsheet to perform the actual calculations.

A Graphic Illustration. The concept of variance analysis is best understood when it is depicted graphically. Consider the example of labor costs. Total labor costs for a given employee or category of employees can be calculated by using the number of hours worked and the wage rate per hour. Assume that the labor budget is $400, resulting from an estimate of 50 hours of work at $8 per hour. Graphically, this can be represented by a rectangle, with the vertical axis indicating the wage rate and the horizontal axis indicating the number of hours.

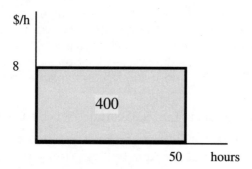

Assume now that the actual labor costs for the period in question were $600. A typical budget report might indicate the variance as follows:

Item	Budget	Actual	Variance
Labor cost	$400	$600	$(200)

Although the report indicates a $200 negative variance, that is, actual expenses greater than budget, it does not indicate *why* the variance occurred. More specifically, in this instance it does not indicate whether the cause was a higher wage rate than anticipated, more hours than anticipated, or a combination of the two.

If the variance were solely the result of a higher wage rate, it could be viewed as shown in the following graph.

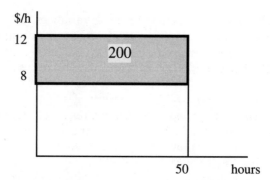

If, however, it was a result solely of more hours than budgeted, it could be viewed as it is depicted in the following graph.

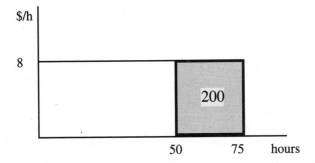

Finally, if it was a result of a combination of both a higher wage rate and more hours, the variance could be depicted by several wage/hour combinations; one example is shown in the following graph.

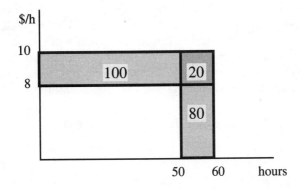

Note that there is a problem here because the small rectangle in the upper right portion of the graph is the result of a combination of both the labor rate (or wage) variance *and* the hour (or use) variance. This combination variance sometimes is referred to as the gray area because it cannot be assigned reasonably to either the higher rate or the higher use but rather to the *combined effect* of the two. In this instance, then, $100 of the total variance can be attributed to the higher wage rate, $80 to the greater number of hours, and $20 to the combined effect.

For ease of calculation, the combined effect ordinarily is included in the rate variance (here the labor wage *rate* variance). Not only does this approach simplify the calculation and presentation of information, it also seems reasonable. Specifically, whoever is responsible for the rate variance is responsible for it over as many units as actually were used. This means that the $20 combination effect described above would be added to the $100 to give a $120 labor rate variance.

Given this approach, the budget report might look as follows:

Item	Budget	Actual	Variance
Labor costs	$400	$600	$(200)
Labor rate (wage) variance			(120)
Efficiency variance			(80)

The managerial utility of this report results directly from the fact that in most organizations different managers are responsible for different elements of a total variance. In line with the need to align responsibility with control, it is important to designate the portion of the total variance that is attributable to each manager. It then becomes possible to discuss the reasons for each variance with the manager who is responsible for it.

In this context it is important to emphasize that a negative variance is not designed to be used as a club. Instead, it is the first step in diagnosing the reasons *why* costs diverged from budget and exploring those reasons with the appropriate managers so that, where possible, corrective actions can be taken to bring costs back in line. Similarly, as will be shown below, a positive variance is not necessarily a cause for celebration. It does suggest, however, that some improvement in operations has been achieved that could be examined for possible transfer to other operating units.

Calculating Variances

The accounting technique used to calculate a variance follows two relatively simple rules with slight differences that depend on whether a revenue or an expense variance is being calculated.

Expense Variances. With expense variances, when actual expenses exceed budgeted expenses, the organization's financial condition is worsened; that is, its income is reduced from what it otherwise would have been. Similarly, when actual expenses are below budgeted expenses, the organization's financial condition is improved. Since we want a variance that lowered income to be a negative number and a variance that increased income to be a positive number, we always deduct actual expenses from budgeted ones. In addition, to make sure we include the combination effect in the rate variance, we use the following rules:

1. For an expense variance related to use, subtract the *actual use* from the *budgeted use* and multiply the result by *budgeted rate*.

2. For an expense variance related to rate, subtract the *actual rate* from the *budgeted rate* and multiply the result by *actual use*.

We can express these rules with formulas:

1. *Use:* $(U_b - U_a) \times R_b$

2. *Rate:* $(R_b - R_a) \times U_a$

where U stands for use, R stands for rate, and the subscripts a and b stand for actual and budgeted, respectively

Revenue Variances. With revenue variances, when actual revenue exceeds budgeted revenue, the organization's financial condition has improved; that is, its income is greater than it otherwise would have been. Therefore, to make sure that an increase in income is a positive number and a decrease in income is a negative number, we reverse the logic and subtract budgeted revenue from actual revenue. To make sure that the combination effect is included in the price variance, we use the following rules:

1. For a revenue variance related to volume, subtract *budgeted volume* from *actual volume* and multiply the result by *budgeted selling price.*

2. For a revenue variance related to selling price, subtract *budgeted selling price* from *actual selling price* and multiply the result by *actual volume.*

These rules can be expressed with formulas:

1. *Volume:* $(V_a - V_b) \times P_b$

2. *Selling price:* $(P_a - P_b) \times V_a$

where V stands for volume, P stands for selling price, and the subscripts a and b stand for actual and budgeted

Doing the Computations. Let us return to the example above and perform the calculations according to these rules and formulas. Since there are no revenue variances, we need not concern ourselves with them; we just need to calculate expense variances.

 PROBLEM Calculate the expense variances in the example above, using the appropriate formulas. It is important to do the calculations before looking at the analysis that follows. Variance analysis can be a little tricky, and making these calculations is an important part of the learning process.

ANSWER The expense variances can be calculated as follows:

Use variance = (budgeted hours − actual hours) × budgeted rate

$$(U_b - U_a) \times R_b$$
$$(50 - 60) \times \$8.00 = (80)$$

Rate (wage) variance = (budgeted wage rate − actual wage rate) × actual use

$$(R_b - R_a) \times U_a$$
$$(\$8.00 - \$10.00) \times 60 = (\$120)$$

Multiple Variances. Note that although this technique was performed in a situation in which only two items were involved, it also could be performed in a situation where several items have a variance. When volume is involved, for example, a flexible budget can be prepared first, and the remaining variances then can be calculated by using the actual level of volume. Let us look at this more complicated situation with another example, this time using materials instead of labor.

 PROBLEM   The Haskell Manufacturing Company has budgeted and actual material costs for one department that are as follows:

	Number of Units of Output	Material per Unit	Direct Material Cost/Unit	Total Cost
Budget	7,000	10 sq. feet	$.20/sq. foot	$14,000
Actual	6,000	12 sq. feet	$.25/sq. foot	$18,000

The factory manager is interested in obtaining a better understanding of the reasons behind the budget overrun. Begin by preparing a flexible budget for the department.

ANSWER   The flexible budget is prepared by changing the volume from its budgeted level to its actual level while holding everything else constant at budgeted levels. We then can determine what the budget *would have been if we had known volume in advance*. This budget then can be compared with the actual results, as follows:

	Number of Units of Output	Material per Unit	Direct Material Cost/Unit	Total Cost	Variances
Original Budget	7,000	10 sq. feet	$.20/sq. foot	$14,000	
Flexible Budget	6,000	10 sq. feet	$.20/sq.foot	$12,000	$2,000
Actual	6,000	12 sq. feet	$.25/sq.foot	$18,000	($6,000)
Total					($4,000)

Note that the volume variance (original budget minus flexible budget) is a favorable $2000 ($14,000 − $12,000). That is, if we had known the volume in advance, we would have budgeted $12,000 rather than $14,000.

Since to calculate the flexible budget we held all other factors at the levels in the original budget (10 square feet per unit and $0.20 per square foot), this $2000 positive variance is due *exclusively* to the lower volume. It is favorable since it reduces expenses, and this, other things being equal, improves our income. (Of course, we have excluded revenue variances from the analysis. Assuming we are paid on a per-unit basis, the fall in volume would have led to a negative revenue variance, indicating a reduction in income.)

As was indicated above, an unfavorable variance (i.e., one that lowers the income of the organization) is shown in parentheses; it sometimes is called a *negative* variance. A favorable (positive) variance does not have parentheses. Sometimes unfavorable variances are designated as UF and favorable variances are designated as F.

The spending variance (flexible budget minus actual results) is an unfavorable $6000 ($12,000 − $18,000), caused, as can be seen from the data, by using two additional square feet per unit and paying $0.05 more per square foot. The combined result of the volume and spending variances is a total unfavorable variance of $4000.

 PROBLEM   We now can calculate the reasons for the spending variance. As was indicated above, a portion of this variance is due to higher use (12 square feet versus 10 square feet) and a portion is due to a higher rate ($0.25 per square foot versus $0.20 per square foot). Spend a few minutes doing the calculations, using the formulas provided earlier.

ANSWER   The expense variances can be calculated as follows:

$$Use = (U_b - U_a) \times R_b$$
$$= (10 - 12) \times (\$0.20)$$
$$= (\$0.40)$$
$$Rate = (R_b - R_a) \times U_a$$
$$= (\$0.20 - \$0.25) \times 12$$
$$= (\$0.60)$$

Note that these are variances per unit of output. To obtain the *total* variance, we have to multiply these unit variances by the actual volume of output, that is, the volume used in calculating the flexible budget, as follows:

	Variance per Unit of Output	×	Actual Volume of Output	=	Total Variance
Use variance	($0.40)	×	6,000	=	($2,400)
Rate variance	($0.60)	×	6,000	=	(3,600)
Total					($6,000)

Alternatively, the calculations could be done in one step, as follows:

Variance	(Budget – Actual) × Other* ×	Actual Volume	=	Total Variance
Use (sq. feet)	(10 – 12) × .20 ×	6,000	=	($2,400)
Rate ($/sq. foot)	(0.20 – 0.25) × 12 ×	6,000	=	(3,600)
Total				($6,000)

* "Other" in the case of the rate variance is the *actual* use of square feet per unit; in the case of the use variance, it is the *budgeted* rate per square foot.

As this example demonstrates, variance analysis can help explain why actual expenses deviated from the budget. In the case of Haskell Manufacturing, we now can see that we saved $2000 in expenses as a result of producing fewer units but that our expenses increased by $3600 because of higher prices for the raw materials and by $2400 because of greater use of raw materials per unit of output.

Mix Variances. The volume variance computed in the problem above assumed that every unit of volume had the same variable expense associated with it. In many organizations, different types of products and services have different unit variable expense amounts. When this is the case, the volume variances are calculated by using weighted averages of the variable expense amounts. If there were a change in the budgeted proportions of the different product or service types, there also would be an *output mix variance.*

Input mix variances also arise with items such as raw materials and labor. This can happen if, for example, a responsibility center manager uses a different mix of raw materials than was budgeted or if the actual skill mix of labor differs from that in the budget. Techniques for calculating input mix variances are described in most cost accounting textbooks.

Many organizations do not calculate mix variances. In these organizations, the output mix variance is automatically part of the volume variance and the input mix variance typically is part of the rate variance (assuming that the different types of raw materials or different skill levels for labor have different rates). For example, in a hospital an output mix variance results from a change in the hospital's case types (e.g., relatively more coronary artery bypass surgery cases than influenza cases). An input mix variance comes about when there is a change in the mix of services used to treat a given case type (e.g., more or different radiological procedures ordered for each patient undergoing coronary artery bypass surgery). A second type of input mix variance could take place if the manager of, say, the radiology department used a mix of technicians to take the x-rays that was different from the budget. Variance analysis can isolate all these factors and attach dollar amounts to them.

Managerial Uses of Variances. An important feature of variance analysis is the ability it gives senior management to link managerial responsibility to changes in revenues and expenses. To provide a summary, Exhibit 10-1 lists each variance and identifies the department or responsibility center manager who ordinarily controls it. Clearly, this linkage may differ among different types of organizations, but the exhibit gives a general sense of where the responsibility lies for each variance.

As this exhibit suggests, operating managers ordinarily do not control the volume or mix of services supplied, set wage rates for employees, or control the rates paid for raw materials and other expense items. Consequently, variance analysis permits management to focus attention on each individual item and the managers who control it.

Simply identifying the separate variances is not enough, however. Senior management needs to know why, say, a large efficiency variance arose and what steps are under way to correct it. Thus, by separating a total variance between budgeted performance and actual performance into its individual components, senior management is in a better position to discuss those steps with the appropriate responsibility center managers.

EXHIBIT 10-1

Types of Variances and Controlling Agents

Variance	Controlling Agent
Volume variance (revenue/expense)	Marketing department/senior management/the environment (depending on the organization)
Output mix variances	Same as above
Selling price variances	Senior management/marketing department/responsibility center managers (depending on who in the organization sets prices)
Raw material price variances	Purchasing department/responsibility center (managers who place orders)
Wage rate variances	Senior management (who negotiate union contracts)/responsibility center managers (who make job offers)
Raw material usage variances	Responsibility center managers
Labor efficiency variances	Responsibility center managers
Input mix variances	Responsibility center managers

Limitations of Variance Analysis. It is important to remember that although variance analysis can highlight the reasons for a deviation between budgeted performance and actual performance, and can do this in terms of volume, rate, use, and mix, it cannot explain *why* a particular organizational unit was more or less efficient than budgeted or why volume was higher or lower than anticipated. As a result, variance analysis can be a useful tool to *assist* managers in asking the right questions and identifying the lower-level managers to whom those questions might be addressed. As with many other management accounting techniques, however, it should be considered only as a means to help managers learn more about the activities of their organizations so that they can take corrective action when it is called for.

In using variance analysis for managerial action, it is important to recognize that few variances can be interpreted independently from all the others. A negative material use variance in the factory, for example, may have arisen because the purchasing department bought some raw materials of lower quality than anticipated. Thus, what appears as a positive rate variance for the purchasing department, may have negative "downstream" consequences in the production effort. Similarly, a production center manager may have incurred a negative rate variance because his or her department needed to work overtime to prepare a rush order for another department, or a negative efficiency variance because there were several recently hired people on the production line.

In summary, when used properly, a negative expense variance (rate, mix, or use) can be extremely valuable. It can help identify areas where operating improvements can take place and allow managers to see the financial consequences of their corrective actions. When used in a clublike way, however, it can be quite threatening and even may lead to unproductive conflict within a department or reduced cooperation between line managers in different departments. Indeed, if the organization's success depends on collaboration between or among these managers, the misuse of variance analysis by senior management or others can have serious negative consequences for performance.

 PROBLEM The Oak Street Inn was a small bed and breakfast in a resort town. The inn charged a nominal fee for a night's stay. The following budgeted and actual figures were available:

	Actual	Budget
Person-nights	10,000	12,000
Revenue	$750,000	$720,000
Expenses	735,000	684,000
Income	$15,000	$36,000

1. Reconcile the $30,000 increase in revenue by using the appropriate revenue variances.
2. Prepare a flexible budget for the inn's expenses. Use it and the revenue variances to reconcile the change in income between budget and actual.
3. What additional information would help explain the difference between the budgeted and actual income figures?

ANSWER

QUESTION 1

To reconcile the budgeted revenue and actual revenue, we begin with a calculation of unit rates:

	Actual	Budget
Revenue	$750,000	$720,000
Person-nights	10,000	12,000
Rate per night	$75.00	$60.00

We now can calculate the price variance and the sales volume variance, as follows:

Price variance	[($75–$60) × 10,000]	=	$150,000 F
Volume variance	[(10,000 – 12,000) × $60]	=	$120,000 UF

To reconcile the $30,000 increase, we begin with budgeted sales revenue and use the variances to convert it to actual sales revenue. The calculations are as follows:

Budgeted revenue	$720,000
Plus: favorable price variance	150,000
Less: unfavorable volume variance	(120,000)
Actual sales revenue	$750,000

Alternatively, we could have calculated a flexible budget, as follows:

	Original Budget	Flexible Budget	Actual Results
Person-nights	12,000	10,000	10,000
Price per night	$60	$60	$75
Revenue	$720,000	$600,000	$750,000
Volume variance	($120,000)		
Price variance		$150,000	
Total variance			$30,000

The flexible budget for expenses can follow the same format:

	Original Budget	Flexible Budget	Actual Results
Person-nights	12,000	10,000	10,000
Expense per night	$57.00	$57.00	$73.50
Total expense	$684,000	$570,000	735,000
Volume variance	$114,000		
Spending variance		($165,000)	
Total variance			($51,000)

To reconcile the change in income, we can make the following calculations:

	Total	Volume	Price/Spending
Revenue variances	30,000	(120,000)	150,000
Expense variances	(51,000)	114,000	(165,000)
Total variances	(21,000)	(6,000)	(15,000)
Plus budgeted income	$36,000		
Equals actual income	$15,000		

Note that the decline in volume had only a $6000 negative impact when the reduced expenses at budget were combined with the lost revenue. The big problem was a spending variance of $165,000. It appears that the inn compensated for this by raising its prices 25 percent ($15 on a base of $60).

The big question that remains is why expense per night increased by almost 30 percent (from $57 to $73.50). Among the items of information we might like to have are the following:

- The breakdown between fixed and variable expenses
- The labor and material breakdown of the two figures
- The wage and efficiency information for labor
- The price and usage information for materials

THE REPORTING PROCESS

Once appropriate data are collected and the necessary variances have been calculated, a key task for the responsibility accounting system is structuring and presenting the data so that managers receive useful information. Indeed, if the reporting phase of the cycle is to be successful in providing responsibility center managers with the information necessary to run their centers effectively and efficiently, it must meet four criteria.

Criterion 1: Timeliness

The information must arrive on a timely basis. In this context, that does not necessarily mean quickly but rather appropriately with respect to the managerial action that may be necessary. In some instances, monthly reports that arrive within a few days of the end of each month may be necessary; in others, it may be feasible for the monthly reports to arrive within a week or two. Similarly, daily, weekly, quarterly, or annual reports may be necessary, and each will have an appropriate time lag between the effective date of the information in the report and the date when it must be received by the managers who must act on it.

Criterion 2: A Hierarchy of Information

Information must be available in various levels of aggregation, from highly summarized to highly detailed. Generally, not all managers at all levels in the organization will find it necessary to have the same level of detail. A plant manager, for example, most likely will not want detailed efficiency information for each worker in the factory. However, he or she may wish to have information about the efficiency of different *sections* within the factory. Generally, the information on sections in the factory would appear at a second level in the hierarchy so that it does not impair senior management's reading of the more summarized information, such as the factory's overall efficiency.

Because of these differing needs, a good reporting system usually has several levels of detail:

- A highly summarized level used by senior management only, generally on a divisional or departmental basis.

- A breakdown of sections (or subdepartments) within a division or department that is used primarily by division or department managers but is available to senior management for reference.

- A breakdown of personnel within sections (or subdepartments) that is used primarily by section managers but is available to division or department managers for reference.

- A transaction listing for both personnel and supplies that generally is not used unless an in-depth reference is needed. This level contains the building blocks for the more summarized information as well as for the financial and full cost accounting systems.

Obviously, the levels of detail must be tailored to the individual organization and its needs. For smaller organizations, where management is intimately aware of the activities, a highly summarized level and a transaction level may be all that is needed. As potential problems are identified, they can be discussed with the individuals involved, using transaction information, as necessary, to answer questions. For larger organizations, all four (or even more) summaries may be needed.

Exhibit 10-2 shows how information might be structured in a multi-divisional company, using the Home Products Division for the more detailed examples. Note that the exhibit contains five levels of information, each of which disaggregates the information above it. For example, the home products division is shown as a single line in the first-level report, a report designed for senior management. In the second-level report, the product lines of the division are broken out, such as major appliances, small appliances, and hardware. The product lines are broken into regions in the third-level report, and regions are broken into facilities in the fourth-level report. Finally, the fifth-level report breaks each facility into its individual products. A report such as this allows a division to trace its profit or loss down through the organizational hierarchy to locate its source(s) in product lines, regions, facilities, and individual products.

The drill-down sequence, as these levels often are called, is by no means standard. Another organization in the same industry might designate *regions* for the second-level report, for example, and *facility* for the third-level report, with *product lines* at the fourth level. The key is that the reporting hierarchy must fit the organization's structure of responsibility centers.

Determining the Number of Summary Levels. Several factors are central to a decision concerning the appropriate number of summary levels: (1) the managerial time associated with using the reports, (2) the kinds of actions that can be taken on the basis of the reports, (3) the amount of responsibility given to individuals at different levels in the organization, and (4) the cost of preparing the reports. A careful weighing of these factors is an essential ingredient in designing an effective and usable reporting process.

Criterion 3: Relevance and Accuracy

An effective reporting process is characterized by the presence of relevant and accurate information. Although accuracy requires no elaboration, the term *relevant* does. In many instances one finds reporting systems with a great deal of information that is of marginal or no use to the managers receiving the reports, while certain crucial information is missing. A good example is year-to-date information, which, although generally of some use to a manager, often is not included in a set of management reports. Conversely, if the organization has a highly seasonal pattern of operations, year-to-date information, unless adjusted for seasonality, may be of little use.

A Reporting Hierarchy

MULTI-DIVISIONAL CONGLOMERATE ($000)

A. Fifth-level report

Division Summary (Senior Management)	Actual June	Actual Year to date	(Over) or under budget June	(Over) or under budget Year to date
Direct Costs:				
Division 1	$2,110	$12,030	$(315)	$35
Division 2—Home Products	24,525	147,280	(710)	(2,590)
Division 3	1,235	7,570	(125)	(210)
Division 4	1,180	7,045	95	75
Division 5	3,590	18,960	(235)	245
Division 6	4,120	25,175	160	(320)
Division 7	2,245	13,680	180	(160)
Division 8	3,630	22,965	(70)	(730)
Total	$42,635	$254,705	$(1,020)	$(3,655)
Controllable overhead	$27,120	$161,970	$3,020	$5,130
Total	$69,755	$416,675	$2,000	$1,475

B. Fourth-level report

Division 2—Home Products Product Line Profit Summary Division Vice President	Actual June	Actual Year to date	(Over) or under budget June	(Over) or under budget Year to date
Product Line				
Hardware	$5,340	$35,845	$(625)	$(1,380)
Major Appliances	3,310	19,605	(30)	(620)
Small Appliances	3,115	18,085	90	(135)
Dietary Supplements	5,740	33,635	(65)	(640)
In-home Repair Services	7,020	40,110	(80)	185
Total profit	$24,525	$147,280	$(710)	$(2,590)

C. Third-level report

Major Appliances Regional Profit Breakdown (Regional Manager)	Actual June	Actual Year to date	(Over) or under budget June	(Over) or under budget Year to date
Region 1	$895	$5,400	$119	$75
Region 2	1,030	7,000	176	(50)
Region 3	760	4,500	(160)	(350)
Region n	625	2,705	(165)	(295)
Total	$3,310	$19,605	$(30)	$(620)

D. Second-level report

Regional Breakdown of Major Appliances (Field Operations Managers)	Actual June	Actual Year to date	(Over) or under budget June	(Over) or under budget Year to date
Region 1				
Facility 1	$245	$1,300	$(35)	$(65)
Facility 2	300	1,775	20	120
Facility 3	150	780	35	165
Facility n	200	1,545	99	(145)
Total	$895	$5,400	$119	$75

E. First-level report

Product Breakdown of Major Appliances (Facility Manager)	Actual June	Actual Year to date	(Over) or under budget June	(Over) or under budget Year to date
Facility 1				
Product A Dishwashers	$90	$560	$(25)	$(50)
Product B Refrigerators	75	350	(20)	(80)
Product C Stoves	45	280	15	95
Product D Microwave Ovens	35	110	(5)	(30)
Total	$245	$1,300	$(35)	$(65)
Facility 2				
Etc.	$170	$1,500	$(55)	$(150)

Unit cost information is another example of information that may be of little utility. If a manager has no control over volume, *total* unit cost information (which includes both fixed and variable costs) is of almost no value and indeed may be quite misleading. Instead, the relevant information would be either controllable or variable cost per unit, which presumably is not affected by volume and therefore includes costs that can be controlled by the manager. Clearly, what is relevant for one organization quite likely will not be relevant for another.

Criterion 4: Attention to Behavioral Factors

To be effective, a reporting system must be taken seriously. It is not sufficient simply to prepare and distribute reports. Unless senior management communicates to managers at various levels in the organization its expectation that the reporting system will be used as a basis for taking appropriate managerial action, the system will have little value.

Senior management can take any number of steps to communicate its intent, including holding regular meetings to discuss the reports, requiring follow-up memos or e-mails by middle managers, and even using telephone calls and hallway conversations. Senior management must not ignore the reports, however, for if it does, line managers likely also will ignore them.

MEASURING AND REPORTING NONFINANCIAL INFORMATION

In addition to reporting on financial performance, an effective responsibility accounting system measures and reports on *nonfinancial* performance. Increasingly, the objectives of many organizations are extending beyond the satisfaction of annual income targets to encompass a variety of nonfinancial objectives as well.

Nonfinancial objectives tend to fall into two general categories: (1) ones that will have an impact on long-term financial performance, such as gaining market share, assuring product quality, improving production or service-delivery processes, or enhancing the capabilities of personnel, and (2) ones that are oriented toward social responsibility, such as providing a safer, more fulfilling workplace for employees; reducing the amount of industrial pollutants; or contributing the well-being of the community. When these kinds of nonfinancial objectives become important to senior management, the measuring and reporting processes must be modified to accommodate them.

Central to the task of measuring and reporting nonfinancial results is the nature of the measures that may be employed. In a nonprofit context, for example, there is a "continuum of output measures" that range from relatively unmeasurable but highly meaningful indicators of performance to easily measurable but not terribly meaningful indicators.[1] Almost all nonprofit organizations would agree that their principal objective is to have an impact on the status of the communities they serve. However, it is extremely difficult to measure a community's status, and even if that status were measurable, the establishment of a linkage between it and the activities of a particular organization would be a futile task.

Just as social indicators are difficult to determine and measure, process measures are rather easy. Number of newsletters produced, number of clients served, and the like, are all relatively easy to measure and report. Unfortunately, they say little about whether an organization is achieving its nonfinancial objectives or having an impact on its community.

It is thus in the intermediate category of results measures that the activity of performance measurement takes place in most nonprofit organizations. In this case the managerial challenge is to develop a set of objectively measurable indicators of performance so that nonfinancial objectives can be established during the budget formulation process and then measured and reported at regular intervals during the budget year.

The dilemma facing nonprofit organizations also exists in the for-profit sector, where the challenge is quite similar: to develop nonfinancial indicators of performance that are built into the budget and then measured and reported at regular intervals during the year.

Clearly, the specific characteristics of nonfinancial reporting in a particular organization depend on the nature of the relationship among customers, programs, and resources. In general, however, nonfinancial reports provide information on items such as minutes spent per activity, the number and kind of customers served, the nature of the services delivered, the results of those services, customer satisfaction, and progress toward overall organizational goals. Exhibit 10-3 shows some examples.

The classic work in the area of nonfinancial performance measures is John Rockart's "Chief Executives Define Their Own Data Needs," which was published in the *Sloan Management Review* over 20 years ago.[2] More recently, Sharon McKinnon and William Bruns have addressed the issue in their book *The Information Mosaic*.[3] The most popular book on this topic is Robert Kaplan and David Norton's *The Balanced Scorecard*,[4] which has generated a great deal of senior management thinking about the kinds of nonfinancial measures that are useful and how they are interrelated.

Kaplan and Norton break the nonfinancial measures into three categories, each of which is related to a different area of importance to an organization and has a causal, usually lagged, relationship to financial performance: customer satisfaction, employee skill development, and internal processes. At Milliken & Co., for example, several internal process

EXHIBIT 10-3

Measures of Nonfinancial Performance

Area	Positive Measures	Negative Measures
Manufacturing quality	First-pass yields	Percentage defects
Vendor quality	Percentage of on-time performance	Percentage returns
Customer quality	On-time delivery	Percentage returns
		Percentage complaints

measures of performance are reported on a regular basis. They include lead, or throughput, time; change, or setup, time; and downtime. As a consequence of these new areas of attention, the company saw positive results in both process and cost control.[5]

Presenting the Information. The presentation format for nonfinancial information is important to its use. With the wide variety of feasible measures in each of several areas of concern to senior management, it is possible for the information to become overwhelming. In response, some companies have begun to use a "spidergram," such as that shown in Exhibit 10-4. This technique helps senior management see several different measures in several different categories at a glance. In the spidergram, the inner circle is the minimum acceptable level of performance, the outer circle is the goal, and the jagged line is actual performance for the period in question.

In this report the organization, a hospital, is looking at four broad areas of performance: customer service, growth, financial results, and internal processes. It has several measures of each area and can use the report to tell at a glance where it is meeting—and failing to meet—its goals.

The organization prepares a report like this with varying levels of detail, depending on the target audience. The report in Exhibit 10-4 is designed for the organization's board, but managers at different levels have modified versions that vary with their areas of responsibility. Senior management can focus on those areas where the jagged line is inside the minimum acceptable line and can use the information to discuss specific remedial actions with line managers and others who have responsibility for the different measures.

Whether an organization uses a spidergram is less important than its recognition that one consequence of developing and measuring nonfinancial results is the need to provide nonfinancial performance reports to managers. To the extent feasible, these reports should be integrated so that

EXHIBIT 10-4

Example of a Spidergram

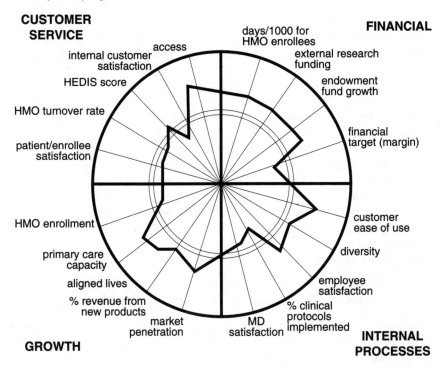

managers can determine the resources being consumed in the attainment of various nonfinancial results. As with financial reporting systems, a nonfinancial reporting system must provide accurate, timely, and useful information to the appropriate managers.[6]

Developing Useful Good Nonfinancial Reports

There are five issues senior management needs to consider in its efforts to develop a useful set of nonfinancial reports: (1) developing appropriate measures of quality, (2) relating inputs and outputs, (3) addressing the needs of external constituents as well as the organization's managers, (4) using surrogate measures of performance, where necessary, and (5) aligning responsibility with control. Let us look at each issue separately.

Issue 1: Measuring Quality

The move toward total quality management (TQM) in many organizations has led to an increased focus on measuring and controlling quality.

Historically, quality was measured through the use of an inspection process at the end of a production line. The TQM movement has shifted this focus to ongoing activities so that the inspection process has been all but eliminated in many organizations that use TQM. For example, Lexus was able to take market share away from Mercedes by making a one-time investment in a manufacturing process that produced nearly defect-free cars, whereas Mercedes was expending considerable resources on an ongoing basis to catch mistakes. Since customers care little about a company's internal processes, only about the end result—an absence of defects in this case—Lexus was able to meet customers' quality needs at a lower cost than Mercedes could.

Eliminating the inspection process does not obviate the need to consider ways to measure quality and report it to managers. For example, many organizations increasingly are relying on their customers as the ultimate judge of quality. When this happens, the reporting system must be designed to accommodate the results of customer surveys and other approaches to gathering customer-based information. This information then must be reported to the appropriate managers so that, where necessary, action can be taken to improve operations.

Issue 2: Relating Inputs to Outputs

Nonfinancial reporting should build on the distinction between inputs and outputs. For example, a well-designed cost accounting system measures total resources consumed (direct labor hours, raw materials, variable overhead costs) by type of product, but this information frequently is not used by managers for control purposes.

Once a manager begins to focus on the relationship between inputs and outputs for control purposes, questions arise about the desired ratios between the two. Although the tendency in some organizations may be to attempt to provide a given level of output with as few inputs as possible, that approach may have negative consequences for an organization's long-run performance. This problem is particularly apparent when the organization receives a fixed dollar amount per product in advance each year and must on the average spend less than that to survive financially. This is the case with, say, a magazine publisher, an insurance company, or a health maintenance organization.

With a magazine publisher, there may be a tendency to focus managerial attention on resources consumed per printed article and to minimize that ratio. This could lead to decisions to eliminate activities that might build subscribership, however, such as articles by highly paid columnists. Thus, once an organization begins to measure ratios of outputs and inputs, it also must begin to establish standards or norms for those ratios and avoid the trap of seeking a low ratio in all instances.

Issue 3: External Constituents' Needs versus Management's Needs

Organizations that begin to develop performance measures and nonfinancial reports oriented toward an external constituency must be careful to avoid having the information needs of the external users fully govern the choice of measures of results. In this regard, many organizations find themselves facing a dilemma in which *their* nonfinancial objectives are inconsistent or incompatible with the nonfinancial objectives of their external constituents. The Occupational Safety and Health Administration (OSHA), for example, may wish to know about the number of job-related accidents, but management may be interested in a measure that indicates an increased or decreased *potential* for such accidents. It therefore may wish to measure, say, the frequency of in-house inspections of hazardous equipment even though this may not be required by OSHA.

Issue 4: Use of Surrogates

It is important to recognize that some nonfinancial objectives are difficult or impossible to measure. This is an unfortunate fact of life in many organizations. In these situations, managers may find it necessary to develop surrogate measures of output. Employee job satisfaction is inherently difficult to measure, for example, but a surrogate such as turnover, absenteeism, or tardiness may be feasible to measure.

Issue 5: Aligning Responsibility with Control

In nonfinancial reporting as in financial reporting, responsibility must be related to control, and a hierarchy of reports must be developed. For example, whereas an employee-by-employee summary of hours spent by client may be appropriate for, say, an account executive in an advertising agency, a client-by-client summary most likely would be more appropriate for senior management.

An Example

An example of a two-level nonfinancial report is shown in Exhibits 10-5 and 10-6. The setting is a business school. Several aspects of this report are worth noting.

Alignment of Responsibility and Control. The report is divided into areas of responsibility. Marketing and recruitment, for example, constitute one aspect of a program, whereas student performance and student satisfaction are two very different aspects. Although it may not be

EXHIBIT 10-5

Commonwealth University Business School: Program Performance Report for the MBA Program

Indicator	Year 1	Year 2	Year 3	Year 4	Year 5

Marketing and Recruitment

1. Number of inquiries
2. Number of applications sent
3. Number of applications received
4. Application rate (= 3 ÷ 2)
5. Number of accepted applicants
6. Admission rate (=5 ÷ 3)
7. Number of matriculants
8. Yield (= 7 ÷ 5)
9. Average GPA for matriculants
10. Average GMAT for matriculants

Student Performance in Program

11. Grade distribution for required courses
    A/A–
    B+/B/B–
    C+/C/C–
    Below C–
Overall GPA
12. Grade distribution for elective courses
    A/A–
    B+/B/B–
    C+/C/C–
    Below C–
Overall GPA
13. Number of students with B+ average or better leaving program in year 1
14. Percent of matriculants
15. Number of Students with C+ average or worse leaving program in year 1
16. Percent of matriculants
17. Number of graduates from program
18. Percent of matriculants

Student Satisfaction/
Overall Program Performance

19. Average instructor rating
19a. for required courses
19b. for elective courses
20. Number of graduates attaining job of choice within 3 months of graduation
21. Percent of graduates
22. Average salary of graduates after 5 years
23. Number of graduates making annual financial contributions to school
24. Percent of graduates
25. Median gift per graduate
26. No. of gifts of $500 or more
27. Percent of graduates

EXHIBIT 10-6

Commonwealth University Business School: Comparative Program Performance Report for the Current Year

T = Target; A = Actual

-------------------Program-------------------

Indicator	1		2		3		4	
	T	A	T	A	T	A	T	A

Marketing and Recruitment
4. Application Rate
5. Admission Rate
8. Yield
9. Average GPA for matriculants
10. Average GMAT for matriculants

Student Performance in Program
Overall GPA for students in
11. Required courses
12. Elective courses

% matriculants leaving program in year 1 with
14. B+ average or better
16. C+ average or worse
18. % of matriculants graduating from program

Student Satisfaction/
Overall Program Performance
Weighted average instructor ratings
19a. For required courses
19b. For elective courses
21. % of graduates attaining job of choice within 3 months of graduation
22. Average salary of graduates after 5 years
23. Percent of graduates making an annual financial contribution to the school
25. Median gift per graduate
27. Percent of graduates making a gift of $500 or more

possible to assign a specific person to each aspect, these aspects neverthe-less indicate areas where action can be taken, frequently by different individuals. The head of the admissions office would be expected to take action concerning marketing and recruitment, for example, whereas the program director would have responsibility for student performance and some responsibility for student satisfaction. The placement and development offices presumably would have responsibility for student satisfaction related to job placement, and the development office would have responsibility for alumni contributions.

Relationship between Outputs and Inputs. In several areas "outputs" could be related to inputs. It would be possible, for example, to determine the cost per admitted applicant, per course, or per graduate. With the latter two aspects tuition might be used as a surrogate for cost so that the program's performance per tuition dollar received could be calculated.

Role of Nonfinancial Objectives. Although not all output measures relate directly to nonfinancial objectives, several do. Presumably the program is interested in attracting well-qualified students. To the extent that its yield (entering students as a percentage of admitted students) is high (assuming it is admitting only well-qualified students), it is doing its job. Similarly, it is likely that the program is interested in retaining only well-qualified students; items 13, 14, 15, and 16 begin to address this issue by asking how many *well-qualified* students (B+ average or better) leave versus how many *less-than-well-qualified* students (C+ average or below) leave. Finally, it is likely that the program is interested in placing its students appropriately and having them satisfied with their education. The last category addresses this issue.

Changes Over Time. Because there is a 5-year series of comparisons (Exhibit 10-5), both the program manager and senior management can see how the program is changing over time. This 5-year series could be supplemented with a set of targets so that it would be possible to measure the program's performance both over time and with respect to the target.

Cross-Program Comparisons. By having the boldfaced items in Exhibit 10-5 for several programs, as shown in Exhibit 10-6, senior management can compare the relative performance for these programs for a given year or compare variances from either a target or prior years' averages.

Linking Nonfinancial to Financial Performance

Although these examples are set in a nonprofit context, readers should not lose sight of their applicability to many organizations in which nonfinancial performance is important. Nonfinancial performance, though frequently not tied directly or immediately to net income, usually has an important relationship to it over time. That is, improvements in, say, customer satisfaction, operational processes, and employee capabilities generally lead to improved financial performance, although perhaps not immediately. Organizations that have begun to focus on TQM have recognized this linkage. To the extent that the linkage is important, so too is the development of a measurement and reporting system that helps the organization manage it.

NOTES

1 For additional discussion of this continuum, see Robert N. Anthony and David W. Young, *Management Control in Nonprofit Organizations*, 7th ed., Burr Ridge, IL: McGraw-Hill/Irwin, 2003.

2 John F. Rockart, "Chief Executives Define Their Own Data Needs," *Sloan Management Review*, March–April 1979.

3 Sharon M. McKinnon and William J. Bruns, Jr., *The Information Mosaic: How Managers Use Information*. Boston: Harvard Business School Press, 1991.

4 Robert S. Kaplan and David P. Norton, *The Balanced Scorecard*. Boston: Harvard Business School Press, 1996.

5 James Don Edwards, Cynthia D. Heagy, and Harold W. Rakes, "How Milliken Stays on Top," *Journal of Accountancy*, Vol. 167, Issue 4, April 1989.

6 For additional discussion of nonfinancial performance measures, see the references cited in earlier footnotes. See also Robert S. Kaplan and David P. Norton, "The Balanced Scorecard—Measures That Drive Performance," *Harvard Business Review*, January–February, 1992; Robert G. Eccles and Philip J. Pyburn, "Creating a Comprehensive System to Measure Performance," *Management Accounting*, October 1992; and Sharon M. McKinnon and William J. Bruns, Jr., "What Production Managers Really Want to Know . . . Management Accountants Are Failing to Tell Them," *Management Accounting*, January 1993.

CHAPTER 11

Management Accounting in Context

Management accounting is not a required activity. In this respect it is unlike financial accounting, which is required in an organization that wants a clean audit opinion. The only management accounting requirement is the computation of the cost of goods sold in manufacturing and merchandising organizations. Thus, when senior management decides to undertake management accounting activities, it does so because it believes the information provided will assist in decision making and therefore will be worth the cost. This is true for full cost accounting, in which the information presumably will be used for pricing and profitability assessments. It is true for differential cost accounting, in which senior management believes that a cost analysis will help it make a more financially beneficial alternative choice decision. It also is true for responsibility accounting, in which senior management believes that the development of an appropriate network of responsibility centers and the creation of a management control process will help it achieve the organization's strategy more effectively and efficiently than otherwise would be the case.

In all three of these areas, especially in the last, senior management must recognize that management accounting does not exist in a vacuum. Instead, it must be an integral part of a wide range of organizational activities that must be well managed if the organization is to be successful. The goal of this chapter is to discuss these other activities and place the material in the first 10 chapters into a broader managerial context.

The chapter begins with a discussion of the idea that different costs are used for different purposes and then outlines the criteria for a good responsibility accounting system. Next, it illustrates the contingent nature of responsibility accounting systems by positioning them as one of several activities that relate to one another in an organization and must be well managed if the organization is to be successful. The chapter concludes with a "Managerial Checklist" concerning those interrelationships.

DIFFERENT COSTS FOR DIFFERENT PURPOSES

Fundamental to an understanding of management accounting is the notion that *different costs are used for different purposes*. For example, Chapters 2 and 3 stressed the fact that differential costs rather than full costs are appropriate for breakeven analyses and alternative choice decisions. Full costs were shown to be inappropriate for these types of decisions. In the same vein, a separate set of information—both costs and revenues—is appropriate for a responsibility accounting system. Specifically, for responsibility accounting purposes we are concerned with the distinction between controllable and noncontrollable items. These three different uses of cost information are shown in Exhibit 11-1.

Two aspects of this exhibit are worth noting. First, it summarizes much of what was covered in the first 10 chapters of the book. Full cost accounting was discussed in Chapters 1, 4, and 5; differential cost accounting was covered in Chapters 2 and 3; and responsibility accounting was covered in Chapters 6 through 10. Second, the goals in the first two categories—improving the full-cost accounting system and assessing cost behavior—ordinarily can be achieved by the accounting staff with, as was discussed earlier, appropriate guidance from senior management to assure that the resulting information meets its needs. However, the responsibility accounting system requires continuing and active involvement from senior management if it is to be effective in helping the organization achieve its strategic goals.

CRITERIA FOR A GOOD RESPONSIBILITY ACCOUNTING SYSTEM

To assure that it has a responsibility accounting system that meets its needs, senior management can focus on the issues discussed in the last five chapters. The criteria for a good system can be grouped into three categories: structure, process, and behavioral aspects.

Structure

Perhaps the most important structural aspect of a responsibility accounting system is the idea that its responsibility centers must be well designed and fit the organization's authority structure. Well designed

EXHIBIT 11-1

Different Types of Management Accounting

Goal	Information Used	Key Activities	Managerial Uses
Full Cost Accounting			
Improve the full cost system	Direct and indirect costs	Choice of cost object	Product line profitability
		Assignment of costs to cost centers	Strategic decisions (programs, facilities,
		Choice of allocation bases	personnel needed to support chosen product lines)
		Allocation of service center costs to production centers	Pricing
		Attachment of costs to products	Some cost control
Differential Cost Accounting			
Assess cost behavior	Fixed and variable	Analysis of cost behavior	Offer a special price
		Contribution analyses	Subcontract for services
		Breakeven analyses	Retain or discontinue an unprofitable program or product line
Responsibility Accounting			
Control costs	Controllable costs versus noncontrollable costs	Determine cost drivers	Cost control
			Motivation
		Budget using cost drivers	
	Variances between actual and budgeted costs		Performance measurement
		Determine responsibility	Assign responsibility to controlling agents
		Programming	
			Cost control
		Reporting and evaluation	

means that the responsibility-control relationship has been assessed and that senior management is convinced that line managers are being held responsible for the factors over which they have a reasonable degree of control.

It also is important that a good decision by a manager be categorized as "good" on the reports that the manager receives; that is, if the decision is good for the organization overall, it also should be good for the manager's responsibility center. To illustrate, assume a company has a central computing facility that senior management wants department managers to use. If a manager decides to use that facility to carry out some work instead of purchasing his or her own computer and hiring staff to perform the work, the responsibility accounting system should have a transfer price that charges the manager's responsibility center no more than it would have been charged if he or she had purchased the system.

Process

The management control process should be characterized by four phases: programming, budgeting, measuring, and reporting. The *programming phase* should assess changes to the organization's product lines and/or programs. Each product line or program should fit with the organization's overall strategic focus, and the objectives for each one should be delineated clearly.

The *budgeting phase* not only should identify the relationship between product lines (or programs) and responsibility centers but also should clarify the financial and nonfinancial expectations for each responsibility center. Managers should be held responsible for setting budgets not only for the dollar amounts associated with their product lines (or programs or other activities) but also for an appropriate set of nonfinancial objectives.

During the *measurement phase* the accounting staff should collect data relating to revenues, expenses, and nonfinancial objectives as identified in the budgetary process. In general, information for responsibility accounting purposes should be organized differently from the way it is organized for cost accounting purposes, and those differences should be incorporated into the measurement phase. Where appropriate, variances should be calculated and made available to the relevant managers.

During the *reporting phase* the information is presented to managers. The reports that do this should (1) be timely, accurate, and relevant to the responsibility center, (2) separate controllable from noncontrollable items, (3) show nonfinancial as well as financial results, and (4) contain information of varying levels of detail appropriate to the managers who will be using them.

Behavioral Aspects

Perhaps the most important behavioral aspect of a responsibility accounting system is that it be taken seriously by senior management and middle management. Senior management's active participation in the system in both the budgeting and reporting phases is necessary if middle- and lower-level managers are to take the system seriously and feel obligated to achieve the expectations outlined during the programming and budgeting phases of the management control process. Additionally, to the extent feasible, the responsibility accounting system should be characterized by goal congruence; that is, the financial and nonfinancial goals of individual managers, as determined by the responsibility center structure, programming decisions, and budgeting activities, should be consistent with the overall goals of the organization.

Finally, to the extent that managers participate in the programming and budgeting phases of the management control process, their participation should be an integral part of those phases. In this way their commitment to programming and budgeting decisions will be appropriate to the organization's needs.

A DESIGN PROBLEM

To illustrate these various aspects in practice, let us look at some responsibility accounting design issues in practice.

 PROBLEM Consider the following two strategic scenarios: A German chemical company prides itself on being a low-cost producer; efficient production is the key to its success. As a result, it seeks economies of scale, focuses its attention on new production methods, and has a highly centralized decision-making process. A Swedish chemical company, by contrast, is constantly seeking new markets and usually is not the low-cost producer in its market. It gains clients and earns profits through innovation and selling, always looking for new ways to help its clients use its products. It has a highly decentralized decision-making process, allowing its divisional managers, who know their clients best, to make decisions concerning new product ideas and production techniques.

Which strategy is correct?

ANSWER Neither strategy is correct or incorrect; they simply are different. Indeed, both strategies can be equally effective if they are in tune with their marketplaces. It even is possible that both companies could compete in the same marketplace, each focusing on a different type of customer. Most important for our purposes here, the two companies would have very different responsibility accounting systems and would need line managers with very different skills and orientations.

 PROBLEM   What might these responsibility accounting systems look like? Specifically, what would be the responsibility center structure, and how would each company design the programming, budgeting, measuring, and reporting phases of its management control process? What role would senior management play in the responsibility accounting system?

ANSWER   Here is one possible scenario:

The German company with its emphasis on production most likely would have designated its factory as a standard expense center, with responsibility for achieving low unit costs for all orders received. The Swedish company, by comparison, probably would have designated its divisional managers as profit centers, since their responsibility is to work closely with customers to determine new ways to market the company's products. They thus have the ability to generate additional revenue. This assumes, of course, that the divisions themselves have production facilities; if they do not, they quite likely would be revenue centers. The divisions might have designated their production facilities as standard expense centers, but given the emphasis on innovation, they also might have made them profit centers.

In the *programming* phase of the management control process one would expect to see the Swedish company developing many new product and service ideas and the German company moving more slowly in this area, concentrating instead on improvements in the production process. Importantly, however, if programming is to work well in the Swedish company, its divisions must be given a great deal of independence. Management cannot intervene to seek the lowest-cost production technique for new ideas generated by a division; instead, divisional managers must be given the opportunity to earn the profits themselves (assuming they are profit centers) without senior management becoming excessively involved in their decision making. In the German company, by contrast, one would expect senior management to be highly involved in much of the decision making.

The same holds true for the *budgeting* phase. Here one would expect to see the German company closely scrutinizing the cost data submitted by production managers, while senior management in the Swedish company most likely would look at overall profits and leave decisions concerning unit costs, marketing costs, and the like, to the judgment of the divisional managers.

In the *measurement phase*, operations most likely would be closely controlled in the German company, and a flexible budget would be used, based on the actual volume of production by type of product. Senior management in the Swedish company, by contrast, probably would focus on actual profits compared to the budget and would care little about changes in volume, mix, or unit costs; the division managers would be responsible for both volume and mix of sales and the cost of producing the products to meet customer demand. Additionally, costs would be measured much more closely in the German company, and there no doubt would be a great deal of detailed information on different types of costs. This might be true at the divisional level in the Swedish company (although this is unlikely, given its more market-oriented strategy), but senior management probably would have no interest in detailed cost data for the divisions.

Finally, one would expect to see a *reporting* system in the German company that focused principally on efficiency. Once adjustments had been made for changes in volume, product mix, the unit prices of supplies, and labor wages, a great deal of emphasis would be placed on efficiency. In fact, one might expect to see the factory divided into several different standard expense centers, each with efficiency standards for each type of product produced. In the Swedish company, by contrast, the reporting system no doubt would focus on profits, but beyond that it probably would attempt to indicate what proportion of profits came from new products and services and the extent to which the division was gaining new customers.

A Contingency Approach

This example illustrates the contingency nature of responsibility accounting systems, that is, why there is no one "right" responsibility accounting system. The system not only must *fit* the organization's strategy, it also must be compatible with the authority structure and the values of senior management. For this reason, even if two companies had similar strategies and operated in the same market, it is still likely that their responsibility accounting systems would be different, depending on, say, senior management's views with regard to the balance between autonomy and central control or on any of several other design-related matters.

In the final analysis, the most important characteristic of a good responsibility accounting system is that it assist senior management in accomplishing the organization's strategic purposes. In this regard its link to several other organizational activities is an important consideration.

LINK TO OTHER ACTIVITIES

As Exhibit 11-2 indicates, there are several linkages between the responsibility accounting system and other organizational activities. Indeed, given the tendency on the part of the accounting staff in many organizations to see responsibility accounting as its exclusive province, and the staff's occasionally limited view of the broader set of organizational issues at work, senior management leadership is especially important in assuring that these linkages are well designed and managed.

Programming Flows from Strategy Formulation

Programs are one of the most readily observable aspects of an organization's strategy. Thus, if new programs and large capital expenditures (the programming phase of the management control process) are to remain

EXHIBIT 11-2

Responsibility Accounting in Context

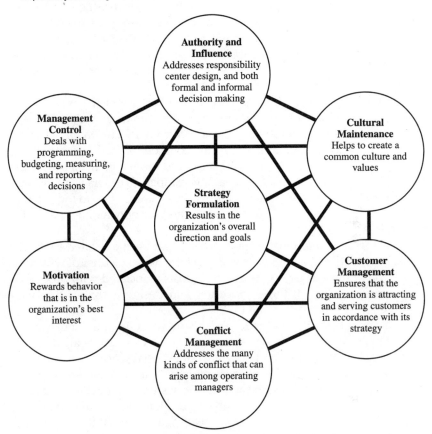

consistent with the organization's strategy, line managers must understand the linkages between their activities and the organization's overall strategic direction. Moreover, if an organization's strategy is to evolve over time because of, say, shifting environmental opportunities and threats or changing organizational strengths and weaknesses, senior management must find ways to monitor and manage the organization's programs so that they remain consistent with and supportive of the evolving strategy.

Even in organizations that have a loosely organized authority structure, such as the Swedish company discussed above, senior management tends to review programming decisions above a certain threshold amount. Thus, whereas individual units in companies such as the Swedish company might be expected to make many programming decisions on their own, they would not be allowed to do so for "big-ticket" items. Since these decisions have a major impact on the overall strategic direction of the firm, senior management generally wants to approve them in advance.[1]

Moreover, as the following example illustrates, a company's cost accounting system (which is part of the measurement phase of the management control process but is closely linked to customer management) also must fit with its strategy.[2]

In the late 1980s, Siemens Electric Motor Works, which was faced with intense competition from newly emerging companies in Eastern Europe, made a radical shift in its strategy. It moved from a focus on large batches (100-plus) of standard motors, where the competition had become strong, toward specialty motors, which were produced in very small batches (1 to 5 motors). Shortly afterward, almost half the company's orders were for a single motor and another 26 percent of the orders were for two to four motors. Orders for 100 or more motors now accounted for only about 3 percent of total orders.

Historically, manufacturing overhead had been allocated to motors on the basis of direct labor hours and machine hours, neither of which did a good job of measuring (1) the one-time costs associated with processing a customer's order, (2) the engineering and design activities that were required for a special order, and (3) the activities needed to handle the special components for the motor(s). As a result, when it added a markup to its total manufacturing costs, Siemens was grossly underpricing its small-quantity orders (where customers were not especially price-sensitive) and overpricing its orders for 100 or more motors (where customers were *very* price-sensitive). Because its cost accounting system had not been modified to measure the costs associated with its strategic shift to manufacturing motors in small batches, Siemens was heading toward a financial disaster.

However, by shifting to an activity-based costing (ABC) system, Siemens was able to gain a much better understanding of the overhead costs associated with motors produced in small batches. It was able to revise its prices accordingly and avert the looming financial crisis.

The message here is not just about the value of activity-based costing (discussed in Chapter 5). Rather, the Siemens example emphasizes the importance of attaining a fit among a company's strategy formulation, customer management, and management control processes. All too often, when a company shifts its strategy and begins to undertake new forms of customer management, it neglects to make the requisite changes in its responsibility accounting system, especially in the measurement and reporting phases of the management control process. As a result, the company comes close to flying blind.

Link to Culture

As was discussed earlier, the way senior management establishes constraints on programming and the way it makes use of the "programming purse" can have a profound impact on line managers' "basic assumptions" about what is acceptable and what is unacceptable in the organization.[3] This, in turn, can help either maintain or change the organization's culture.

Similarly, the design of the network of responsibility centers can affect the organization's culture. Centralizing revenue and establishing expense centers, for example, promotes a somewhat centralized culture, whereas the use of ETOB (every tub on its bottom) profit centers is more consistent with a decentralized culture. Profit centers with cross subsidization—sometimes called the "portfolio approach"—lie somewhere between these two extremes.

Finally, the types of nonfinancial information senior management decides to measure and report can have an important impact on the culture it wishes to establish. For example, if a company collects and regularly reports on matters of customer satisfaction and holds line managers responsible for achieving certain minimum scores, it can expect to have a culture that emphasizes customers more than does the culture of a company in the same industry that does not collect and report such information.

Link to Customer Management

The link between responsibility accounting and customer management is an especially important one in that customer behavior patterns drive an organization's revenues. Moreover, the shortening of product life cycles and ongoing efforts at quality improvements in some companies mean that the measurement and reporting phases of the management control process will have to undergo constant revisions if they are to provide line managers, professionals, and others, as well as senior management, with timely information on a company's performance in these arenas. Also, of course, nonfinancial reports are needed to provide managers with information on matters of customer satisfaction: number of customers served, quality of the goods or services delivered, complaints and/or reworks, and so forth.

Link to Conflict Management

One goal of many programmatic reports is to assess performance at various points in the customer management process so that managers can review whether goods and/or services are being delivered as expected and whether customers are satisfied with them. However, when action is called for on the basis of a report, there may be different views on what should be done and how it should be carried out. Thus, in addition to needing a conflict management process during the programming phase of the management control process (as was discussed earlier), an organization will need to manage the conflict that arises in the measurement and reporting phases of the process. A key task for senior management is to determine the places where conflict may arise and design appropriate mechanisms to manage it.

Link to Motivation

In general, senior management seeks a fit among the motivation process, the responsibility network, and the measuring and reporting phases of the management control process. The combination must encourage managers to make decisions that are in both the short-run and long-run best interests of the organization, and the reports that managers receive must allow them to determine the results of their decisions. Clearly, this is a complex endeavor.

In addition, there must be a clear policy set by senior management about the kinds of actions it expects line managers to take on the basis of the management control reports and a carefully designed set of incentives to encourage line managers to abide by those policies. Otherwise, the feedback loops shown in Exhibit 6-3 may not further the organization's progress toward its strategy.

And Back to Strategy Formulation

To complete the loop, some of the decisions senior management makes during the strategy formulation process will depend on the kinds of information it receives from the management control process. Depending on its design, the motivation process can encourage line managers and others to propose new investments, new programs, or new products and, more generally, to act in the best interest of the organization overall. Or it can discourage them from doing this.

A MANAGERIAL CHECKLIST

The information in this chapter and earlier chapters implies a variety of actions that senior managers might take with the responsibility accounting system. Here are a few items of special importance to consider:

1. In what ways does the programming phase of the management control process reinforce the organization's strategy? What changes seem to be called for?

2. Are cost drivers used to both formulate the budget and report the results to managers so that the reports that emerge from this process are linked to the customer management process? If they are not, how can we begin to align these activities and processes?

3. Does the financial measurement and reporting phase of the management control process measure fixed and variable costs for different mixes of products and compute the relevant variances? Do the resulting reports help managers assess their financial performance against the budget in meaningful ways?

4. Are the financial reports used as part of the motivation process? If they are not, how can these two processes be better linked?

5. How does the information being measured and reported relate to the goals of the programs as defined in the strategy formulation process and the programming phase of the management control process?

6. How do nonfinancial reports help managers assess their performance (e.g., outcomes and quality measures)? In particular, do the reports, together with the financial reports, help managers assess the effectiveness and cost-effectiveness of their programs? If they do not, what changes are needed?

7. Is the responsibility accounting system updated as needed to accommodate the new demands and information requirements created by new strategic directions? If it is not, how might it be?

8. Are midlevel managers involved in determining the kinds of activities that are measured and the way that information is structured and presented on reports? If they are not, do we wish to develop mechanisms to allow them to express their concerns about the measurement and reporting phase of the management control process?

N O T E S

1 For additional discussion of this issue, see David Solomons, *Divisional Performance: Measurement and Control.* Homewood, IL: Dow Jones Irwin, Inc., 1965.

2 For details on this situation, see Robin Cooper and Karen Hooper Wruck, *Siemens Electric Motor Works, Inc. Harvard Business School case 9-191-006.* Boston: Harvard Business School Publishing, 1991.

3 Schein characterizes "basic assumptions" as the essence of culture. See Edgar H. Schein, *Organizational Culture and Leadership,* 2d ed. San Francisco: Jossey-Bass, 1992.

The Reciprocal Method of Cost Allocation

To see how the reciprocal allocation method works, let us assume that we want to allocate an overnight mail delivery company's two service center costs of maintenance and administration to its two production centers: next-day delivery and 2-day delivery. Management has decided to allocate maintenance costs on the basis of the square footage in each department and to allocate administration costs on the basis of the number of hours worked by the employees in each of the respective departments. Exhibit A-1 shows how the initial data for the company might look.

Note that there are no square feet shown for maintenance and no labor hours shown for administration. Since we are using square feet as the basis of allocation for maintenance and labor hours as the basis of allocation for administration, we therefore exclude those measures from those two departments. In effect, we do not calculate the cost of maintaining the maintenance department or administering the administration department.

EXHIBIT A-1

Basic Information for a Reciprocal Cost Allocation

	Adminis-tration	Main-tenance	Two-Day Delivery	Next-Day Delivery	Totals
Basic information					
Area occupied (square feet)	1,000	—	1,000	3,000	5,000
Labor hours	—	100	100	400	600
Production center costs ($000)			$1,500	$4,000	$5,500
Service center costs ($000)	$1,200	$2,400			3,600
Total costs ($000)					$9,100

To perform a reciprocal allocation, we must develop a set of simultaneous equations; the number of equations in the set must equal the number of service centers to be allocated. In the above example, we must set up two equations with two unknowns; the unknowns are the amount of administration to be allocated (designated as A) and the amount of maintenance to be allocated (designated as M). Then, since maintenance costs are allocated on the basis of square footage and administration occupies one-fifth ($^{1000}\!/_{5000}$) of the square footage,

$$A = \$1200 + \frac{1}{5}(M)$$

In effect, the amount of administration to be allocated is the sum of its direct costs and its share of the maintenance costs.

Since administration costs are allocated on the basis of hours worked and maintenance uses one-sixth ($^{100}\!/_{600}$) of the hours,

$$M = \$2400 + \frac{1}{6}(A)$$

That is, the amount of maintenance to be allocated is the sum of its direct costs and its share of the administration costs.

We now can substitute terms as follows:

$$A = \$1200 + \frac{1}{5}[\{\$2400 + \frac{1}{6}(A)\}]$$

or

$$A = \$1200 + \$480 + \frac{1}{30}(A)$$

Therefore,

$$A = \$1738$$

And since $M = \$2400 + \frac{1}{6}(A)$,

$$M = \$2690$$

To complete the reciprocal allocation, we remove $1738 from administration and allocate it to the remaining three cost centers on the basis of labor hours and then remove $2690 from maintenance and allocate it to the three other cost centers on the basis of square footage. The result is that the service center costs are fully allocated to both the other service centers and the production centers and the full $9100 in costs now resides only in the production centers. These allocations are shown in Exhibit A-2.

EXHIBIT A-2

Allocation of Service Center Costs to Mission Centers

	Adminis- tration	Main- tenance	Two-Day Delivery	Next-Day Delivery	Totals
Initial costs ($000)	$1,200	$2,400	$1,500	$4,000	$9,100
Maintenance allocation*	538	(2,690)	538	1,614	—
Administration allocation†	(1,738)	290	290	1,158	—
Total costs	—	—	$2,328	$6,772	$9,100

*$2,690 from formula. Allocated $1/5$ to administration, $1/5$ to Two-Day Delivery, and $3/5$ to Next-Day Delivery
†$1,738 from formula. Allocated $1/6$ to maintenance, $1/6$ to Two-Day Delivery, and $4/6$ to Next-Day Delivery.

As might be imagined, once the number of cost centers exceeds three or four, solving the set of simultaneous equations becomes quite complex for a person, although it can be done easily with a computer. Moreover, even the stepdown method can benefit from the use of a simple spreadsheet application that carries out the allocations automatically. If it is designed properly, the computer program will allow an analyst to determine how the costs of each mission center are affected by different cost center structures, different allocation bases, and different stepdown sequences.

The Concept of Present Value

The concept of present value rests on the basic principle that money has a time value. For example, $1 received a year from today is worth less than $1 received today. To illustrate this concept, consider the following situations.

 QUESTION A colleague offers to pay you $1000 one year from today. How much would you lend her today?

ANSWER Presumably, unless you were a good friend or somewhat altruistic, you would not lend her $1000 today. You could invest your $1000, earn something on it over the course of the year, and have more than $1000 a year from now. If, for example, you could earn 10 percent on your money, you could invest that $1000 and have $1100 in a year. Alternatively, if you had $909 and invested it at 10 percent, you would have $1000 a year from today.

Thus, if your colleague offered to pay you $1000 a year from today and you were an investor expecting a 10 percent return, you most likely would lend her only $909 today. With a 10 percent interest rate, $909 is the present value of $1000 received 1 year hence.

 QUESTION Under the same circumstances as those in the previous question, how much would you lend your colleague if she offered to pay you $1000 two years from today?

ANSWER Here we must incorporate the concept of compound interest, that is, the fact that interest is earned on the interest itself. For example, at a 10 percent rate, $826 lent today would accumulate to roughly $1000 in 2 years, as shown by the following:

$$\text{Year 1 } \$826 \times 0.10 = \$82.60$$
$$\text{Year 2 } (\$826 + \$82.60) \times 0.10 = \$90.86$$
$$\text{Total at end of year 2} = \$826 + \$82.60 + \$90.86 = \$999.46$$

Thus, you would be willing to lend her $826.

261

QUESTION   The previous question consisted of a promise to pay a given amount 2 years from today, with no intermediate payments. Another possibility to consider is the situation in which your colleague offers to pay you $1000 a year from today and another $1000 two years from today. How much would you lend her in this case?

ANSWER   We now must combine the analyses in each of the two questions above. For the $1000 received 2 years from now, you would lend her $826, and for the $1000 received 1 year from now you would lend her $909. Thus, the total you would lend would be $1735.

Our ability to make these calculations is facilitated by present value tables. Two abbreviated tables are included at the end of this appendix. Table A, "Present Value of $1," is the one we would use to determine the present value of a single payment received at a specified time in the future. For instance, in the first example above we could find the answer to the problem by looking in the column for 10 percent and the row for 1 year; this gives us 0.909. Multiplying 0.909 by $1000 gives us the $909 we would lend our colleague. Similarly, if we look in the row for 2 years and multiply the entry of 0.826 by $1000, we arrive at the answer to the second question: $826.

Table B, "Present Value of $1 Received Annually for *N* Years," is used for even payments received over a specific period. Looking at Table B, we can see that the present value of 1.736 (for a payment of $1 received each year for 2 years at 10 percent) multiplied by $1000 is $1736. With a minor rounding error, this is the amount we calculated in the third example above. We also can see that 1.736 is the sum of the two amounts shown in Table A (0.909 for 1 year hence and 0.826 for 2 years hence). Thus, Table B simply sums the various elements in Table A to facilitate calculations.

TABLE A-1

Present Value of $1

Years Hence	1%	2%	4%	6%	8%	10%	12%	14%	15%	16%	18%	20%	22%	24%	25%	26%	28%	30%
1	0.990	0.980	0.962	0.943	0.926	0.909	0.893	0.877	0.870	0.862	0.847	0.833	0.820	0.806	0.800	0.794	0.781	0.769
2	0.980	0.961	0.925	0.890	0.857	0.826	0.797	0.769	0.756	0.743	0.718	0.694	0.672	0.650	0.640	0.630	0.610	0.592
3	0.971	0.942	0.889	0.840	0.794	0.751	0.712	0.675	0.658	0.641	0.609	0.579	0.551	0.524	0.512	0.500	0.477	0.455
4	0.961	0.924	0.855	0.792	0.735	0.683	0.636	0.592	0.572	0.552	0.516	0.482	0.451	0.423	0.410	0.397	0.373	0.350
5	0.951	0.906	0.822	0.747	0.681	0.621	0.567	0.519	0.497	0.476	0.437	0.402	0.370	0.341	0.328	0.315	0.291	0.269
6	0.942	0.888	0.790	0.705	0.630	0.564	0.507	0.456	0.432	0.410	0.370	0.335	0.303	0.275	0.262	0.250	0.227	0.207
7	0.933	0.871	0.760	0.665	0.583	0.513	0.452	0.400	0.376	0.354	0.314	0.279	0.249	0.222	0.210	0.198	0.178	0.159
8	0.923	0.853	0.731	0.627	0.540	0.467	0.404	0.351	0.327	0.305	0.266	0.233	0.204	0.179	0.168	0.157	0.139	0.123
9	0.914	0.837	0.703	0.592	0.500	0.424	0.361	0.308	0.284	0.263	0.225	0.194	0.167	0.144	0.134	0.125	0.108	0.094
10	0.905	0.820	0.676	0.558	0.463	0.386	0.322	0.270	0.247	0.227	0.191	0.162	0.137	0.116	0.107	0.099	0.085	0.073
11	0.896	0.804	0.650	0.527	0.429	0.350	0.287	0.237	0.215	0.195	0.162	0.135	0.112	0.094	0.086	0.079	0.066	0.056
12	0.887	0.788	0.625	0.497	0.397	0.319	0.257	0.208	0.187	0.168	0.137	0.112	0.092	0.076	0.069	0.062	0.052	0.043
13	0.879	0.773	0.601	0.469	0.368	0.290	0.229	0.182	0.163	0.145	0.116	0.093	0.075	0.061	0.055	0.050	0.040	0.033
14	0.870	0.758	0.577	0.442	0.340	0.263	0.205	0.160	0.141	0.125	0.099	0.078	0.062	0.049	0.044	0.039	0.032	0.025
15	0.861	0.743	0.555	0.417	0.315	0.239	0.183	0.140	0.123	0.108	0.084	0.065	0.051	0.040	0.035	0.031	0.025	0.020

Notes:
1. Tables A-1 and A-2 are truncated versions of most present-value tables, which typically have factors for up to 50 percent and up to 50 years.
2. Tables A-1 and A-2 use 4 decimal places only; calculators and spreadsheet packages with present-value functions use many more decimal places and thus will give slightly different results.

TABLE A-2

Present Value of $1 Received Annually for N Years

Years Hence	1%	2%	4%	6%	8%	10%	12%	14%	15%	16%	18%	20%	22%	24%	25%	26%	28%	30%
1	0.990	0.980	0.962	0.943	0.926	0.909	0.893	0.877	0.870	0.862	0.847	0.833	0.820	0.806	0.800	0.794	0.781	0.769
2	1.970	1.941	1.887	1.833	1.783	1.735	1.690	1.646	1.626	1.605	1.565	1.527	1.492	1.456	1.440	1.424	1.391	1.361
3	2.941	2.883	2.776	2.673	2.577	2.486	2.402	2.321	2.284	2.246	2.174	2.106	2.043	1.980	1.952	1.924	1.868	1.816
4	3.902	3.807	3.631	3.465	3.312	3.169	3.038	2.913	2.856	2.798	2.690	2.588	2.494	2.403	2.362	2.321	2.241	2.166
5	4.853	4.713	4.453	4.212	3.993	3.790	3.605	3.432	3.353	3.274	3.127	2.990	2.864	2.744	2.690	2.636	2.532	2.435
6	5.795	5.601	5.243	4.917	4.623	4.354	4.112	3.888	3.785	3.684	3.497	3.325	3.167	3.019	2.952	2.886	2.759	2.642
7	6.728	6.472	6.003	5.582	5.206	4.867	4.564	4.288	4.161	4.038	3.811	3.604	3.416	3.241	3.162	3.084	2.937	2.801
8	7.651	7.325	6.734	6.209	5.746	5.334	4.968	4.639	4.488	4.343	4.077	3.837	3.620	3.420	3.330	3.241	3.076	2.924
9	8.565	8.162	7.437	6.801	6.246	5.758	5.329	4.947	4.772	4.606	4.302	4.031	3.787	3.564	3.464	3.366	3.184	3.018
10	9.470	8.982	8.113	7.359	6.709	6.144	5.651	5.217	5.019	4.833	4.493	4.193	3.924	3.680	3.571	3.465	3.269	3.091
11	10.366	9.786	8.763	7.886	7.138	6.494	5.938	5.454	5.234	5.028	4.655	4.328	4.036	3.774	3.657	3.544	3.335	3.147
12	11.253	10.574	9.388	8.383	7.535	6.813	6.195	5.662	5.421	5.196	4.792	4.440	4.128	3.850	3.726	3.606	3.387	3.190
13	12.132	11.347	9.989	8.852	7.903	7.103	6.424	5.844	5.584	5.341	4.908	4.533	4.203	3.911	3.781	3.656	3.427	3.223
14	13.002	12.105	10.566	9.294	8.243	7.366	6.629	6.004	5.725	5.466	5.007	4.611	4.265	3.960	3.825	3.695	3.459	3.248
15	13.863	12.848	11.121	9.711	8.558	7.605	6.812	6.144	5.848	5.574	5.091	4.676	4.316	4.000	3.860	3.726	3.484	3.268

Notes:
1. Tables A-1 and A-2 are truncated versions of most present-value tables, which typically have factors for up to 50 percent and up to 50 years.
2. Tables A-1 and A-2 use 4 decimal places only; calculators and spreadsheet packages with present-value functions use many more decimal places and thus will give slightly different results.

INDEX

ABOUT THE AUTHOR

David W. Young, D.B.A., is a professor of accounting and control and former accounting department chair at Boston University's School of Management. A principal in The Crimson Group, Inc., a small firm specializing in customized in-house management education programs, Professor Young is the author of *A Manager's Guide to Creative Cost Cutting* and coauthor of *Management Control in Nonprofit Organizations*. He has consulted with a wide variety of organizations on management control system design, and lectured and taught throughout Europe, Latin America, Japan, and the Middle East.